CW01239526

WHEN NOBODY'S LISTENING

WHEN NOBODY'S LISTENING

Inside Sweden's Drug Gangs

DIAMANT SALIHU

Translated by Jan Salomonsson

polity

Originally published in Swedish as *När ingen lyssnar*. Copyright © Mondial and Diamant Salihu, 2023. Published by agreement with Mondial

This English translation © Polity Press, 2025

The cost of this translation was supported by a subsidy from the Swedish Arts Council, gratefully acknowledged.

KULTURRÅDET

Polity Press
65 Bridge Street
Cambridge CB2 1UR, UK

Polity Press
111 River Street
Hoboken, NJ 07030, USA

All rights reserved. Except for the quotation of short passages for the purpose of criticism and review, no part of this publication may be reproduced, stored in a retrieval system or transmitted, in any form or by any means, electronic, mechanical, photocopying, recording or otherwise, without the prior permission of the publisher.

ISBN-13: 978-1-5095-6463-7 – hardback

A catalogue record for this book is available from the British Library.

Library of Congress Control Number: 2024947775

Typeset in 11.5 on 14pt Bell MT Pro
by Cheshire Typesetting Ltd, Cuddington, Cheshire
Printed and bound in Great Britain by CPI Group (UK) Ltd, Croydon

The publisher has used its best endeavours to ensure that the URLs for external websites referred to in this book are correct and active at the time of going to press. However, the publisher has no responsibility for the websites and can make no guarantee that a site will remain live or that the content is or will remain appropriate.

Every effort has been made to trace all copyright holders, but if any have been overlooked the publisher will be pleased to include any necessary credits in any subsequent reprint or edition.

For further information on Polity, visit our website: www.politybooks.com

You follow drugs, you get drug addicts and drug dealers. But you start to follow the money, and you don't know where the fuck it's gonna take you.
— Lester Freamon, *The Wire*

CONTENTS

Preface to the English Edition ix
Main Characters xxii

Prologue xxxi

Part 1: Pandora's Box
February 2020 – April 2020
1

Part 2: The Chain
March 2020
37

Part 3: D-Day
May 2020 – June 2020
57

Part 4: Foxtrot
March 2020 – August 2020
113

Part 5: The Honey Trap
September 2020 – June 2021
169

Contents

Part 6: The Fox Hunt
September 2021 – December 2022
251

Part 7: When No One Listens
January 2023 – March 2023
303

Afterword 338
Thanks 342

PREFACE TO THE ENGLISH EDITION

At the time of writing, a year has passed since this book was originally published in Swedish, and I've long since lost count of all the children who have been systematically exploited to carry out bombings and shootings. When I went on parental leave, I kept in touch with gang members and family members of victims on my phone during visits to playgrounds. One of the people I was in contact with was a grandfather called Ömer. His son had been shot dead in his home in the south of Stockholm. According to sources in the criminal underworld, the victim's son, Ömer's grandson, had been accused of shooting at Rawa Majid's relatives in Uppsala, and the murder was an act of retribution. When I met with Ömer later on, he was beside himself with grief. He told me how his family had worked hard to earn an honest living since leaving Turkey four decades ago.

'My son had a good life here', he said, with tired eyes. 'What's happening in Sweden right now is more than just a conflict between gangs. It's terrorism.'

The charges against Ömer's grandson and his suspected accomplices were eventually dropped.

Another parent I spoke to told me about how she had tried to convince the local social services to take her son into care, but that they had determined that he wasn't sufficiently involved in criminal activity for such a measure to

Preface to the English Edition

be taken. The police barely knew who he was. His mother, however, had seen how quickly things were heading in the wrong direction. He had suddenly begun to spend a great deal of time with some new friends, and he was very evasive in responding to her anxious calls and messages. One day, the police stormed their house. Her anxiety grew into a panic when she realized that her son was being arrested on suspicion of murder.

After participating in a panel discussion on recent developments in Swedish society in a crowded church, I was approached by a grandmother who told me how she'd been babysitting her daughter's baby when some youths fired a hail of bullets at her front door.

During an onstage interview at the Gothenburg Book Fair in the autumn of 2023, I stressed the point that the criminals I speak to don't usually blame society or their parents. Rather, they tend to insist that they actively chose their lifestyle. I told the audience about a girl I'd met, who went to university and had gone on to serve on various boards, while her brother had been convicted of murder and handed a life sentence.

'We had the same opportunities. But when we reached a certain crossroads in life, and I went right, he went left', the sister had told me.

I noticed a woman at the back of the crowd, who had clearly been moved by this. During the book-signing after the interview, that woman was in the line, accompanied by a young woman, her daughter. They both burst into tears when we met. The story I had just told onstage had resonated deeply within them. The woman's daughter was pursuing a degree in public health sciences, but her brother was an alleged gang leader who was currently serving a long prison sentence. When they told me that her convicted brother's young son had pointed and said that 'That's where daddy lives', when they passed by the police station one day, I found myself overcome by emotion, too.

Preface to the English Edition

The mother had tried, as parents in her situation often do, to figure out what had gone wrong and what she might have done differently.

Later, lying on the bed in my hotel room, I called a therapist who specializes in helping criminals change their lives and deal with their trauma. My reason for calling was that I had recently come into contact with young women who had been victimized by male gang members and gang-raped. It immediately dawned on me that, being a journalist, I was unable to take on the role of their therapist. Instead, they needed somebody who had experience of giving long-term treatment to trauma and PTSD sufferers.

The therapist could hear how tired and exhausted I was over the phone, and before he answered my questions, he asked me one, instead: 'What about you, Diamant? Who are you talking to about all this stuff?'

*

When I first began working on *When Nobody's Listening*, Rawa Majid – the Kurdish Fox – was virtually unknown in Sweden. By the time I was finalizing the book, he was everywhere. His name and picture were in all the newspapers, alongside articles declaring him to be a notorious Swedish drug lord who sent children out to commit acts of violence in the name of the Foxtrot network. This was in the spring of 2023, when the first of two major waves of violence that year was in full swing. I had to update the book constantly, right up until I submitted the manuscript for publication, as new, highly publicized acts of drug- and honour-fuelled violence were being committed every day. The Foxtrot network was at war with the Dalen network, and the situation seemed to escalate with every bombing, every shooting and every victimized participant or innocent bystander.

Preface to the English Edition

Things would soon grow even worse, as even more lines were crossed. That autumn, the second wave of violence of 2023 began and, this time, the conflict was an internal one. Ismail Abdo – also known as the Strawberry – was on one side. His mother was shot dead with a single bullet in her home in Gränby, Uppsala. Her son hails from a family of entrepreneurs, but ended up pursuing a criminal career in the drug trafficking business. He allied himself with Rawa Majid, who also came from Uppsala. However, their loyalties had begun to unravel several months earlier. I've received various accounts of why this happened from sources who had previously been members of the network's inner circle. Rawa Majid had become a megalomaniac, and was ordering an unreasonable number of killings in his highly publicized conflict with the Dalen network during the spring of 2023.

Some sources told me that the turning point for many had been when family members on both sides became targets in the conflict. Others accused Rawa Majid of having claimed too large a portion of the profits from drug trafficking, which was his network's main source of income. By committing acts of violence and offering guaranteed drug deliveries, Foxtrot had managed to gain influence in many Swedish cities, from north to south, as well as to establish varying degrees of presence in both Norway and Finland. Anybody who was allied with Foxtrot was allowed to sell the drugs the network delivered in their name, enjoying their protection. Anybody who opposed them might end up being the next in line to be murdered. This threat was levelled at rival criminals and their family members alike.

Now, though, a war had erupted within the network. Its leaders had long resided in Turkey, where many of them felt sufficiently secure to settle in the luxurious Maslak neighbourhood in northern Istanbul. Rawa Majid was living there with his family, and had also bought a house just a stone's throw from the sea in the coastal town of Bodrum. This prop-

Preface to the English Edition

erty had cost him more than 20 million kronor, according to Foxtrot members.

Allegedly, he borrowed some of the money from his contact within the unofficial banking network known as Hawala, which operates internationally. This individual, who was actually an Arabic-speaking man, used the alias 'Jenny' in encrypted chats.

Mention of money changers like this individual became increasingly common during that dark autumn. During September 2023 alone, twelve people were killed, two of whom weren't even indirectly involved in the conflict.

Foxtrot, like other gangs, had come to depend on Hawala bankers, who took a percentage for processing the gangs' criminal proceeds from drug sales and fraud. In other words, the gangs' practice of using money changers who operated bureaux de change offices had been discontinued after it was uncovered during the police operation that followed the hacking of the secret Encrochat communications network. Instead, individuals who used the informal Hawala banking system were helping the gangs transfer their funds to countries such as Turkey, the Netherlands, Iraq and the United Arab Emirates. The whole procedure was completely anonymous, and didn't involve any digital transactions at all. Once they had been handed the cash, it was entirely up to the money changers and their partners to decide how to handle and launder the money.

The money changers were paid to accept the risk of the money being seized. However, there were so many millions being moved around every day that any such loss would be quickly recouped thanks to the fees the gangs were paying. Long before the internal strife began, Foxtrot had also begun to suffer the consequences of a series of successful police operations leading to major drug seizures. The gang had used credits offered by 'Jenny' and other money changers to buy a lot of the drugs that were seized. A well-organized criminal

Preface to the English Edition

network would have managed to quickly repay these debts, but as the internal rivalries intensified and the justice system achieved more successes, the debt held by Rawa Majid alone is alleged to have grown to tens of millions of kronor.

The police were also growing more effective in combatting the gangs.

The Swedish Police Authority had expanded its operations, and called in extra staff to the regions where there had been a particular uptick in violent crime. Since many of those recruited to perpetrate the violence were children who had never held a gun or planted a bomb before, they made a lot of mistakes, too. Besides accidentally bombing or shooting the wrong targets, they left a tremendous amount of evidence behind: DNA and gunpowder residue on clothes that they never had time to burn; video clips in which they filmed themselves committing murders and attempted murders. The police's 'blue wave' of extra personnel produced a large number of arrested suspects, both girls and boys. A record number of these were minors who had been caught red-handed with murder weapons and unlocked phones in their possession. Often, the Signal app on these phones would be full of plans for crimes, and orders given in voicemails from leaders who were in hiding abroad.

*

When even the most influential Foxtrot members began to evacuate their families from their known addresses – as they had become targets in the blood feud that was sparked by the murder of Ismail Abdo's mother – these former friends began to hunt each other in Turkey and Iraq, instead.

Rawa Majid's time in Turkey came to an abrupt end when he was forced to flee the country. A few days after he escaped, information began to pour in from sources within both the rival factions. Rawa Majid had been detained in Iran, which

Preface to the English Edition

he had entered with a false ID. This information reached both the Swedish police and the Swedish prime minister, Ulf Kristersson, who announced it during a televised party leaders' debate.

Since then, Rawa Majid has been silent. Strangely, Iran, which could plausibly be expected to seek to use him as a bargaining chip to secure a prisoner exchange, has not confirmed his arrest at the time of writing. Despite the uncertainty surrounding his fate, several independent sources have long maintained that the internationally wanted Rawa Majid is, in all likelihood, in Iran. In an interview in *Aftonbladet*, his father also stated that his son had been arrested in Iran, and that he had been released during the spring of 2024.

One of the people who claimed to have helped the Fox get to Iran was Mustafa Aljiburi, or 'Benzema', as he called himself – a reference to the former Real Madrid footballer. This former friend and ally of the Fox, who was a member of Foxtrot, had started an Instagram war against the Ismail Abdo faction – while also mocking and distancing himself from the network's absent leader, Rawa Majid.

In front of thousands of social media followers, he presented himself as a new gang leader with huge ambitions. He declared that his goal was to unite all the criminal networks in Sweden, and share the profits fairly so 'everyone can eat'. Even more significant was his claim that he wouldn't tolerate acts of violence against family members, which had previously been a common practice in Foxtrot. He was media-savvy, and maintained communications with several journalists, including myself. He wanted me to interview him, preferably in a live broadcast. I explained that I am a journalist, not a 'gangland influencer'. The latter term was a reference to the various accounts that gave completely unfiltered and uncritical reports on the activities of Swedish criminals.

Before our first conversation, which had taken place earlier that autumn, Mustafa Aljiburi had been told that his rivals

Preface to the English Edition

had offered a million-dollar reward for his murder. However, he managed to turn the hitman they'd hired over to his side, and cooperated with him to fake his own death. The people who had ordered the hit were sent pictures in which Aljiburi appeared to have been abducted, and then a video of him, bloodied, sitting in a car with the engine running. His allies in the Bro network posted social media posts with pictures of him and the letters 'RIP', to convince his enemies and us journalists that the murder had actually been carried out. This ruse did successfully deceive many people, but, fortunately, no mainstream media channels took the bait. Instead of publishing the story, they all awaited confirmation from the Iraqi authorities or Swedish police. That confirmation never came.

Allegedly, after faking his own death, Mustafa Aljiburi even sent couriers to collect the money his enemies had put up for the hit, paid out in dollars by various Hawala-connected money changers in Iraq. Among other things, he's said to have spent this money on a new black Mercedes, but it was also allegedly used to buy drugs and pay for crimes ordered in Sweden. He presented himself in two very different ways. On the one hand, he claimed to be opposed to acts of violence targeting family members. On the other hand, he didn't think twice about threatening to kill opposing gang members in Upplands Väsby and Västerås if they resisted his army of soldiers. This army largely consisted of children and young adults who had been recruited by a team of young allies who had joined his new faction. Many of these children, who came from a great variety of towns and backgrounds, were arrested by the police when they were armed and ready to kill people who had sided with Ismail Abdo. One thing many of them had in common was that their recruitment had taken place through social media, often initiated by a simple invitation: 'Write to me if you want to work.'

Vulnerable children, some of whom were living in residential centres at the time, responded to this request. They knew

Preface to the English Edition

exactly what it meant. They were directed on to a Signal Chat where a job interview of sorts might be conducted by a masked teenager of their own age. This individual had never met Mustafa Aljiburi in person, but had reached out to him simply because he believed that his side was the right one to join in the ongoing gang war. The teenage recruiter looked up to him like an older brother, and Mustafa Aljiburi was very good at pulling his strings with praise. As a result, the boy's loyalty to him strengthened even further.

The teenager asked the new recruits if they were absolutely sure they wanted to carry out the shootings.

'Yes, bro, I'm ready', he might be told.

He instructed them to go and stay in specific flats, which they shared with others who had responded to the same message. The people in this murder squad were called *klivare*, or 'steppers' – because they were prepared to step up. They were added to Signal groups in which the recruiter and the leader could give them instructions in group chats.

Another individual who was in contact with these child soldiers claims that recruiting them hadn't taken any effort at all. They had volunteered, without even asking for payment, because they wanted to 'make a name for themselves'.

'They're morons', this gang member said.

Some of the children had never used a weapon before, and it was necessary to explain how the weapon they were to use for the murder worked before their missions. After this training, the *klivare* were sent into enemy territory to carry out their tasks. They might be instructed to make video calls, so that one of the leaders could identify their targets in real time, and give them quick orders: 'There, there! Shoot the people in front of you!'

In one such attempted shooting in Upplands Väsby, it's alleged that two inexperienced *klivare* panicked, and ended up being shot at themselves, before escaping unharmed.

Preface to the English Edition

Death lists were drawn up with names of people tied to various groups, all of whom were considered legitimate targets. This means that the task of the recruiters, some of whom were children themselves, was to order other children to kill specific individuals. One person likened the whole process to a computer game, and explained that the fact that the shot callers were abroad made it easier for them to issue life-and-death orders, as they never had to look either the perpetrators or the victims in the eyes.

Neither the *klivare*, who had been recruited directly from residential centres, nor the recruiters ever knew exactly what it was their targets were supposedly guilty of. All they knew was that they were legitimate targets, as they had been declared enemies. The question of whether a certain target was actually guilty of any offence, or really belonged to an enemy network, was settled as soon as Mustafa Aljiburi or someone else at the top of the organization said so.

My long conversations with people who had deep involvement in these events painted a frightening picture. It revealed how older criminals were manipulating vulnerable children who were desperate for a sense of belonging.

In the months since Mustafa Aljiburi had appointed himself the new leader of Swedish organized crime, he watched on as his allies were arrested in Tunisia, Iraq and Norway, from what seemed to be an increasing state of isolation in his home town of Baghdad. A friend of his, Harris Österdahl, who had also been a leading member of the Foxtrot network, was soon shot dead in Sarajevo by *klivare* sent there from Sweden.

During a series of conversations with Benzema, plans were made to interview him in Iraq. The interview, which was to be about the money changers, would be made for *Uppdrag granskning*, an investigative-reporting television show that I work for. This trip never happened. In early January, Benzema was slowly driving along a multi-lane, busy street

Preface to the English Edition

in Baghdad in his Mercedes. A shooter, a nineteen-year-old from Hudiksvall, approached his car from the right. A large number of shots were fired through the passenger window, several of which hit Benzema in the head.

The shooter and his accomplices were arrested soon thereafter, and are now facing a potential death penalty in Iraq. One of the nineteen-year-old's fellow prisoners in Baghdad claims that he was offered 1.5 million kronor to carry out the murder by a contact in Malmö. After accepting, he received assistance from people on the ground in Baghdad, who had been watching Benzema and secured weapons for the hit.

I've received accounts from inside his cell, which he shared with many other prisoners, of torture and exceptionally harsh treatment of those suspected of involvement in the murder. According to reports, the nineteen-year-old was apparently on a group call with ten or so members of various networks in Sweden at the time of Benzema's shooting. These individuals were allegedly involved in the murder plot and all chipped in to raise the fee to have it carried out.

I was told by the person who claims to have spoken to the nineteen-year-old in prison that 'They wanted to make sure they wouldn't be deceived again.' Another person involved was allegedly paid 100,000 kronor to video the murder from a car behind. The footage went viral immediately after Benzema was killed.

His enemies celebrated on social media – most notably, a happy picture of Ismail Abdo and two close allies was posted. Both Mustafa Aljiburi and his friend Harris Österdahl had been killed. According to the indictment that was filed in mid-February 2024, the two had been in contact with the young recruited hitmen, aged fifteen and nineteen, who were suspected of having murdered Ismail Abdo's mother. The teenagers, however, deny all wrongdoing.

Preface to the English Edition

According to sources in the criminal underworld, Rawa Majid remains a target in the blood feud triggered by that murder. The final reckoning is likely to come eventually, in some foreign country, unless the two sides somehow manage to arrive at a reconciliation.

But 'That's never going to happen', according to an ally of Ismail Abdo.

At first, there were some on his side who had their doubts that Rawa Majid had actually been involved in the murder of Abdo's mother. Had he really been prepared to cross that line, which most criminals keep well clear of? The court case that followed the charges made couldn't provide a definitive answer, as the investigation never managed to tie Rawa Majid to the murder. Several Signal aliases that communicated with the shooters remain unidentified, including the alias Killerforce, which gave a series of instructions to the recruited shooters. Among other things, this alias provided them with an address where they were supposed to meet. After the murder, Killerforce arranged for one of the shooters to be sent 1,000 kronor so he could buy pizza. Moments later, Killerforce asked the fifteen-year-old who was later charged with the murder if he was absolutely sure the woman had died.

'Yes, brother, we're one hundred per cent sure', the boy replied.

'Ok bro', Killerforce wrote back.

Former allies of Rawa Majid claim that some of the aliases mentioned in the investigation are ones they believe he was using at the time. Two independent sources from what was once the Foxtrot network have told me this. However, the police and the prosecutors have so far been unable to verify this.

Many have also suggested to me that, while the blood feud united various rival criminal groups against Rawa Majid and Mustafa Aljiburi, everybody is expected to go back to

Preface to the English Edition

focusing on their own interests as they did before. However, members of some organizations have expressed the hope that everybody will realize that they have nothing to gain from more blood being spilled, particularly when it's family members and innocent bystanders who end up getting hurt. Meanwhile, our prisons are overcrowded, our legislation is constantly being tightened to allow law enforcement to reach both the recruiters and the hitmen and we're seeing new laws being proposed to facilitate the pursuit of the enablers such as the Hawala money changers, who manage and launder illicit proceeds, including profits made from drug crimes and fraud.

That's where we are now. *When Nobody's Listening* is the story of how we got here.

Diamant Salihu
June 2024

MAIN CHARACTERS

Police officers/lawyers

Putte. Intelligence officer at the Department of National Operations (Noa) and Europol during the encrypted chat operations.
Cattis. Lead intelligence officer at Noa.
Emil Eisersjö. Operational manager of Noa's intelligence department during the encrypted chat operations.
Linda H. Staaf. Head of intelligence at Noa during the encrypted chat operations.
Solveig Wollstad. Sweden's representative at the European Union Agency for Criminal Justice Cooperation, Eurojust, during the encrypted chat operations.
Lise Tamm. Chief prosecutor at the National Unit against Organized Crime (Rio) when Sweden gained access to the encrypted chats.
Henrik Söderman. Prosecutor at Rio and Noa's contact during the encrypted chat operations.
Ted Esplund. Section head at the intelligence department in the Bergslagen region. Later, national project manager for the encrypted chat operations.
Stefan Olofsson. Head of police operations in the South region during Operation Rimfrost.

Main Characters

Erik Åberg. Deputy local police district commander in the South region.

Patrik Andersson. Section head of the regional intelligence service in the South region – one of the few people to be given early knowledge of the Encro operation.

Richard. Detective in the South region.

Helena Ljunggren. Public prosecutor at Rio in Malmö.

Jacob. Team leader at the Serious Crime Department in the North Stockholm police district. Lead investigator on the attempted murder in Viksjö and the hunt for the Fox and his network.

Denny. Head of a team of detectives in the Järva local police district.

Erik. A detective colleague of Denny's.

Thorbjörn. A response officer who joined the hunt for the Fox and his network as a detective.

Niklas. A response officer who joined the hunt for the Fox and his network as a detective.

TEAM FOXTROT

Patrik Zanders. Lead investigator on the case of the murder of Shad, the Fox's cousin. Worked at Noa on the encrypted chat operations.

Vera. Noa's liaison officer at Europol when Encrochat was cracked. Coordinated the Trojan Shield operation with the FBI.

Stefan Reimer. Justice of the Supreme Court.

Lisa dos Santos. Prosecutor in the Årstabron Bridge murder case against Abdul, Toj and Kevin.

Anders Rissel. Chief of police in the North Stockholm police district.

Lisa Granqvist. Head of the Serious Crimes Department in the North police district.

Martina. Police officer who previously worked in Rinkeby, now working in Norrköping.

Main Characters

Christoffer Bohman. Coordinator of the encrypted chat operations in the North Stockholm police district during the autumn of 2021.
Thomas Olsson. Lawyer who criticized the use of encrypted chats as evidence, and questioned the legality of how the evidence was provided to Swedish police.
Ester Herlin-Karnell. Professor of EU Law at the University of Gothenburg. Specializes in EU criminal law.
Marie Lind Thomsen. Senior prosecutor at Rio during the encrypted chat operations.
Magnus Sjöberg. Head of the National Tactical Council at Noa.

Malmö/Skåne

The Boxer. Leading criminal in Malmö, real name Amir Mekky. Used the alias Airwalnut on Encrochat, according to the police. Thought to be a leading figure in Los Suecos.
Salle. A criminal in Skåne. Loyal to the Boxer, and thus an enemy of Danni. Encountered Danni at the hotel in Ängelholm.
Danni. A leading criminal in Malmö and enemy of the Boxer ever since his brother was kidnapped in 2018. Used the alias Waterbee on Encrochat, according to the police. Encountered his rival Salle at the hotel in Ängelholm.
Niff. Had ties to the criminal underworld of Malmö. An ally of Danni. Used the alias Stiffherb on Encrochat, according to the police. Cohabited with intern physician Karolin Hakim.
Karolin Hakim. Intern physician murdered in 2019. Had a child with Niff.
Sadking. Criminal from Malmö. Loyal to Danni. Communicated with Ftpftp from the Jakobsberg network in Stockholm.

Main Characters

Juggen. Young man in Malmö who brokered services between criminals. Has been linked to the alias Valuedox on Encrochat.
Kitekiller. The Encrochat alias of a young man who committed crimes for pay. Was involved in the murder plot against Salle at the hotel in Ängelholm.
Haraketamal. Encrochat alias with ties to Skåne's criminal underworld. Loyal to Danni. Participated in the assassination plot against Salle.
Atte. 41-year-old from Helsingborg who was murdered when the preliminary investigation against his brother was made public.

The Stockholm area

Maykil Yokhanna. From Vårby. Has been identified as the leader of a criminal group. Enemy of the Vårby network after several years of conflict.
Orhan. Suspected of involvement in the murder of Adriana. Currently avoiding prosecution in Turkey.
Chihab Lamouri. Leader of the Vårby network and an enemy of Maykil. Used the alias Mujaheed on Encrochat, according to the police.
The Captain. One of Lamouri's 'captains' within the Vårby network. Helped plan the assassination plot against Maykil.
Donvar. Drug distributor in Stockholm.
Sara. Girl in her twenties who sold drugs in Stockholm.
Maja. Social worker who had been using drugs recreationally for years.
Rolex man. Encrochat alias that was involved in planning the attempted murder in Viksjö.
Ftpftp. Encrochat alias that was involved in planning the attempted murder in Viksjö. Connected to the Jakobsberg network. Also in contact with Sadking.

Main Characters

The Fish. Involved in the murder plot in Viksjö. Has been linked to the Headshot Gang.

The 16-year-old. Young individual from Rinkeby who carried out the attempted murder in Viksjö. Reportedly, his services were brokered by a senior member of the Death Squad.

Peter. The victim of the attempted murder at the bus stop in Viksjö.

The Money Changer. Operated the World Exchange in Södermalm. Has been connected to the Encrochat alias Muteherder.

Shad. Cousin of the Fox, friend of the Death Squad and, according to the police, a leading member of the Headshot Gang. Murdered in 2018.

The Mask. Thought to be vengeful and a loner. Was accused of involvement in the murder of Shad.

The Death Squad Leader. Man from the Järva area, who is serving a long prison sentence at Kumla. Accused of involvement in a murder plot against the Mask.

Leopardmaster. Encrochat alias used by a man from the Järva area who is said to have been involved in raising money to have the Mask murdered.

Berno Khouri. Leader of the Södertälje network who has been sentenced to life in prison. Has been accused of involvement in a murder plot against the Mask.

Ekrem Güngör. Former lawyer who was referred to as the King and has been tied to the Encrochat alias Literalbeetle.

Amir Amdouni. Former lawyer who was referred to as the Prince and has been tied to the Encrochat alias Literalbeetle.

The Fox. Leader of extensive drug networks. Rose to notoriety under the name 'The Kurdish Fox'. Thirty-six years of age, real name is Rawa Majid. The police have linked him to the aliases Foxkurdish, Foxplanet and Animal.

Albin. Mule who worked for the Fox and was arrested at the Elite Hotel in April 2020. Used the alias Buckradio on Encrochat, according to the police.

Main Characters

Roger. Small-business owner from Ekerö who worked for the Fox as a mule, and delivered drugs in Sollentuna to Mesut.
Mesut. A man from Sollentuna who received a drug delivery there from Roger.
Wilhelm. A man from Åkersberga who worked for the Fox as a mule, and drove cargo to an industrial area in Vallentuna.
Darthvvader. Encrochat alias used by an individual who held a significant position within the Fox's network.
The Coach. Suspected of being the Fox's logistics manager in Sweden. Organized transportation of drug shipments to stash locations using freight companies.
Rodrigo. Holder who worked for the Fox. Kept a stash of drugs in a hotel room in central Stockholm, and took a taxi to Märsta.
Jerker. Major drug dealer who made the delivery in Märsta.
Oliver. Man from Årsta who worked as a mule for the Fox, and made the delivery by the train station in Bro.
Lars. Gave Oliver missions to perform. Used the Encro alias SAS.
The Blacksmith. A father of young children from southern Stockholm. Was in business with the Fox.
Teemu. Finnish citizen and leader of a criminal network in his home country.
Robin. Construction entrepreneur and former Foreign Legionnaire. Bought drugs from Rivkin and engaged in drug deals with the Blacksmith.
Kent. Construction worker and mule who worked for Robin. Received drugs from Oliver in Bro.
The Fox's mother. The mother of the Fox. Lives in Uppsala.
The Fox's father. Father of the Fox and brother of Shad's mother.
Hasse. Friend of the Fox's family. Used to be in a relationship with the Fox's mother.
The Pensioner. Volunteered at the Fox's family's ice cream parlour in Uppsala.

Main Characters

Abdul Haleem. Leader of a criminal network in southern Stockholm. Former friend of Sascha.

Sascha Viklund. Former friend of Abdul. Had a long history of criminal behaviour. Was targeted by Abdul.

Kevin. Young man from southern Stockholm who has been linked to Abdul's network.

Toj. Former friend of Sascha.

Shayan Gaff. 22-year-old trainee teacher who police suspect was shot dead by mistake, because of his resemblance to Gee, an enemy of the Vårby network.

Gee. Linked to the criminal underworld, and, according to the police, in conflict with the Vårby network and Abdul Haleem's network, among others.

Carina. Sascha's mother.

Susanne. Adriana's mother.

Efficientbonsai. Encrochat alias that has been linked to leading figures of the Dalen network. Convicted of masterminding the Einár kidnapping.

The Greek. Leading figure in the Dalen network. Has been in a highly publicized feud with the Fox since the beginning of 2023. Is currently in hiding abroad.

Rest of Sweden

Hamid. The leader of the Örebro Cartel.

The 47-year-old. A man who held a leading position in No Surrender. Former friend of Hamid, later his enemy.

Ako. A man who held an important position in No Surrender. Was shot dead outside his home in Örebro.

Jappis. Encrochat alias for the suspected leader of a squad that carried out attacks in different parts of Sweden.

Silverear. Encrochat alias of a man who had been registered at the same address as Jappis, and was part of his network.

Main Characters

Rebecca. A drug courier in her twenties from the Stockholm area. Visited the Money Changer. Picked up a large quantity of cocaine from the Hockey Player.
The Hockey Player. Holder in Gothenburg who passed on drugs to Rebecca.
The Boss. The Hockey Player's employer, who used to socialize with criminals in Biskopsgården.
Maximilian Rivkin. Malmö man and 'criminal influencer' whom the FBI used to distribute ANOM. Has been tied to the ANOM alias Microsoft.
Rikard. Man in his fifties with prior convictions. Operated an amphetamine lab with Rivkin, and sold drugs on the Flugsvamp website.
Piotr. Mule and amphetamine lab worker. Worked for Rikard and Rivkin.
Lennart. Mule who worked for Rikard and Rivkin.
The Gothenburgian. 33-year-old man who had a leading position in the Bergsjön network in Gothenburg. Smuggled hashish in marble tiles.
The Plumbing Contractor. Man in Kungälv who was initially named as the recipient of the marble tiles filled with hashish.
The Man in Kinna. Small-business owner who had hashish sent to him inside marble tiles.

Overseas

Alexandre. French prosecutor who led the operation against Encrochat.
Hanski. Finnish police officer at Europol, who insisted that Swedish police be included in the Encrochat operation.
The Angel of Death. Nickname for Ridouan Taghi, a Moroccan-Dutch mafia leader. Believed to have controlled a large share of the cocaine market in Europe. Said to have been an affiliate of the Boxer.

Main Characters

Hakan Ayik. Turkish-Australian drug smuggler and 'criminal influencer' used by the FBI to distribute ANOM.
Ali. Park worker in Turkey who found a bag of money that belonged to the Fox.
Timur Soykan. Award-winning Turkish journalist.
Ibrahim Kalin. Spokesperson for the Turkish President Recep Tayyip Erdoğan.
Peter R. de Vries. Dutch TV personality and crime journalist who was murdered during the trial of the Angel of Death.

PROLOGUE

'Are you alone?'

'Yes', I answer.

He gave the stairwell a quick glance before letting me into his flat. A mildly fragrant, but distinctive, scent emerged. If you've ever smelt cannabis before, there's no mistaking it. He told me that he smoked to soothe his nerves, because he got the jitters. He said it was probably ADHD, a diagnosis he had given himself after taking several tests online.

'Come here', he said, watching his dog run across the carpet that was littered with bits of stray tobacco.

He bought the dog with his girlfriend before she moved out. Purple curtains hung down in front of the windows, to keep the sun out.

'So, you're writing about Encro?' he said, without looking up at me.

While he said this, he opened the window, sat down next to it, and lit a cigarette. He took a deep drag and blew the smoke out through the opening.

I had come to see him because of his past convictions, which included ones for weapons offences. He told me he had also smuggled drugs into the south of Sweden, but was never convicted for that.

At the time, Encrochat had been the most popular encrypted service by a wide margin. In countless raids, police officers all over Europe found these adapted phones. They were marketed as a safe channel that 'guaranteed anonymity'.

'I used it to smuggle drugs', the young man told me in his flat in a suburb in the south of Sweden.

He bought his Encro phone for 13,000 kronor from a friend who had come across a whole batch of them from one of his contacts in the Netherlands. The phones could also be bought in ordinary little mobile phone repair shops.

All it took was the right connections.

'Lots of people could sort a phone for you.'

Most Encrochat users agreed that there was no way the police could access the system's contents.

'That's why people discussed drug deals, murder plots – anything illegal, basically – openly on there.'

He told me that he had been careful despite the encryption. Many other users sent each other pictures of expensive designer clothes, watches and jewellery, plane tickets and selfies with weapons, cash and drugs. That was the lifestyle he used to dream of, but he had started to have second thoughts now, he told me. He showed me the scars on his body, which had been left by injuries that could have taken his life. He never really answered my question about how he was earning a living today. 'Savings', he assured me, and quickly changed the subject to what I was really there to talk to him about.

'I remember what things were like before Encrochat', he said, pacing around in the flat as though looking for something he couldn't seem to find. One moment, he was adjusting the cushions on the couch; the next, he was filling up his dog's feeding bowl.

'What was it like, then, before Encrochat?' I asked, somewhat tentatively.

'It was harder for people to kill each other.'

PART 1
PANDORA'S BOX

FEBRUARY 2020 – APRIL 2020

1

In a house in the French countryside, not too far from the Channel, prosecutor Alexandre waited. His laptop was open on the table in front of him. The flickering blue light of the screen was reflected in his eyes as he glanced over at his phone. He was expecting word any minute now.

Alexandre was tired. Work had been busy lately. Violent crime had grown increasingly extreme, and its perpetrators had been quick to adapt to the digital world. Encrypted chat services were at the heart of this unfortunate development. They were used to plan murders, revenge, and weapon and drug trafficking, all sheltered from outside view.

For police and prosecutors, this had led to a frustrating game of cat and mouse, in which they had been constantly one step behind.

In 2017, phones with the Encrochat encryption service began to appear in more and more criminal investigations, after the servers of several competing services were seized. The first of these phones were sold on websites like eBay, but over the years, it became increasingly common for them to be traded through personal networks that reached all across Europe.

Encrochat had created two operating systems for these rather cheap Android phones. The first one was just like the home screen of an ordinary Android phone, but this dummy system was only there to avoid raising any suspicions. It had no features for making calls, sending text messages or surfing the web. The other operating system had the Encrochat service. On the earliest phones, this was opened by simultaneously pressing the volume and power buttons. After this, a password had to be entered, and then you would be magically transported to an encrypted space from which you could send secure messages. The location service features were deactivated, but the phone did have to connect to the mobile data network and to the nearest base station to send messages. There was also a safety feature, to be used if the owner was raided by the police: if a panic code was entered, all data on the phone would be erased.

According to French authorities, Encrochat had more than 60,000 users at its peak, the majority of them located in Europe.

When the C3N cybercrime department of the National Gendarmerie of France carefully analysed the Encrochat phones they had seized, they made a remarkable discovery. All the data traffic related to this encrypted service appeared to pass through a server room in Roubaix. This French town, which won global renown in the nineteenth century for its textile production, is located in the district of Lille. Alexandre was the head prosecutor for organized crime cases in that district, and that was how this case had ended up on his desk.

After receiving indications that the company behind Encrochat was facilitating serious organized crime, Alexandre and his team had decided to initiate a preliminary investigation.

French prosecutors, unlike Swedish ones, can also initiate investigations against legal persons – in this case, the Encrochat business. The main legal issue here concerned the fact that the unknown individuals who ran the business were offering an undeclared, illegal encrypted communications service in France. On top of this, they were doing it in full awareness of the fact that their customers used the service to commit serious crimes.

Alexandre called in technical expertise from the French national intelligence agencies, and now, here he was, waiting by his computer for a report on the status of this secret operation to come in. He looked out the window and dragged his hand through his cropped, dark hair. Then, Alexandre's phone rang. He held it to his ear, his hand trembling ever so slightly. The voice on the other end belonged to a member of the French cybercrime police unit.

'We're in. Now what?'

Alexandre realized that this was a breakthrough, but he couldn't yet imagine how major it would eventually prove to be.

'This is an unprecedented operation', he thought to himself.

After a few hours of rather lively conversations with representatives of a few selected Europol member nations, Alexandre had arranged access for himself and a team of his colleagues to the ongoing planning of tens of thousands of criminals. This was a huge win. Even so, Alexandre felt uncomfortable. The messages in the chats displayed a ruthlessness that most people would find alarming.

Also, there wasn't much time.

If this discovery was to be of any real use, they needed to obtain as much evidence as they possibly could before it became obvious to the users that their phones were no longer secure. However, this priority had to be weighed against the urgency of preventing the murders that they were now watching suspects plotting in real time.

And there were a lot more of these plots than anybody could have imagined.

2

In early 2020, the Swedish police officer Putte was posted to the Europol headquarters in The Hague, the Netherlands. Like most case workers within the Department of National Operations (Noa), he preferred to keep a low profile. People who remembered Putte from working with him in the field, on the other hand, described him as sociable, fit, tall and balding.

Between 1994 and 2004, he served as a neighbourhood police officer and narcotics investigator in the Västerort suburbs of Stockholm. These included Rinkeby, Tensta and Husby, all residential areas that the police had classified as 'especially vulnerable'. One day, he would be out patrolling the squares, and the next day, he would be conducting surveillance operations targeting some suspect or other. These frequent highs and lows were part of what he enjoyed about the job. Maintaining a presence like that was also a way of commanding a degree of respect from the drug dealers. They all knew how the game was played, and they knew that the police were always on their tails. Back then, though, the seizures were usually grams and hectograms, and it was simply unheard of for minors to be working as mules, carrying 5 kilos of cocaine in a backpack, with a street value of up to 4½ million kronor.

One important reason why Putte was here, in The Hague, was that more and more Swedish criminals were establishing themselves on the international stage. Their networks had tendrils in Greece, the Netherlands, Morocco, Somalia, Turkey and South America – but above all, they were in Spain. At one point, up to 200 representatives of the Swedish criminal underworld were in Spain, far away from the watchful eyes of the Swedish authorities.

Besides offering warm weather and a healthy distance from the Swedish police, the Swedish Enforcement Authority and other similar bodies, Spain was also an ideal hub for anybody who wanted to do business in the illegal drug trade. Europe had become a sufficiently important market for the cartels and mafias to have posted representatives of their own in several different countries, but their presence was particularly large in Spain. They actively sought out buyers of cocaine from South America, cannabis from Morocco, and amphetamines and ecstasy from the drug factories in the Netherlands. In ports all over Europe, corrupt dockworkers and officials were allowing drug shipments to slip through, usually for a fee. However, even for honest dockworkers, it would have been impossible to inspect all the millions of containers that arrived each year. The drugs were concealed in shipments of fruit and other goods that were picked up by shipping companies and transported on to 'holders'. These, in turn, delivered the drugs to customers who had pre-ordered specific quantities, often using the encrypted phones to place their orders.

According to a report published by the EU, the European cocaine market alone was worth up to €119 billion annually. South American cartels had also begun to send their own chemists over here, to get local production of synthetic drugs up and running.

For a long time, the Swedish police had been facing difficulties in their attempts to cooperate with their Spanish counterparts on drug enforcement efforts – 100 kilos of hashish, shipped across the Strait of Gibraltar on fast boats from

Morocco to be transported on to Sweden, wasn't the kind of case that would be considered a priority in a country where efficient, well-organized smuggling rings were bringing illegal drugs in by the tonne.

The Swedish police were keen to change this.

In the early spring of 2018, Putte and other representatives of the Swedish justice system had arranged a meeting with their Spanish colleagues at the Europol headquarters. Their aim was to convince the Spanish to agree to deepen their cooperation on efforts that targeted the Swedish criminal networks that had established themselves along the Costa del Sol.

After a few months, Putte and his colleagues travelled to Málaga to further develop this relationship. The timing had been fortunate: at that particular time, there was a major investigation under way, targeting an international drug smuggling ring that involved around twenty Swedes. The Spaniards wanted to know more about who they were dealing with, and the individuals in question were easily identified by Noa. Almost all of them were members of the Swedish criminal elite, and were linked to some of the most notorious criminal organizations in Sweden: Bandidos, the Bredäng network and the Death Squad from Stockholm. However, there were also a number of high-profile criminals from the Malmö region.

'You've got your hands full with this lot. Many of them are potential murderers', they warned the Spaniards.

Just a few months later, the Swedish police were proved right when their Spanish colleagues asked them for help with a stalled investigation into a series of brutal violent crimes involving suspects that had ties to Sweden.

The crimes under investigation included murders, kidnappings and bombings. One of them was the execution of a man who had visited western Marbella to celebrate his son's confirmation. In August, the police had found two men from the

Stockholm area in a house in Mijas. One of them had been bound and stabbed, but had managed to break free and alert a neighbour. The other man had been strangled and shot dead. A few days later, another person died after being shot nine times by a masked man who had ambushed him from behind a rubbish bin.

This wave of violence involving Swedes garnered a lot of media attention in Spain, and the suspects soon came to be referred to as Los Suecos, the Swedes. During this same time, the Spanish police also became aware of a gang leader who had fled Malmö after an attempted murder there. This was Amir Mekky, a Danish citizen of Palestinian descent who had grown up in Malmö and eventually became one of the city's most notorious criminals.

He was later identified as the leader of Los Suecos, the group that was wreaking havoc all along the Costa del Sol. He was also a priority target for Putte and the others at Europol.

*

When he was younger, Amir Mekky, now twenty-six, had been a promising boxer. There was an old photo of him as a young fighter, 171 centimetres tall, in a blue tank top and blue shorts. He was raising his hands in triumph after winning his debut fight at the age of nineteen. His dark hair was cut short, and his body was compact, with highly defined muscles. Later on, after he injured his hand, the nickname 'the Boxer' stuck, although his rivals in Malmö usually referred to him as 'the Dwarf'.

The Boxer was known to social services from an early age, and he first started travelling to Spain in his teens. According to several sources in the criminal underworld, he made connections there with suppliers of cannabis from the farms in Morocco. Soon, he was challenging Malmö's established drug traffickers. He offered lower prices, and subjected any competitors who objected to his activities to brutal violence. By the time he reached his late teens, he had already been a person of interest in several murder investigations, but no charges had ever been brought against him. While all this was happening, he forged alliances with a new generation of criminals who were known to be extremely violent. These new friends included the Death Squad, to whom the Boxer offered sanctuary in Malmö when they were run out of Rinkeby after two teenage boys, Izzy and Maslah, were shot dead. These two unsolved murders marked the beginning of the highly publicized spiral of vengeance between Shottaz and the Death Squad.

The Boxer was described by many in his orbit as an 'ice-cold' operator, who was fiercely loyal to his own people. While he was settling in Spain, suspicions arose that he and his friends were setting up a large-scale drug smuggling operation. Somehow, according to police sources in several countries, he also began to do business with the Moroccan-Dutch mafia leader Ridouan Taghi, also known as 'the Angel of Death' – this nickname came from the fact that he was said to call the shots when it came to who would live and who would die.

Taghi has also been identified as a key connection for the South American cartels. He allegedly controlled up to a third of all the cocaine smuggled into Europe, and had amassed a personal fortune of more than €1 billion.

*

The deepened cooperation between the Swedish and Spanish police forces bore fruit immediately. They were able to arrest people within the Los Suecos network, as well as other individuals who had ties to the Bredäng network and the Death Squad. Several suspects were also apprehended in Sweden, and quickly extradited to Spain to be tried in court. The Boxer, however, remained at large.

In any case, these successes proved that international cooperation was a vital approach when it came to going after the top-level players within the criminal networks.

In February 2020, during Putte's stationing with Europol, this was one of his main objectives: to further improve the Swedish police's chances of catching individuals who were remotely coordinating serious crimes committed in Sweden.

The benefit Europol offered was that it allowed participating countries to pool intelligence on persons of interest between their respective police forces. This allowed them to look up the most recent known addresses, telephone numbers and overseas business partners of various suspects, all in a single database.

Putte's role was to give Europol insight into the Swedish criminal world, to draw up network charts and explain what kinds of crimes each group engaged in. Swedish police produced a shortlist of about ten 'high value targets', who were to be prioritized if they turned up in other Europol member countries' investigations. Almost all the people on the list were known gang leaders, whose violent crimes and drug trafficking had been highly publicized.

Naturally, the Boxer was on that list.

He was also a priority target for Spanish law enforcement, as he was wanted for murder in Spain. According to Swedish sources, he might have been in Morocco or Thailand, but their best guess was that he was in Dubai. Wherever he was, the police suspected that he was remotely ordering and coordinating murders and drug smuggling operations.

For more than a year, Putte had been collaborating closely with his Finnish colleague Hanski, who was an analyst at Europol. They both had the same drive to go after serious criminals. Soon, Putte's friendship with this blonde Finn, who seemed to be available at all hours, would prove crucial for Sweden's involvement in the operation that the French police had started in Lille, under the leadership of the prosecutor Alexandre.

3

Starting in early March 2020, Europol's headquarters grew increasingly vacant. As the pandemic spread through Europe, Europol made a mid-month announcement that all non-regular staff were to work from their respective home countries. Being an external resource, Putte had to hurry back to Sweden. He wasn't even given time to fetch his work computer before the premises were closed down.

However, the lockdown wasn't complete. Unbeknownst to Putte, there was a secret operation under way in one of the larger meeting rooms on the ground floor. Representatives from various countries were planning how to distribute the data from Encrochat if Alexandre the prosecutor and the French police actually managed to hack their way into the company's server. They hadn't cracked the service yet, but they were well on their way.

Meanwhile, Putte flew back home to his wife and house in western Stockholm. Hanski didn't contact him until a few weeks later, in April. Putte was sitting with his computer in the living room when he received a message on Signal, an encrypted app used by police officers, human rights activists and journalists. And by criminals.

'Could you send me some Swedish slang terms for murder, drugs, things like that?' Hanski asked.

These kinds of questions were common in their work, and Putte quickly sent over a list of words.

'What words might Mekky have used in these contexts?' Hanski continued.

What Putte didn't know when he was being asked these cryptic questions was that his Finnish colleague was part of a covert operation at Europol. He had been putting in sixteen-hour days, sitting in front of screens in a face mask and trying to track communications between criminals in all corners of the world. Because there were tens of thousands of different user aliases on Encrochat, Europol was using AI software to help their analysts identify messages related to cases of 'TTL', or threat to life – ongoing conspiracies to commit murder. However, the software could only interpret posts written in English, so Hanski had been specifically asked to help out with the Nordic languages. He didn't speak Swedish, but he used the glossaries that Putte and other colleagues from the Nordics provided him with to carry out manual searches in the long logs of messages.

Every day, at least one new TTL alert came in from somewhere in the world, and the analysts would have to evaluate it before proceeding to quickly alert the police in that specific region. It was vital that none of the recipients of this intelligence realized that the data had been mined from Encrochat. Murder plots were being hatched all over Europe, but the Swedish users were particularly industrious in this regard. They were extremely violent, and highly inclined to murder. This was further underlined by the fact that Sweden had recently climbed to the top of the European statistics for shooting deaths per capita.

Because of the large number of ongoing high-priority cases, it didn't take many days for Hanski to convince the other parties involved in the operation to grant access to the project to a few select colleagues in Sweden, in the hope that this might help prevent murders. He assured the team that the Swedes would never leak the information they were given. Putte was the first person that Hanski and a French colleague reached out to.

The intelligence that was passed on to Putte was never to be disseminated further, not even within Noa. Putte accepted these terms without hesitation. Hanski and the Frenchman also brought in two of Putte's colleagues, who were based in Malmö and Gothenburg, two cities where Europol had uncovered several potential TTL cases.

Putte was overwhelmed by what he learned, and promised to provide all the help he could from his home office.

Meanwhile, his colleague in Gothenburg received intelligence from Europol about an arms smuggling operation involving members of a family that the police were very familiar with, since many of its male members had been convicted for offences in the past.

On Good Friday, 10 April, Putte and his wife had just opened a bottle of wine when his mobile phone started ringing, at about quarter to seven in the evening.

Putte received another piece of valuable intel.

'Do you know who this is?' Hanski asked, and sent over a picture of a couple of newlyweds.

The man Europol was trying to identify was wearing a dark suit, a white shirt and a white bow tie. In the photo, he was embracing his wife as they both made happy faces at the camera. Putte didn't recognize the man, but since he had been asked a series of questions about the Boxer over the last few days, he suspected that this might be somebody who was connected to him.

*

In June 2018, some friends of the Boxer were accused of kidnapping the half-brother of Danni the Jew, another influential individual in the criminal circles of Malmö. He was a few years older than the Boxer, but despite his nickname, he wasn't Jewish. Word in Malmö's underworld had it that he was good for millions and millions. While others usually spent all their money on cars, watches and designer clothes, Danni had a reputation for being good at managing his criminal earnings.

'He has more money than anybody else, because he's a smart bastard', a source loyal to the Boxer told me.

Allegedly, a ransom fee in the millions had been paid to secure the release of the brother, who, it was claimed, was subjected to humiliations and violence during his time in captivity. However, several sources close to Danni would deny that any payment had been made.

'They never paid a single fucking krona', one of them told me.

They claimed that the kidnapping had occurred after the Boxer approached Danni about a proposal for a joint venture. Allegedly, the Boxer asked for help with 'certain things', and when Danni declined, he didn't take it too well. Shortly after this, Danni's half-brother was abducted while Danni was in Spain. Rumours began to circulate that Danni had been arrested, so the kidnappers delivered their ransom demand of 20 million kronor to Danni's friends instead. Then, the Boxer stepped in to 'act the hero', according to somebody who was present for the negotiations. According to this person's account, the Boxer picked the kidnapped brother up and drove him home. He had been hoping that Danni might repay this favour.

'But even a ten-year-old could have seen through that ruse', my source told me.

In any case, the kidnapping provoked a retaliation. Just before Midsummer, the Boxer and several of his friends were leaving their regular haunt, the Galaxy Café in Värnhem, where many young boys went for online gaming. The moment the group walked out the door, they were met by a volley of shots. The group of heavily armed men who were firing at them had been waiting for them outside. Apparently, the Boxer was the main target, and he did receive minor injuries. However, three of the people who had been there with him, two of whom were brothers, were shot dead.

During the summer of 2018, this triple killing outside the Galaxy Café led to three further slayings within the same conflict. One of those shot was one of the individuals who had been arrested for kidnapping Danni's brother. After that, Malmö was fairly quiet for a year, until the next murder occurred. That case would end up shaking all of Sweden to its core.

*

One morning towards the end of August 2019, a friend of Danni's, known as Niff, left his home in central Malmö with his partner, an intern physician called Karolin Hakim. They had their newborn daughter with them. When the couple walked out through the front door, two masked men approached them and opened fire. The first two shots were aimed at Niff, but missed. Running for his life, he dropped his daughter, whom he had been holding, in the chaos. He disappeared around a corner with one of the gunmen following him, while Karolin ran to her daughter to pick her up. Several witnesses who had heard the shots had come out onto their balconies, and saw the second masked gunman turn to face the mother and her child. Without any hesitation, he walked over to her and fired several shots. Karolin turned her body as the first bullets hit her, as if to protect the child, and then collapsed to the ground. Her daughter slipped from her hands and landed by her side on the pavement.

Several witnesses heard the spent cartridges clatter against the ground. In the next moment, they saw the man who was standing at Karolin Hakim's feet point his gun at her head, and pull the trigger.

Many have wondered why she, who wasn't involved, had been executed in such a ruthless manner. It's been claimed that it was because she recognized the shooter, and called his name as she pleaded with him to stop.

'He didn't want to leave any witnesses behind', an informed source explained to me.

The murder added further fuel to the already deadly conflict between the Boxer's and Danni's networks.

'Killing women just proves what filth they are', one of the Boxer's enemies told me.

Two months later, one of the Boxer's close friends was shot dead on Munkhättegatan, a street in Malmö. The police announced that the attack was carried out by rivals of the Boxer's.

An individual who was involved in this conflict would later tell me that the escalation of the violence was fuelled by strong desires for vengeance, first for the kidnapping and then for the killings that followed it, most of which remained unsolved.

'It's not at all related to any drug trafficking, although the police still say it is, to get more resources. Any human being would feel hatred and want revenge if their best friends or someone's partner was killed', the man told me.

Another source claimed that it started out as a conflict over drugs and jealousy, but that 'after that, it was all about seeking revenge for earlier acts of revenge'.

When the Boxer's friend was killed on Munkhättegatan, there were already plans in place for the murder of one of Niff's closest friends. These plans were put into action on Christmas Eve 2019. A 36-year-old expat from Malmö, who the police claim was still engaging in drug-related business with Niff and Danni, was slain in the upmarket London district of Battersea. When he returned home from dinner on

Christmas Eve, a shooter who had travelled in from Sweden was waiting for him in a skin-like latex mask. The shooter fired ten shots at the man, who died in front of his wife and his two-year-old son.

The whole conflict seemed like a deadly game of chess, in which both sides did everything in their power to remove the most important pieces on the other side from the game.

*

While Hanski was waiting for Putte to tell him the identity of the person in the picture he sent, time passed by in the largely empty Europol headquarters. Analysts worked in shifts, searching through criminals' chats to make sure they didn't miss any murder plots that had been planned for the upcoming weekend. Intelligence continued to be passed on to colleagues all over the world. New murder plots were always appearing on their screens. Now, it was Malmö's turn. In several chat threads, they saw plans to avenge the death of Karolin Hakim being made, and an investigator who was working on the case in Malmö was quickly fed intelligence from Hanski that revealed that there was a credible threat to somebody's life.

'It keeps coming so frighteningly close. We manage to put the right measures in place to prevent the murders, but the people whose lives we've saved never even find out that it happened', the investigator explained.

It was difficult for local police and the intelligence officer Putte at Noa to follow all the developments in this complicated conflict within the criminal underworld of Malmö. While the police did know that about ten murders and several attempted murders had been committed over the last two years, they seldom got much in the way of detailed information. In any case, Noa had decided to declare a so-called 'special national event' in response to the escalating violence in Malmö. This measure freed up about 100 police officers from all over the country to be deployed to the South region, where they would reinforce local police and help reduce the number of shootings and bombings. This operation, which was codenamed Operation Rimfrost, targeted about 80 key individuals in the region, who had all been identified by police intelligence as the main instigators of the violence.

Putte knew that the Boxer and his closest allies were on that list. He took another look at the picture he had been sent by Hanski, his Finnish colleague at Europol. After looking at the photo for a while, Putte was reminded of a co-worker of his in Malmö who might be able to recognize this person. Perhaps they might be able to get one step closer to finally catching the Boxer.

*

It wasn't unusual for Swedish police to receive surplus intelligence from international collaborative operations. The formal route this was supposed to take required a prosecutor or court to file a European Investigation Order. However, this could be time-consuming, and mostly happened in the context of preliminary investigations. As a result, intelligence professionals had made a habit of forming what they referred to as 'circles of trust'.

This approach allowed police officers in the intelligence services to help prevent major crimes by quickly sharing confidential information with trusted contacts. This system was why the Finn had been given permission to share the photo with Putte.

Relationships like the one between Putte and Hanski were often forged at conferences and international meetings. Leadership would grumble occasionally about these conferences, as they tied up highly skilled staff for extended periods of time. But the meetings were beginning to prove increasingly fruitful, as they allowed officers to connect with colleagues and engage in mutually beneficial collaborations.

An unwritten law governed all these interactions: any information shared to prevent an offence had to be treated with care, and the source was never to be revealed. Data wasn't to be passed on to prosecutors, or included as evidence in criminal investigations. Instead, the details were 'cleaned up' and presented among analyses and searches performed using Swedish databases before ever being passed on to any investigative teams. The local investigators didn't need to know where the information actually came from.

This approach wasn't entirely unproblematic.

Any Swedish police officer who received information about a crime in Sweden would normally be legally obliged to file a report. However, confidentiality in foreign affairs took precedence over this principle, and thus the source had to be kept secret. This was a case where two separate pieces of legislation contradicted one another, but in which foreign policy considerations ultimately took priority.

For Putte, so far, this all seemed like a routine case in which he was helping a colleague identify an individual who lived at a certain address. However, despite knowing about this secret operation, he had no idea how serious the matter really was.

Even though it was Easter, Putte sent the picture on to his colleague in Malmö, hoping that it might be somebody who was close to the Boxer, a potential lead that might help bring about an arrest. But it wasn't.

At this point, the Boxer had been able to keep himself off the police's radar for a year and a half. Putte sent the disappointing news that he couldn't identify the person in the picture to Hanski, who sent more information back a few moments later. This time, Putte received a screenshot of a map of a part of Västerås.

'Do you know of anyone interesting who lives here?' Hanski asked.

Putte entered some street names from the centre of Västerås into the hitta.se, a Swedish directory website, and proceeded to cross-reference the names that appeared with various police databases. At first, he didn't find anything that seemed interesting, but when he repeated this procedure on some of the neighbouring streets, he came across something.

An interesting name turned up on a street called Treklövergatan.

The wife of a man named Maykil Yokhanna lived in a flat on that street, in a light-brown brick building. Maykil was a prominent criminal in Vårby gård in southern Stockholm who had a reputation for being good at forming relationships and getting people to join him. He was often seen sporting a man bun and sideburns, and was considered potentially violent. He and his wife had recently been involved in a high-profile shooting that the police had gathered a lot of intelligence about.

Just a few months earlier, at least twenty-six rounds had been fired at the couple's car at a petrol station at Kungens kurva in Stockholm. A friend of theirs was in the car with them. The real target was Maykil, but it was the driver, Maykil's friend, who ended up taking several shots to the head, neck, chest and back. The friend would later die from these injuries, while Maykil escaped unscathed. His wife was hit in the head, and suffered serious injuries.

The shooter had ties to Maykil's mortal enemies in the Vårby network. This conflict had been going on for quite a few years, and it had already resulted in several murders and attempted murders.

If his wife lived at this address in Västerås, it seemed likely that Maykil might also be staying there.

Putte took another look at the wedding photo. When he compared it to pictures of Maykil and his wife from the police's internal files, he was convinced. The person in the photo was Maykil.

4

Just before midnight, Putte received an encrypted email from Hanski. It contained a secret intelligence report that put all the seemingly random questions he had received from Europol that evening into context.

The dossier included information from Encrochat, and explained that the map image that was shared with Putte was discovered in messages sent by criminals who were trying to locate a specific target: Maykil Yokhanna, the man Putte had identified in Hanski's picture.

Had they found him? Putte wondered to himself as he browsed the file.

He paused when he read one of the messages, and quickly realized that the answer to his question was right in front of him. Maykil's enemies had located the address.

'My soldiers are ready', an individual who was using the alias Mujaheed wrote.

As Putte read on, he learned that weapons and a hideout near Maykil's home on Treklövergatan had been provided. The hideout was a flat that they would escape to right after the hit, where they could lie low and avoid the police.

Putte also noted that someone had posted a photo of a car a few days earlier. It was taken at a car park in the residential area where someone was hoping to catch sight of Maykil.

'We'll head out and hide with our weapons', the other person wrote to Mujaheed.

The answer he received was three flexing-arm emojis.

As Putte read more of these chat logs, he realized that the murder was actually being plotted at this very moment.

He put his glass of red wine down immediately, and logged on to his police computer to check the records. His wife had grown used to having the phone ring at all hours of the day. She quickly realized that he was working on another serious case, and left him to it at their large dining table, which was decorated with tulips and Easter branches.

Within a few minutes, Putte was beginning to relax.

The target, Maykil, wasn't home. He was safe, in jail. He had been arrested six days earlier in the company of two other suspects, for possession of two handguns.

However, Putte's anxiety from a few moments ago began to return when he realized that he didn't know where Maykil's wife was. She had just survived an attempt on her life. He wondered whether she was in danger now.

Because of the strict confidentiality involved, Putte had to tread lightly. Accidentally revealing the source would have been a disaster.

He called his contacts in the police forces of Västerås and Uppsala, and made it clear to them that he had reliable intelligence that suggested that there was an ongoing threat to life.

'How would you rate your source?' one colleague asked him.

'My source is highly credible', Putte replied, and left it at that.

His colleagues appreciated how serious the situation was, and soon a large detail of police officers was sent out to scout the area and maintain a presence of marked patrol cars. The hope was that this would discourage any would-be assassins from carrying out their plot.

Pandora's Box

Before Putte went to bed, he received assurance that the situation at the couple's home was 'under control'.

*

However, Putte was completely unaware of the drama that had been unfolding between the would-be shooter and the people who had planned the hit on Maykil. Chat logs that wouldn't come to light until much later reveal that the seventeen-year-old boy who had been sent to Västerås to shoot Maykil had come down with a serious case of cold feet. It was the boy's father's birthday, and he wanted to go home to celebrate it.

'I love you with all my heart, but it's my dad's birthday on Friday and I have to go', the seventeen-year-old wrote to his superior.

The teenager insisted that he was confident that the other guy he was there with would be fully capable of getting the job done on his own.

Then, the answer arrived:

'Brother, I told you! No babying out. This is serious.'

The person who was writing this was a captain of the Vårby network, a criminal group that was organized according to a military-style hierarchy. Chihab Lamouri was the leader of the organization, and had a group of captains below him who took responsibility for things such as managing cars and weapons, as well as controlling the drug trade in their respective neighbourhoods in the south of Stockholm. The bottom tier was populated by young soldiers who carried out the tasks their elders assigned to them. It wasn't really too surprising that the group worked this way. When Lamouri was growing up, many of the older criminals in the area had backgrounds in various motorcycle gangs, which are known to have highly hierarchical organizations.

The captain told the seventeen-year-old to stay where he was, and offered to buy a present for his father. This didn't convince the teenager, who apologized, but continued to beg to be allowed to go home. At this point, the captain told the boy that he was embarrassing him. The teenager panicked, and continued to express his doubts about the mission. The leader, Chihab Lamouri, soon learnt what was going on.

'You can't decide to just run away when you're in the middle of something, that's not OK', wrote the Encro alias Mujaheed – which has since been linked to Lamouri – to the adult shooter who was there to carry out the mission with the teenager.

'Brother, who is this brat?' Lamouri wrote to the captain who had been contacted by the seventeen-year-old.

The captain grew angry, and told the teenager off for being a coward and making him look bad.

'You fucking freak.'

'Listen, you have to stay there, brother.'

'This is more important than anything else.'

Then, in capitals:

'YOU'RE EMBARRASSING ME.'

'STOP BEING SUCH A BABY.'

'FINISH THIS.'

A few minutes later, relieved, the teenager reported that he had just learned that Maykil was in police custody, and that he wouldn't need to do any more 'babying'.

It was never revealed whether the seventeen-year-old was ever given some kind of punishment for defying his orders. But whatever else happened, no murder was committed that evening or on Good Friday.

5

On the night of Good Friday, Putte called his immediate superior, the lead intelligence officer Cattis. He wanted a meeting with her. Cattis ran day-to-day operations, and was highly experienced. Putte told her that big things were coming down the pipeline, but that he wasn't able to discuss them over the phone. Emil Eisersjö, head of the Noa intelligence section and manager of operations there, was also invited to their meeting, along with a close, long-time colleague of Putte's.

The next day, they all gathered in Emil's office. They left their mobile phones outside the room in a noisebox, which was supposed to prevent other countries' intelligence services from listening in on their conversation. Then, Putte, Cattis, Emil and their colleague all sat down in a room with windows that overlooked Kronobergsparken.

'This is big, really big', Putte began, taking in the little group around the table.

He didn't often get too excited, but he was definitely excited now.

'It's like opening Pandora's box', he continued, without elaborating on how he acquired the intelligence on Maykil that Hanski had sent him.

He was interrupted by Emil Eisersjö, who wanted a clear idea of what was going on. The four of them had worked together for a long time, and they all had a great deal of trust in one another, and so the operational manager of the intelligence department felt entitled to insist on knowing more.

'We need to be able to talk openly here. We need to put all the cards on the table, and I need to know what it is we have', Emil Eisersjö said in his strong, Gotland accent. 'What is the source of all this intelligence?'

Not until then did Putte tell the others what his contacts at Europol had revealed to him: the Encrochat platform's encryption had been broken. They looked at each other, all realizing how huge this was. This could give them a proper opportunity to go after the main users of encrypted phones: the leaders of Swedish organized crime.

'This is going to be bigger than anything else. We have to cancel all other operations. This is a once-in-a-lifetime chance', said Putte. 'This is as good as it gets.'

'It's like Enigma in the Second World War', Emil added.

'We'll need to prepare for this', Putte pointed out. 'There's going to be more of this intelligence coming in.'

*

Five years before this, Emil Eisersjö had spent his entire police career working in the field. When he was an undercover officer, he took part in extensive efforts to disrupt the criminal networks that operated in the southern parts of Stockholm. He had gone out to look for members of groups that were embroiled in bloody conflicts, stopped them for checks when they were driving around in the streets, and joined the task forces who broke down their doors to carry out raids. He had done it all, many times over.

Policing wasn't his job; policing was his life.

As time went by, he grew more and more keen to work in police intelligence. When the police force was reorganized in 2015, he applied for a leadership position with the intelligence department in the Stockholm region, but ended up going for an interview with the head of Noa's intelligence section, Linda H. Staaf. She suggested to Emil that he apply for a position with her department, instead of the one at the region. This was a bit strange, considering the fact that Emil had once slated the whole department she'd recently been made head of, insisting that 'They never produce anything useful.'

After some persuasion, however, he agreed.

*

When Emil learnt that Encro had been cracked, he immediately began to ponder the next big question: how could they set up an organization that was capable of handling a continuous flow of intelligence like the one the Europol contact had promised them? The data might contain information related to violent crimes, and in those cases, the police would need to be able to respond quickly. However, enthusiastic colleagues and high hopes wouldn't be enough to convince Noa management to redirect all available resources to the intelligence department.

Emil Eisersjö wondered how he should approach this. He didn't have a single official document to present to Noa leadership about this operation.

The Swedish police were already under an extreme amount of pressure due to all the shootings and murders they were dealing with. All over, resources were constantly being called in to carry out whatever tasks were at the top of the current list of priorities.

Sweden wasn't yet directly involved in the main Encro operation, which was being managed by the French police at Europol. So far, the whole Swedish operation was Putte and his two colleagues in Gothenburg and Malmö, who were being sent specific intelligence by Hanski. How many serious violent offences might they learn about? Could Noa handle this on their own, or did they need to bring in every regional police force in the country, as well?

Before the meeting was over, Putte had been instructed to let Europol know that Sweden wanted to participate in the operation, and that any intelligence shared by Europol would be treated as strictly confidential, and used only to take preventative action against serious crimes that were uncovered.

'Make it clear that we're very grateful for anything we can get, and that we're capable of handling the information', Emil said.

Putte was also tasked with finding out all he could about the operation, without pushing his contacts at Europol too far. It was a delicate mission, to say the least. He wouldn't want to be too nosy and accidentally close the door on a collaboration that could make such a huge difference for Swedish law enforcement.

6

A few days after briefing his colleagues about Encrochat, Putte received new intelligence from Hanski. The Boxer, who had fled the country after his bloody conflict with Danni, had finally been located. He was no longer in Spain.

'He's in Dubai.'

Putte felt his hopes rekindle when he heard Hanski's words. Finding the Boxer was a top priority, for Noa and Europol alike.

Putte had been suspecting that the Boxer might have left Spain for some time, as he was wanted by the police there for bombings and contract killings. Thanks to information from the Encrochat server, Europol had been able to identify an individual who wrote in Swedish and was in regular contact with people in both the Costa del Sol in Spain and the Malmö region.

However, before the police could act on the intelligence they had on the Boxer, Putte and his colleagues were already busy preparing for a Swedish Encrochat operation.

On Friday 24 April 2020, Noa held a meeting to discuss how to proceed with the intelligence they would soon be receiving from Europol.

One of the people in the meeting was the lead intelligence officer, Cattis. When the meeting ended, she wrote a cryptic note on her computer.

'New case: Robinson.'

This would become the Swedish codename for the Encro operation, because it happened to be Friday when Noa began its work in earnest, and Friday was the name of Robinson Crusoe's friend in the novel by Daniel Defoe.

In recent weeks, Hanski, Putte's contact, had been moved up in the chain of command and began to make the case that Sweden ought to be invited to join the operation. This wasn't just a matter of his having faith in the trustworthiness of the Swedish police – it was also necessary, as it soon became apparent that there were almost 800 Encrochat users in Sweden. The growing Encro material exposed the activities of hundreds of Swedish criminals who would go on to demonstrate an extreme capacity for violence.

Involving the Swedish police was going to be necessary to save lives.

*

In the previous few days, Cattis had been in touch with Solveig Wollstad, Sweden's representative at Eurojust, the European Union Agency for Criminal Justice Cooperation.

Cattis briefed her on the operation and asked her the following questions: 'Are we able to participate in this? Is it legal for us? What legal justification would we have for this operation?'

'I advised them that using the material was allowed', Solveig Wollstad would later tell me.

According to Cattis, Solveig explained that this was a French case, and that a French court had authorized the surveillance activities, so it was up to them whether they wanted to share intelligence from their own ongoing criminal investigation through Europol. However, the understanding was that any data shared in this way was not to be used in preliminary investigations at this stage. A European Investigation

Order could be filed later to request the materials, and any requests of that kind were to be sent to Sweden's representative at Eurojust – Wollstad herself. She was the one who would have to assess the legitimacy of any investigation order before forwarding it to the French Eurojust representative, who would then, in turn, contact the relevant judge in their own country.

Cattis double-checked this with Head Prosecutor Lise Tamm at the National Unit against Organized Crime, or Rio. The two of them had known each other since the mid-1990s, and Tamm came to the same conclusion, by similar reasoning. Everything had been done by the book.

In addition to this, Swedish courts utilize a principle of free examination and evaluation of evidence, something that would prove very important for the Encrochat operation. The point of this principle is that all parties in a trial can present any evidence they manage to obtain, and the value of the evidence they present is to be assessed by the court as it sees fit. This applies even to evidence that has been obtained by questionable means, as long as there hasn't been torture involved. In other countries, such as the United States and the United Kingdom, the admissibility of evidence is regulated very differently.

The head of Rio appointed his colleague, prosecutor Henrik Söderman, to serve as a Swedish contact person for the international Encrochat operation. He was fearless, tech-savvy and very experienced. He drew the same conclusion regarding the legality of the operation as his boss had done before him. His role, then, would be to prepare for the day when it became possible to request the chat logs themselves from France, so that they could be used in preliminary investigations.

Noa's Linda H. Staaf acknowledged that this approach – tapping a server in France to access the communications of Swedish citizens – was controversial. Nobody had ever done that kind of thing in Sweden before. This aspect of the operation would indeed be challenged by defence lawyers and others, who would argue that the operation constituted an 'indiscriminate act of mass surveillance' of communications in another state, in violation of Swedish law.

'Whether it would be legal or not in Sweden is beside the point, because the information was obtained in the course of a French investigation, in compliance with French law', Solveig Wollstad explained to me.

She pointed out that the EU operates under a principle of mutual recognition of national legislations, and that this serves as the basis for all judicial collaborations between member states. Law enforcement cooperation would be very difficult without this principle.

Even though it meant exposing herself to potential criticism, Staaf decided to go ahead. This was a rare opportunity for the police to make a move against the criminals 'who are causing so much misery in our society'. She would rather find herself answering questions about why the police chose to access the chats than questions about why they decided not to. The fact that doing this could save lives outweighed any fear she might have had of facing criticism, and, besides, the prosecutors in Rio had informed her that French law had been observed.

'Too many people are too anxious, too afraid of making mistakes. I wanted to go on the offensive, but within the confines of the law, of course', she told me when we met much later.

Another argument that was put forward was that Swedish law enforcement wasn't allowed to feign ignorance of ongoing plans to commit violent crimes.

'Turning down this opportunity to get intelligence simply wasn't an option', prosecutor Henrik Söderman explained to me.

*

Just a few days later, Noa received an invitation to a digital meeting with Europol. Putte, Cattis and two other colleagues from Noa participated.

The Swedes were informed that a secret data-interception operation of some kind had been under way since 1 April, targeting Encrochat's server in northern France. Encrochat had been cracked as the result of a collaboration between France and the Netherlands, and the other countries that had already been invited were Spain, the UK, Germany and Norway.

French prosecutor Alexandre, who was directing the operation from Lille, explained that his team had learnt of several active murder conspiracies in Sweden when they observed where Encrochat users were connecting to the network from. Neither France nor Europol had the legal authority or resources to prevent crimes in Sweden without the assistance of the Swedish authorities. Because of the seriousness of the crimes in question, inviting the Swedes to join the team had become a top priority.

The Finnish Europol investigator Hanski had already been making this case. Alexandre also had a great degree of trust in the Swedish justice system, after past cooperations with Swedish police and prosecutors. To be allowed to participate in the operation, the Swedish team members would be expected to observe the same special conditions as other participants. Strict confidentiality was demanded, without exception. The UK would soon learn this the hard way. British police were expelled from the collaboration after a court case in which details concerning international meetings at Eurojust had been revealed.

'They violated the confidentiality agreement', Alexandre explained.

The intelligence gathered from Encrochat was only to be used to prevent serious crimes, such as murder, and even the officers who took part in apprehending potential murderers weren't to learn where the intelligence came from. All they were to be told was that a certain individual would be carrying a weapon at a certain time. The suspect would be arrested on suspicion of possession of a firearm. The real reasons for the arrest mustn't be revealed to prosecutors or police officers involved in the case until the international Encrochat operation came to an end and France officially shared the secret chat logs.

Once the delegates at the meeting had worked out all the legal issues involved, a member of Europol's senior management began to speak. He gave the small, Swedish delegation an uncertain look.

'Is that all of you?' the Europol chief asked them.

'Yes', Cattis replied tentatively.

'You might want to rethink that', he said, with concern in his voice. 'You're going to be getting thousands of chats.'

PART 2
THE CHAIN
MARCH 2020

7

When he was in Stockholm, Donvar got around in a new Volkswagen Passat. He couldn't drive overly luxurious cars, or the police would hassle him. He didn't even have a driving licence, but he still kept a car for his friends and relatives to drive him in when he needed a lift. Whenever he walked around in Stockholm, he was careful not to wear expensive designer clothes and watches that cost a decent yearly salary to buy. He only wore things like that during trips abroad.

His goal was to earn 20 or 25 million in the drug business. After that, he'd be able to retire, ideally in a warmer country.

It was towards the end of upper secondary school, when his interest in his studies had begun to wane despite his occasional moments of brilliance as a student, that he began to think seriously about how to make big money. He'd prefer to have it as soon as possible, too, without having to grind his way through classes at the adult education centre and then go on to some demanding university programme. He got in touch with one of the older guys in his neighbourhood, and bought 20 or 30 grams of cocaine to start with. He sold this on to customers. The work suited him perfectly: he was charming, articulate and sociable.

He sold out quickly, and then managed to secure a supply of good cocaine from his connection. One day, he made up his mind: if he was going to be doing this at all, he would have to go all-in. The more risks he took, the more money he would be able to make. He wanted to play the game at the highest levels. The older guys always used to say that for any single unlucky moment, which might earn them some time in prison, they always had ninety-nine lucky moments.

He liked those odds.

'Why should I sell 20 grams when I could sell a kilo?' Donvar thought to himself. His business was growing quickly, and he soon brought people in to work for him, many of whom he paid monthly salaries to hold drugs for him in their homes.

When he got an Encro phone, his whole world changed. All it took was being prepared to trust your friends. He had recruited a team of loyal workers to handle the drugs and money for him, all to minimize the danger of getting caught. If the police took one of his shipments, he was confident that his workers would never snitch on him.

He was also careful to stay well clear of anything that might get him arrested. He'd hardly even met most of the people who worked for him in real life. Many of them came to him by recommendation, and sometimes he would have a trusted friend meet with them to determine if they were up to the job. Some of them were local kids from his neighbourhood, and others were ethnic Swedes. Donvar preferred workers who had legitimate incomes, homes of their own and driving licences. They would be able to transport and hold drugs for him, and take care of themselves without arousing any undue suspicions. And Donvar paid them well.

Like most drug-dealing networks, his had a lot of young people on the payroll. They were about seventeen years old and up, and most of them were hungry lads who were dedicated to the goal of making money. He felt particularly responsible for them, because some of them were from his own neighbourhood, or even the younger brothers of his own friends and acquaintances. Donvar never felt any obligation to turn somebody away when they approached him for work, just because they were young. He sometimes told them not to waste their money, to stop walking around in Adidas, and even encouraged them to stay in school.

'Don't be a monkey – be an Einstein!' he would tell them.

He didn't feel that he had taken advantage of those kids; as he saw it, all he did was channel their ambition.

'I've never met anyone who was forced to hang out on the square, anyone who *had* to do these things. Except, of course, people who had debts to work off. But everyone down on the square is there of their own free will', he said.

After a moment's reflection, however, he added that many did end up in debt. This often happened after the police seized a stash of drugs. Some chose to leave the country, disappearing for a while in the hope that their debts would be forgotten. They were wrong, though. Sooner or later, they would have to make things right. That's where the violence entered the picture. You had to set the odd example here and there, or people would start trying to exploit your good nature, and refuse to pay for your goods. This was the paradox of the police's fight against gang crime: every time they seized some drugs, thus removing goods from the market, somebody would inevitably end up in trouble as a result, and this might well seed further conflict.

'I don't care. I want my money', Donvar explained.

He's serious. I asked him, delicately, what he might be prepared to do to somebody who failed to clear a debt.

'I don't think it's worth killing people over drugs or money. But that person would just have to find some way or other to pay their debt.'

Donvar had the caution he has maintained for all these years to thank for having managed to keep his criminal record so clean. As a result, he was free to move around relatively undisturbed. He had worked his way up, and was now running a well-organized operation that turned over many millions. By the spring of 2020, he was exclusively selling his customers half or whole bricks of cocaine at a time. He bought it by the kilo from his supplier, who took care of the smuggling operations. A brick is 1 kilo, and a *gubbe*, 'old man', is 1 gram. The pandemic was in full swing, and the borders were closed, but the drugs kept flowing all the same. The mules always found a way in. Having the best supply chains gave you a great opportunity to make big money. Sometimes, a shipment of, say, 80 kilos of hashish would arrive; another time, 200 kilos was hauled over by lorry, all the way from Spain. But Donvar's preferred product was cocaine, because it tended to yield the best returns.

The buyers were most anxious before the cargo had crossed the French border, where, according to Donvar, the Customs checks are the most rigorous. However, of the transports that got through to France, which was the majority of them, up to 90 per cent would end up crossing the Öresund Bridge, he claimed. The checks there were easy to pass through.

Which shipments made it past the first checks and entered Europe was mainly a matter of luck, assuming you hadn't bribed the Customs officials. But that kind of thing was only ever done by people who operated on higher levels than he did. They were the big players, who brought in large quantities of cocaine from South America and had huge amounts of cash to spend on bribes for corrupt port and Customs workers. According to the police's own intelligence reports, there were eighty-four major drug traffickers whose operations reached Sweden. It was estimated that around forty operators each were bringing in more than 1 tonne of drugs each year – some of them up to 8 tonnes. Many of them were based in Spain and the Netherlands. Donvar told me that this might be true, but that these individuals were probably only the faces of their organizations, the people who had attracted the most attention. Behind them, he estimates that there are probably another hundred or so like him, who have money

The Chain

and share the risk of bringing in the drugs. Most of these individuals evaded police attention completely.

He painted me a picture of Sweden as a place where there were numerous operators at work, who were all in business with each other in various ways. It all sounded a bit like a team of superstar real estate brokers who worked together. The only difference was that the business these people were in involved trading large quantities of drugs and distributing them to smaller operators through various channels. Donvar told me that if he'd started selling drugs ten years earlier, and had more time to grow his network of contacts, he 'would have been Pablo Escobar by now'.

He had invested the money he had made in real estate, in Sweden and abroad, which he still rented out. To eliminate any connections to himself, the properties were registered as belonging to his relatives and family members. He also owned several expensive watches, including a rose gold Rolex Daytona that was worth more than 400,000 kronor. Despite this, he told me that 'Money can't buy happiness.' The criminal lifestyle was burdensome, too: trust issues and stress were constant strains. It wasn't so much that he was worried about getting caught, since he always avoided socializing with other criminals. What got to him was the constant pressure of having to bring in the new goods that his workers and customers were eagerly waiting for.

His parents had long suspected that their son might be involved in something illegal. Where else could all that money come from? Nonetheless, they had turned a blind eye to his business, despite their absolute abhorrence of anything related to drugs. They hated drugs more than anything else.

'Anybody who takes drugs is selling their soul', Donvar's parents had told him, in their native language.

'I don't sell drugs', Donvar assured them, sincerely.

He was always able to milk the fact that he had never been sent to prison.

'It seems like your blood has been poisoned by money. When money gets a hold on you, it can be a drug worse than heroin', his parents had told him.

Donvar told me that he thought they might actually be right about this. That was exactly what had happened to him. He wasn't proud of making his money by dealing drugs, but he couldn't see himself earning an income like that from a regular job.

Who ended up buying his goods was none of Donvar's business, as he saw it. They were all adults. If they hadn't bought from him, others would gladly have sold to them.

8

One of the people who bought drugs from the networks in Stockholm was Sara, a girl in her twenties who had managed to stay under the radar and avoid attracting the interest of the police. She had done her best to operate with caution. She dressed neatly, and always tried to blend in with her surroundings.

One day, she had wandered around the Farsta shopping centre for two hours, waiting for a customer she had been supposed to be selling 2 kilos of cannabis to. She wore glasses and a veil, even though she was actually an Orthodox Christian. The idea was to avoid attracting any undue attention. Business was good. She thought of herself as an entrepreneur, although her plans to go to university and pursue a career as an accountant or lawyer had been shelved.

Life got in the way.

After upper secondary school, she had been depressed and started spending most of her time at home, numbing her anxiety with cannabis and cocaine. She would smoke 50 grams of cannabis a week. It was a costly habit, and she had no income besides the benefits she received from the Social Insurance Agency. When she had paid her rent, she had just 3,000 kronor left in her account. A friend of hers, who knew her life story – with two destructive parents and a father in prison – had asked her this:

'You've got more balls than anyone I know. You grew up in this life, and now you're broke. Why don't you just start dealing?'

*

Having grown up with criminal parents, she had always felt contempt for people who dealt drugs or engaged in other criminality. There were plenty of events she thought she had dreamt that later turned out to be actual memories from her childhood. Her dad, high, digging for drugs he'd hidden in a cemetery. Or the time when they hid a gun in her clothes during a car ride, hoping that if the police stopped them, they might not search their daughter.

If someone had told her that she would become a criminal when she was fifteen, she would never have believed them. It was unthinkable. She remembered one time when she threw a party in her home, and some guy lit a joint.

'I picked up a chair and bashed him over the head with it.'

'"Don't do drugs in my flat", I yelled at him.'

The pendulum swung quickly, however. Being both attractive and sociable, she had always had an easy time making new friends. Before she realized it, she was attending lots of parties around Stureplan with the heirs of wealthy families. Moving in those circles and going to those parties had begun to give Sara the idea that she was also going to live in a big expensive flat or a fancy house in Danderyd one day.

'I thought that spending time with rich people would somehow make me rich, too.'

She soon developed more tolerant attitudes to partying and taking drugs. And the lines faded completely when she followed her friend's advice and began dealing. At first, it was just cannabis, and her only customers were ten of her closest friends. She bought cheap 'dirt weed' and sold it on. Within three months, though, she had more money, better cannabis, a list of 266 customers in her phone book, and orders coming in every day. She could move half a kilo of cannabis in a week, and earn a total of 70,000 kronor. About 30,000 of that was profit that she could pocket for herself. She believed that what allowed her to get her business up and running so quickly was the fact that she was a girl in an industry dominated by men.

'My number was being passed around all over the place. Everyone wanted to buy from a girl. They thought it was kind of cool, and more discreet. I never gave anyone a headache. I spoke good Swedish, and I had sophisticated manners.'

At first, she continued to socialize with her new, rich friends. She never told them that she made her money selling drugs – the only person she told was a former boyfriend. He went on to become one of her best customers, ordering 5 grams of coke every Friday.

'The rich ones were the worst', Sara explained, telling me how her ex-boyfriend would sometimes tell her to bring a friend, so they could 'make it a threesome'.

One night, he tried to lick her ear. It made her feel 'like dirt, like a whore'. She was only there to do her job. She felt everything turn black.

'Touch me again, and I'll slit your throat and take all your money. Are we clear?'

The man paid for his goods and left.

Another time, she was invited to a club to deliver drugs to a group of financial bankers. Deep inside, she could feel all her self-esteem draining away. In upper secondary school, she'd always felt that she could do anything she wanted, even though her grades were rather mediocre. Now, she was just a kid from the ghetto, 'Farsta glitter', as they used to call girls from the suburbs who ventured into the city to mingle with the jet set.

But when she was conducting business, when she met with her customers, she would experience that rush that she had heard others talk about. Planning purchases of large quantities of drugs was exciting. The trip had to be planned in minute detail. After that, it was all about getting into the right frame of mind. She needed to stay vigilant and keep her wits about her. She never listened to gangster rap when she was driving to a meet to buy drugs. Instead, she would play ABBA in the car. She figured that if she was stopped by the police, it would be impossible for them to suspect that somebody who was listening to that kind of music might have kilos of drugs stashed away in the trunk.

Having a lot of customers, though, came with a greater risk that one of them might end up getting caught and set the police on the trail back to her. Because of this, she moved her business over to the encrypted app Wickr, which her drug suppliers had told her about.

*

Whenever she brought in a new batch of product to sell, she would send a message to the hundreds of customers who soon joined her Wickr channel.

'Hi everyone, hope you're all well! Here's the menu', she began, and then went on to describe strains of cannabis with phrases like 'aromatic notes of earthy pine and lemon'. 'Great coke' was available, at a cost of 800 kronor for 0.7 grams. Larger quantities could be arranged, too, of course. At the end of the menu, her customers would find Tramadol listed. She charged 300 kronor for a blister pack of pills, but offered a discount for larger purchases.

At the end of her message, Sara would inform her customers that home deliveries could be arranged for an added fee. She encouraged them to get in touch with any questions, and ended the message with 'all the best' or 'best regards'.

When she sent her menu out, it never took long for the notifications to start pouring in from the app. She logged in and saw that a customer had placed an order. It was a man she knew, and she confirmed that she could come and make a delivery outside his workplace.

She usually took the metro, but this address was close enough for her to get to by electric scooter instead. Fifteen minutes later, she arrived, parked the scooter, and walked over to her customer, who was happy to see her. She hugged him, and as she did so, she dropped the drugs off in his left pocket and withdrew the cash that was waiting there for her.

'How are you doing? It's great to see you!' she said.

'You too! How are you?' the customer asked.

They walked to a more secluded location. To outsiders, this all looked like two friends meeting. Nobody could ever have guessed that she was a drug dealer making a delivery to a customer.

After her move to Wickr, her income grew quickly, and she soon found herself raking in amounts that she had only dreamt of before. She shows me a picture from those days, in which she's reclining on a black couch in a tracksuit under a pile of 500-kronor notes, staring straight at the camera with a Calippo ice lolly in her hand.

Back in her flat, she sorted her cash into various shoeboxes from Gucci and Louis Vuitton. Each box would contain the profits she had made from a certain drug. She had studied business administration in secondary school, and had developed an elaborate system for her cash management. Most of the profit was to be saved. However, she allowed herself to spend the profits she had made from cocaine freely, reserving this money for impulse purchases. It was 'quick money', and coke was easy to sell. Emergency expenses, like when her dishwasher broke down, would be covered with cash from the ecstasy box. That was her emergency fund. Whenever a shoebox had more than 20,000 kronor in it, she moved that cash to the home of an acquaintance, a customer whom Sara provided with free drugs in exchange for letting her keep her savings there. She kept an 'office', as she calls it, in the home of another customer. This was a flat where she kept her stash, and packed the deliveries she would be making to her customers.

*

One Friday night, during the time when her earnings were at their greatest, and her life was at its best, she was in a seedy bar at Skanstull in Södermalm with one of her girlfriends. They were drinking beer, and talking about their lives. Even though she was raking in cash, she didn't feel that she was really making any progress in life.

'I have plenty of money, but I never treat myself to anything.'

A short while later, a black limousine pulled up outside. The two friends got in, and the driver poured them each a glass of champagne. Then, they just drove around the night-time streets of Stockholm. They listened to Yasin, snorted cocaine and drank bubbly. For a moment, she felt like a big-time drug kingpin. After driving for a while, the driver stopped and asked the girls: 'Aren't we going to pick up your friends?'

'No, no, this is just for us', Sara replied, handing him several 500-kronor notes and telling him to keep driving. He was surprised. He wasn't used to driving two young girls who were out on their own.

'What do you do for a living? Are you a stripper?' the driver asked.

Sara was annoyed at this, and her brash, ghetto attitude came out in full.

'Strippers are my customers. They come to me for a little something for their anxiety', she explained, giving the driver a look that made it clear to him that he'd better shut up and do his job.

During this time, she was in a destructive relationship with a guy who was a member of a criminal network. They needed a flat, and Sara knew someone who said he wanted to rent them one, but then changed his mind before they could move in. Her boyfriend's friends decided to fine Sara a significant amount of money, because they knew she would be good for it. Her own boyfriend threatened to break up with her if she didn't do as his friends demanded. But she refused.

Following this, the network issued her a temporary 'dealing ban', and she was no longer allowed to buy drugs from them. She was devastated by this. She suffered a panic attack, and began to worry what might happen next. This was supposed to be her path to a better life, she thought to herself. But the truth was that she was working in a business full of macho men who viewed women as possessions.

'Many girls who leave relationships like that after several years have been beaten half to death', she told me.

The ban was lifted when a friend of hers paid the arbitrary fines. When the time came for her to get back on her feet, she reached out to several different networks who had wares to offer her. She travelled to Tensta, where she was robbed of 80,000 kronor during a meet where she was supposed to be buying hashish. However, she recognized one of the robbers, and phoned some people she knew, and they managed to get her money back for her.

Another time, she was involved in ripping off somebody else, a guy who used to receive 2-kilo packages of hashish from Morocco by mail order. He had been promised a 'salary' and threatened Sara when she didn't pay him for a delivery. He hadn't realized that she had shared the order with a group of other, more violent, individuals. In response to his threats, she and two guys locked him inside a wardrobe. With a gun to his head, he was forced to take off her sock and suck on her right big toe to apologise. This was her way of letting the world know what the consequences would be if anybody else tried to mess with her like that.

Robberies, violence and threats were just part of the lifestyle of the people she did business with. Because of this, she was always keen to stay on good terms with her suppliers, the people who brought in large quantities of drugs, so that she would always be able to meet her customers' demand.

Occasionally, though, she still had to approach new suppliers. When she was heading to a meet with a friend, they received word that the whole thing was a set-up, and that they were going to be robbed. Because of this, she never showed up for the exchange.

One night, her phone rang. She answered it, and found herself talking to that supplier, who was demanding that she come outside to resolve the situation. Still in her pyjamas, she put on a winter jacket, a hat and a pair of Uggs. Outside the building, she was held at gunpoint and taken to a wooded area where her male partner, the guy who was supposed to have gone to that meet with her, was kneeling in the snow with a gun pressed to his face.

A small group of teenage boys stood around him. Sara had never met anyone who had such darkness in their eyes as the man who held the gun.

'I don't want any trouble', she said, with tears running down her cheeks, shivering from both the cold and her fear.

After this, she and her friend were allowed to stand back up and go home.

*

After the incident in that wooded area, Sara received some news that would bring her to decide, once and for all, that this life wasn't going to work out for her: she was pregnant with her new boyfriend's baby. Someone close to her, an ex-criminal himself, helped her realize that dealing drugs and parenting were incompatible. Her own childhood was proof enough of that.

'I'm going to save all the money I make until the baby arrives, and then I'll stop', she told one of her oldest customers.

One summer's day, she was contacted by a customer through Wickr. Sara was due in just a few weeks, and she felt heavy. It felt as though every joint in her body was about to give out. The customer wanted to buy 10 grams of cannabis. Because he was a regular, she let him come to her house rather than meeting him down by the shopping centre.

She was happy to have someone to talk to, and having him over was just like having a friend visit. Almost all of Sara's friends from before had abandoned her once word began to get out that she was selling drugs. They were happy enough to take the drugs, but they didn't want to socialize with somebody who made a living dealing them.

While the customer was in her home, her contractions suddenly grew stronger. She recorded them with a pregnancy app, which soon prompted her to start packing a bag and prepare to go into labour.

'Stay here until my boyfriend gets here. He's stuck in traffic', she told the customer.

He was excited, and seemed almost prepared to deliver the baby himself. After a while, he sat down on the floor and placed his bag in front of him.

'Do you mind if I skin up? So I can smoke it later?' he asked, hesitantly.

'Yeah, you can smoke if you want. It's fine', she groaned, and watched him start rolling a joint.

This would be her last sale. After her boyfriend got home, the customer headed on. At midnight, Sara went to the maternity ward, where she gave birth to her baby. Later, with the softness of her child resting against her chest, she arranged to sell her Wickr account to a friend, who took over the 920 customers and the 40 criminal contacts she had accumulated.

9

Maja was a social worker who worked with young people who struggled with drug abuse. She had also been using drugs herself ever since she attended upper secondary school. Now, she was almost thirty, and tonight, she was at a dinner party in a friend's home. They cooked pasta carbonara, listened to music and drank red wine, but as their inebriation began to give over to fatigue, they gave each other a look they knew all too well.

'Let's buy some fucking coke!' one of the guys exclaimed.

It was Maja's turn to place an order on Wickr this time. She usually bought from a girl who was a few years younger than her, who sold a variety of different drugs, but specialized in cannabis. Tonight, though, she chose a different dealer, who usually had good cocaine. Maja already knew what he had on offer after having been sent a long advertisement with a price list earlier that week. At the end of the message was a list of instructions and rules for how the transaction was to occur. No Swish payment app or credit. Have the cash ready. Deliveries were made at 'quiet, peaceful locations, where we won't have to worry about the police'. The final instruction read: 'Sample our wares at home, away from our place of business.'

Half an hour later, she received a message that informed her that the car was outside. Maja hurried down the stairs

The Chain

and spotted a taxi. She climbed into the back seat on the right, where she was met by a girl in her twenties, who was sitting behind the driver. This triggered Maja's curiosity, but it also eased her. Female dealers made her feel safer. That was probably the idea. She handed over a 1,000-kronor note, and received a ball of plastic wrap with the cocaine inside it. She exited the car and headed back to her friends, who cheered when she walked in.

Inside, on the kitchen table, they laid out the white powder on a serving platter. Maja went through the familiar motions of chopping herself a line with her bank card. Her friend, who worked in advertising, turned up the music as Maja rolled up a 500-kronor note and lowered her nose down over the dish.

*

One day in the springtime, I met Maja in a cafe on Södermalm. She was hung over, but she had made the effort to come and see me because she wanted to give me her point of view as a consumer. It felt particularly important to her because her work involved helping people whose lives had been ruined by drugs in different ways.

When I asked her what she thought about her own responsibility in all this, what it meant to be a social worker who bought drugs, she shrugged.

'I think there's something of a double standard to my behaviour, but I don't think I want to give that too much thought', she began.

The reason why she kept doing it was that it was so much fun, and the fun outweighed the downside of doing something that conflicted with her values on a deeper level.

'Those two roles are actually opposed to one another, and so far, I haven't been prepared to take full responsibility for that', she said, and took a sip of tea.

She cared about her clients. They were young kids who had either been selling drugs or ended up in trouble in some other way. They were highly motivated to change their lives.

'But the people I buy my cocaine from are just the same', she said, noting that, of course, she did feel responsible for them to some degree, but also for herself, for breaking her habit.

Maja didn't believe that the blame for the problems that drugs can bring lay solely with the individual. As she said this, she seemed to realize that this might all just be her way of justifying her own drug use.

'I don't think that one person not buying any more would have any impact at all – the market would still be there. This is a major social issue, and solving it will take a lot more than any individual can do', she said.

I asked her for her professional opinion on how we ought to address the current situation, with all the shootings and gang violence, and the addiction and suffering that drugs cause. She told me that she blamed the politicians for the way things have turned out. She would have preferred to see earlier interventions in deprived areas, better funding for schools, better access to housing, and more job opportunities. That would have eliminated many of the causes that send kids down the path to a life of crime and dealing drugs, she claimed.

'Would that reduce the demand for drugs, though?' I asked.

She was quiet for a few seconds.

'That's a difficult question . . .'

PART 3
D-DAY
MAY 2020 – JUNE 2020

PART 3

D-DAY

10

On the morning of 1 May 2020, Putte and three other intelligence officers and directors gathered for a meeting at Noa. The sun was shining in through the meeting room windows, reminding them that summer was near, but the hallways inside Noa were silent and deserted. Many of the staff had been told to work from home as the virus kept spreading. One colleague from the South region had travelled up to Stockholm, and a fifth colleague from the West region was attending remotely by video. They couldn't add any more people to the early part of the meeting, because Noa only had a handful of logins to the platform that hosted their video conferencing. Their Finnish colleague, Hanski, connected from Europol, and gave them a demonstration of how to navigate the chat logs.

Putte soon realized that the material was more detailed than he could have ever imagined. It was like sitting right next to the criminals while they discussed murders, kidnappings, bombings and huge drug shipments. 'We're finally going to be one step ahead of them', Putte thought to himself, but, just as quickly, he realized how enormous the responsibility that now rested on him and a few of his colleagues really was. His initial euphoria gave way to horrific anxiety when he began to read the chats.

Misinterpreting just a single one of these messages could mean getting somebody killed.

They spent the first few days setting up an organizational structure, so that they could process the materials more methodically. An early challenge would be figuring out who the real people behind all the different aliases were. Putte and his closest colleagues would be focusing on identifying people who lived abroad.

They quickly identified the leader of the Vårby network, Chihab Lamouri, as Mujaheed. There had been increasingly frequent sightings of him in Spain lately, and he had appeared in Spanish police surveillance photos in the company of other known criminals from Sweden. Besides sending selfies taken in front of the mirror, Lamouri had been issuing orders to his underlings in Sweden from Spain, including orchestrating the Easter weekend assassination plot against his arch-rival Maykil Yokhanna. As the officers needed to be able to talk without endangering the secrecy of their work, the team set up a call centre in a conference room. They installed screens and computers, and settled into what would be their workplace for the next few months.

To help the team keep up with the huge influx of material, Cattis set up a rotating schedule whereby one member of staff would always be searching for specific search terms among the hundreds of thousands of messages delivered to them by the French.

Before long, they were learning expressions that were new even to experienced police officers.

What the hell is a *japp*? And what's a *goare*?

They soon gathered that *japp* meant that someone was going to be shot, and that a *goare* was a person who lured a target into a trap.

*

On the evening of 4 May, pictures of the rapper Einár begin to circulate on social media. *Aftonbladet* published an article on their website. The rapper had been anonymized in the article, but the pictures showed the seventeen-year-old tied up, beaten and humiliated. That same evening, Einár commented on the kidnapping in a video on his Instagram account.

'Walla, I just have something to tell you. Anyone out there could get kidnapped, anyone out there could get beaten, anyone out there could get . . . I don't know . . . but brother, *benim* is fine. You can see, I'm alive.'

Neither Putte nor his colleagues had noticed the pictures when they were sifting through the chat logs. But, just like everyone else, they saw the pictures that were being sent around. Eventually, after searching through the Encro materials, they found unedited images that had been sent back and forth between certain users a few weeks earlier. Among other things, the pictures showed Haval Khalil, a rapper and Einár's friend at the time, who was said to have been the person who lured the seventeen-year-old to the flat in Vårby where the kidnappers were waiting for him. After further investigation, the police realized that plans had been made to kidnap Einár at a much earlier point in time, with the aid of another rapper, Yasin, but that the whole thing had been called off for some reason. Since there was already a complaint filed regarding the abduction, all they could do for now was gather evidence that might prove useful.

At this point, they also decided to include the seven police regions in their work. There were far too many ongoing conflicts and assassination plots, and there were local intelligence officers working in the various regions who would be more familiar with their local criminals. Keeping track of all the thousands of chats that Europol delivered each day was an insurmountable task for this small team of Noa officers.

However, bringing more people into the operation was also a source of concern. If a single leak reached the criminals, or a tip-off was made to a newsroom, that could potentially ruin all their work – not to mention the harm it would do to the Swedish police force's international reputation.

*

The police officers found themselves in a constant state of worry. Every criminal plot they failed to detect in time was potentially a failure to prevent a death. The caseworkers told me that they spent countless sleepless nights searching through the chats in a state of 'dreadful anxiety'. The first thing Putte, Cattis and their colleagues in the intelligence department did when they woke up in the morning was to browse the news sites: had anyone been shot? Had there been another bombing? Finally being able to follow criminal plots as they were being made, before the actual crimes were committed, turned out to be a source of constant fear.

Most mornings, there wasn't any bad news. But on 19 May 2020, a headline in *Aftonbladet* sent chills down their spines: 'Man hospitalized after shooting'.

Around eight o'clock that morning, at a bus stop in Viksjö in north-west Stockholm, a man in his twenties had been shot multiple times. According to the newspaper, he had ties to a criminal network. The suspected offender was reported to have fled the scene on an electric bicycle, and the police announced that a major operation involving police cars, a helicopter and an ambulance was under way. Beneath the article, there was a photo of a bus shelter with cracked panes of glass.

When they arrived at the office that morning, they discussed the shooting. However, since this particular offence had already taken place, ordinary investigative measures were being carried out by the local police. There were so many other serious crimes being plotted that had yet to be committed, and they had to prioritize those cases.

It wasn't until a few weeks later that Putte discovered the chats in which the Viksjö shooting had been planned in

D-Day

detail. Searching for different variations of the term *japp*, he found messages from the very night when the crime was committed. An individual linked to the Jakobsberg network, who goes by Ftpftp, was writing to Rolex man, an individual who once lived in Malmö and knew Ftpftp from serving time with him in prison. The team soon figured out that they were mocking the shooter for having failed in his mission.

From older chat logs, Putte learned that a flat had been prepared. It was what they called a *tryckarkvart*, a hideout. The fridge was stocked with microwave meals, so that the shooter could keep out of sight there for a few days after the hit. With the assistance of a friend, Rolex man had found a 'kid' from Rinkeby who was prepared to do the job. The would-be assassin was 'totally loyal' and wasn't even 'asking for *para*' – he was prepared to do the job for nothing! (*Para* is slang for cash.)

The police believed that his motive was simply to demonstrate his loyalty and gain approval.

He should at least be given a watch afterwards, one of the plotters suggested.

'Yes brother, this guy is 100 per cent for real', Ftpftp wrote back.

The day before the shooting, they were tense with anticipation.

'Yes brother, I just want it to get done tomorrow, I've been waking up every hour all night to check the time, haha', Ftpftp wrote to Rolex man.

The night before the assassination, the two continued writing to each other. The shooter had impressed them. He may have looked like any other kid, but 'looks are definitely deceiving'.

'Your friend has fostered a true soldier, who looks like a sweet little kid, haha', Ftpftp wrote to Rolex man, whose wife was in the late stage of pregnancy at the time.

The friend who had vouched for the kid was thought to be a member of the inner circle of the Death Squad, according to several sources, and, like his friends, he spent most of his time in Spain, where he would eventually be arrested. The Death Squad, a gang from Rinkeby, had earned a reputation for using impressionable teenagers as soldiers to carry out their hits. If one of them should go missing, there were always plenty of other young kids who were prepared to step up and prove themselves as a *hundragubbe*, 'someone 100 per cent dedicated', and demonstrate their absolute loyalty.

Rolex man laughed at the kid.

'Haha poor guy, they've ruined his life.'

'Hahahaha', came the reply.

*

The shooter in Viksjö would eventually be discovered to be a sixteen-year-old from Rinkeby. This teenager's problems had been mounting ever since he came back to Rinkeby from his parents' native country of Somalia. His whole family, eleven people in all, disappeared off to Somalia for three years, in violation of Swedish compulsory schooling regulations. In the Järva area, it's not uncommon for students to disappear to their parents' home countries for extended periods of time.

In Somalia, the sixteen-year-old attended a religious boarding school for more than a year, and social services suspected that he was traumatized by his experiences there. After the family returned, and the boy enrolled at the Rinkeby school, the staff at the school quickly notified social services. There were serious gaps in his knowledge, but he refused all offers of extra support.

Instead, he left.

He changed schools nine times in his last two years of lower secondary school. He left the compulsory school system without achieving the minimum grading requirements. After

D-Day

that, he and one of his older brothers began to be seen more and more frequently in the company of a younger generation of guys who were loyal to the Death Squad. He was found to be abusing cannabis and Tramadol, and his parents couldn't seem to get through to him. A few days before Christmas Eve 2019, the police discovered him in a flat in Sundsvall, accompanied by some older members of the Death Squad. At that point, social services took him into their care.

In May 2020, he was sent to a residential care home for young people in Smedjebacken, Dalarna. But just a week later, he escaped through a window.

The investigators would eventually learn all this from a report that was filed at a later date. Leading this investigation would be Jacob, an experienced lead investigator who would go on to play a vital role in the encrypted chats operations.

The chat logs revealed to the police that the sixteen-year-old had gone to the hideout that Ftpftp had arranged for him, and received a loaded gun from him. That was where he was going to prepare for his mission. Thanks to a person who went by the name of Fisken, 'The Fish', the plotters had learnt which bus stop the target was going to be at, and at what time. The Fish had known the victim since they did time together in Kumla prison in 2019, but he double-crossed his friend and tricked him into telling him about his morning routine.

'I thought he was happy for me, because I had found a job and turned my life around. It's hard to believe that someone could be so deceitful', said Peter, who is now almost twenty-six years old.

At dawn on 19 May 2020, he left his home and walked through the tunnel under Viksjöleden. He noticed somebody sitting on a bench next to the opening, but didn't pay too much attention to him. Peter was facing the road when he felt a sudden, burning sensation in his body.

It was one or two shots. He turned and saw what looked to him to be a 'little kid'. It wasn't anybody he recognized.

At first, he thought it must be some kind of joke, but he quickly realized that this was serious and started running. The kid chased after him. His body felt incredibly heavy, and after running barely 20 metres along a path, his legs couldn't carry him any farther, and he collapsed.

He had been hit with multiple shots, but because of all the adrenaline that was rushing through him, he couldn't feel any pain yet. Witnesses saw a young black man, with his hood pulled up and a turquoise face mask on, approach Peter.

As he lay there bleeding, with the young hitman towering over him, he gathered the last of his strength and raised his right hand to shield his face and beg for mercy. He never managed to produce any words, but he did have time to think, 'Is this how my life ends?'

Then, another shot was fired. Smoke and blood gushed from his hand. It had caught the final bullet, which had been meant to take his life.

In a weak voice, he managed to cry out: 'Help!'

The shooter disappeared, and several people approached him. Everything was turning black. All the people talking annoyed him, but he managed to stay conscious. The ambulance arrived, and somebody cut his clothes open to remove them.

While he was at Karolinska University Hospital, receiving treatment for life-threatening injuries, his brother came to visit. He brought along a friend for moral support. It was the Fish, who had helped arrange the attempt on his life. He had tried to convince Peter that certain people were behind the attempted hit.

'But it made no sense. I had no quarrel with anyone', Peter told me.

After a series of operations and a long stay at the hospital, he was discharged, although his injuries would affect him for

D-Day

life. He spent most of the first two years in bed, his weight plummeting from a muscular 94 kilos to just 52 kilos. Later on, he would realize that his former friends, people he had known since childhood, had hired a sixteen-year-old who had agreed to kill him for free.

'It's almost humiliating', he said, 'but that's what it's like on the streets these days.' The rules had all changed when people began to use teenagers to commit murders. They did it to climb the ranks, and all they risked was two or three years in prison.

'I'd get a life sentence if I killed someone, but a sixteen-year-old kid has nothing to lose', Peter explained.

He couldn't understand why they would want to kill him, and he hoped that he would be able to get answers at some point. If he'd been given a chance to talk to his former friends, he doesn't think that any of this would ever have happened. But people were so paranoid now, too afraid to even meet with somebody.

During the trial, Peter said that he sometimes wished that he had been shot in the head instead, because he would never be able to live a normal life again.

Now, he was on his way to recovery, but his injuries would remain with him for life, and his loved ones had been very afraid since the attack. Many people had told him that they were plotting revenge for him, but the last thing he wanted was for anyone to do something that would cause more problems. What Peter, who had a criminal past and had served prison sentences for drug offences, saw in all this, rather, was a chance at a new beginning.

'You never realize what you have to lose until it's too late', he told me, adding that, although he was recovering, ever so slowly, there was a part of him that would always be 'dead and wounded'.

11

By now, the various police regions were regularly monitoring the chats that were flooding in. One of the many locations in Sweden where this was putting a new strain on the police was Örebro.

It was late May, and the scents of the Sibylla fast-food joint outside the local police station were wafting through the air. This place had been here for decades, and was still called 'The Hole in the Wall', its original name. Many police officers seemed to favour the same menu item: the halloumi burger.

'They think it's healthy', one of the staff members laughed.

Most days, Ted Esplund stood in line here, waiting to buy his lunch. However, in recent weeks, he had hardly even left the office. Since the seven police regions had been invited to join the Encro collaboration in early May, intelligence officers all over the country had been monitoring criminal plots and rumours that were being passed around in criminal circles. Ted headed one of the intelligence sections at the Bergslagen region, and had spent much of the last few weeks keeping up to date on everything that was going on in the region he was responsible for. Even before the Encro operation went national, there had been another operation, codenamed Rimfrost. That was an investigation of and response to a series of recent bombings and shootings in Linköping, Norrköping and Örebro.

D-Day

The ongoing operation already involved surveillance and bugging measures targeting key individuals that the police suspected of being prepared to use lethal force.

One of the biggest conflicts revolved around two childhood friends who had gone on to become leading members of rival gangs. One was a 47-year-old who has been identified as the leader of a recently formed Swedish chapter of No Surrender MC, an outlaw motorcycle gang that originated in the Netherlands. His former friend, now his mortal rival, Hamid, was a few years younger, and the leader of a criminal network called the Örebro Cartel.

According to police intelligence, Hamid's network was involved in extensive trading and distribution of drugs, and was said to be working with international contacts in Spain, Serbia, the Netherlands and other countries. According to police sources, Hamid had been running things remotely from Spain for the last year or so. The rivalry between these two friends was said to have begun on New Year's Day 2018, when an argument had got out of hand. When the police responded to a complaint at the scene, and asked them what had happened, the No Surrender leader shouted: 'Did anything happen here, boys?'

Then, he turned to Hamid, and said, loud enough for the police to hear: 'You fucking cunt!'

*

After this, the conflict intensified. In essence, what the sides were battling over was the drug market, but they were also fighting for something even more important than that: honour and pride. The disagreement had spiralled into a series of retaliatory actions, including bombings, shootings and several murders. This tangled web of violence was further complicated by the fact that, as No Surrender had established their presence in the Mellansverige region of Sweden, they were also in conflict with X-team, a Bandidos supporter group.

In June 2019, a bomb made of up to 25 kilograms of dynamite was set off next to a residential building in Linköping, at an address where a No Surrender member was registered. The blast caused massive damage to nearby properties, and many of the residents had to be evacuated for a long time. According to the National Bomb Squad, this was one of the worst bombings in Sweden in several decades, in terms of the damage caused, the danger posed to the public and the number of people impacted.

A few months later, a leading member of No Surrender was shot dead, along with one of his friends, outside the Hugos restaurant in the centre of Norrköping. The next attack occurred in the spring of 2020. Somebody shot at the No Surrender member who had been the target of the previous bombing, and another member of the same motorcycle club, his friend, was shot dead near a petrol station in Norrköping.

*

One month after the murder of the No Surrender member at the petrol station, Ted Esplund found himself sitting wide-eyed at his desk, reading a backlog of Encrochat messages. The most influential criminals in his area were openly discussing their various murder plots.

It was just too good to be true.

The Encrochat material allowed Ted to piece together the events that had taken place last spring between No Surrender and the Örebro Cartel, and get the full story. When he went back through the chat history, he could see that there had been several hitmen at work at the same time. They were prepared to take on contract killings for money. He scrolled past lines and lines of chats between different people, and figured out that the shooters who carried out the murder at the petrol station didn't even know what their target looked like.

That was why pictures of the victim had been sent to them before the hit.

'Here's some evidence that'll hold up in court', Ted thought to himself as he sat there in front of his computer.

He determined that an individual who went by the name of Jappis on Encrochat seemed to be the leader of a group of hitmen, and that this person had been deeply involved in the murder at the petrol station. The chat contents led the police to suspect that Jappis had been taking on contracts all over the country, and then passing instructions on to his various hit squads to let them know who they were supposed to take out.

In the posts after the murder at the petrol station, Jappis demanded an account of what had happened. The two targets stopped for petrol and then, as they were driving out of the petrol station, they saw the shooters roll up next to their car.

'So, I had to drive, but we happened to drive a little too far ahead, and they ended up just behind me', the alleged shooter wrote.

Multiple rounds were fired at the No Surrender members, but the driver of the shooter's car had ended up in a spot that gave both of the victims an opportunity to get out of their car and run off.

'Walla brother! They were saved by a single metre', the shooter wrote, explaining that the hitmen had to drive away after this happened. Apparently, they weren't yet aware that one of their targets' injuries had been serious enough to kill him.

It wasn't until later that night that Jappis received the news from *Aftonbladet* that one of the men had died. Several Encrochat users expressed their satisfaction.

'He's dead', a friend of Jappis wrote, and followed this with three smiling emojis.

'I know, congratulations brother', he replied, and added four smiley emojis and the same number of heart emojis.

*

Ted Esplund realized that there were a lot of people who had been keen to see this murder succeed. According to messages on Encrochat, eleven people had agreed to pay a fee of 300,000 kronor for the hit.

It was chilling reading. Several hitmen were out there, prepared to take any job for the highest bidder. Human lives had no value to them. At the other end were the people who ordered the hits and pooled the money to have their rivals murdered. The raw cold-heartedness of the chats horrified Ted. But he also gained insight into the minds of these criminals that would never have been available to the police without these chat logs. The murders were planned in detail, and the *goare* method, where friends of the victims lured them into death traps, was used frequently. He began to understand how Jappis and his friends perceived themselves: in their minds, they were soldiers fighting a war. They jokingly used the North Korean flag and pictures of the North Korean leader, Kim Jong Un, in several of their messages to each other.

Jappis's shooters weren't the only crews mentioned. There were other hitmen, including members of the Shottaz network from the Järva area in Stockholm. Apparently, this team had been hired once before, but failed, and, as a result, there were doubts about their ability to get the job done this time.

Ted and his colleagues realized that there was an imminent threat to someone's life. The next intended victim, apparently, was a man called Ako, who had ties to No Surrender. He had refused to accept police protection in the past, even though he was clearly under serious threat. The police refused to give up, and reached out to him on several other occasions.

'I know there are people who are out to get me. I can handle it myself', he told them.

Ted was disappointed, but not at all surprised. Not talking to the police was simply a part of the criminal code, and criminals stuck to it even when all the police wanted was to save their lives. The people who lived this life know the rules, and they know that cooperating with the police was also likely to put them in life-threatening danger. However, Ted still hoped that Ako and many of the others whose lives were under serious threat would come to their senses eventually. The last thing the police wanted to see was more murder victims and grieving families. Ted knew that even the most hardened of criminals could change their ways and become productive members of society.

At this stage, the police were only allowed to act on Encro intelligence to prevent violent crimes, even though they were seeing a constant stream of evidence regarding serious drug offences. Several police officers at Noa described their frustration at seeing drugs being sold by the kilo, without being able to do anything about it.

Violent crimes were to be prioritized, above all else.

Even if they were to pass on a tip to colleagues somewhere in the country about 3 kilos of cocaine that were being transported in a certain car, to a certain address, there were still far too many deliveries just like that one being made. Taking action on every crime wouldn't only risk raising suspicions among the criminals; it would also mean committing practically every resource the police had at their disposal. For now, they had to settle for compiling evidence that would eventually secure long prison sentences for the people who had committed these offences.

*

A while later, Ako had returned to Örebro after spending some time away. He was sighted in a pub in the city, and news of this soon reached his enemies. This time, though, the police were also following the messages they were writing, almost in real time.

'Is there a shooter ready?' the alias Silverear asked the Örebro Cartel's Hamid on Encrochat.

When he didn't get a reply, he contacted Jappis instead, telling him that he hadn't been able to reach Hamid. Silverear repeated his demand that Hamid have a shooter ready outside when they left the restaurant, but received no response. Apparently, there was nobody available to carry out the planned assassination at that moment.

Situations like this would arise from time to time, when targets suddenly appeared after having been in hiding for a while. Even though there was a reward to collect, the hitmen were too slow to respond. Because of this, the idea of bringing in Shottaz was mentioned again on Encrochat. Hamid spoke to a friend in Södertälje, who had been heavily involved in drug trafficking, and they discussed whether they might be able to find somebody who could lure Ako and the other No Surrender men into a trap. As it happened, they found someone. There was a potential *goare*, a girl, who was prepared to do the job.

'I want to look that son of a whore in the eye and send him to Allah', the man from Södertälje wrote to Hamid.

'They can't fail this time, we're going to serve him up to them. But make sure to tell them not to leave the place until he's dead and they've emptied the whole clip in his face', Hamid replied.

The two of them also made plans for what to do once they had taken their rivals off the board.

'I want to sit on a beach with you after this is done, sucking on a pair of tits', Hamid wrote.

He later suggested that they should offer the shooters 'an extra fifty grand' to take the head of one of the targets, or blow the body up.

'Hahaha! OK!' his friend replied.

*

That summer, Ako continued leading his normal life in Örebro, even though he knew that there was a price on his head. Rather than going underground, he stayed visible, out and about on the town. In a chat with one of his friends in No Surrender, Ako showed clear signs of fatigue and paranoia. He said that he stayed out as long as he was able, until he was exhausted enough to go home and pass out.

'I have to keep myself busy, so I won't have time to think', he wrote.

He didn't know who to trust any more.

The police had also been devoting huge resources to preventing a series of shootings. But taking somebody into custody for their own protection simply wasn't an option. Protection could only be given on a voluntary basis. Previously, the police had even discussed the possibility of installing CCTV outside Ako's home, but as there had been no violent crime at that particular location, the situation didn't meet the necessary criteria to justify a surveillance operation.

Eventually, Ako came to a grisly end. He was shot dead as he was returning to his home in Örebro one night in mid-July. A moment later, Ted Esplund's phone rang. It was one of his colleagues, who informed him of what had happened.

'What the hell!', Ted exclaimed, and drove to the office immediately.

Hamid would later be charged for his participation in the discussions on Encrochat, where he had plotted to kill members of No Surrender. He was also convicted of serious drug and firearm offences, but the Court of Appeal acquitted him on three charges of preparation and conspiracy to commit murder.

12

Throughout the spring, a constant stream of new intelligence from the encrypted chats made its way to the Swedish police, thanks to the French investigation that Sweden had been invited to participate in. At the intelligence department of Noa, the Department of National Operations of the Swedish police force, more information had been uncovered concerning the conflict between the Boxer and Danni. These findings were shared with the intelligence department of the police's South region office.

The analysts there realized that three criminal networks had formed an alliance to bring about the death of the Boxer together. A death list had been drawn up, which included everybody who was close to him or on his side of the ongoing gang war that had already cost ten people – including Karolin Hakim – their lives.

Everybody on the other side had a price on their heads, and a reward of 2 million kronor had been promised to anybody who revealed the Boxer's whereabouts. A user wrote about this to the Encro alias Waterbee, which has been linked to the 38-year-old Danni, whose half-brother had been kidnapped by individuals loyal to the Boxer two years earlier. To raise funds for all this, they would need to sell more drugs.

'We need gear and cash for this war', Waterbee wrote at the end of April, just days before Noa gained access to

D-Day

the chats and was able to begin following them in real time.

Later, the police would realize that allies of Danni and Karolin Hakim's partner Niff had also found out where the Boxer's hiding place was. Somebody going by the alias Sadking, who had previously discussed the price of the location of the Boxer, wrote to Niff in mid-May: he had found out where the Boxer bought his Encro phones.

'His phones are from Dubai. That means he's there.'

Sadking suggested a trip to Dubai as soon as the pandemic restrictions were lifted. Police forces all over the world have noted that criminals tend to congregate in Dubai, both for recreational visits and as a permanent place of residence. Several criminals I've spoken to feel that the United Arab Emirates is a safe country to be in, as few people dare to carry firearms or carry out attacks on each other there. The death penalty serves as a strong deterrent.

That was also why Sadking and Niff didn't want to kill the Boxer themselves.

'If we kill him ourselves, it could ruin our lives there, you know', Niff wrote. Since the death of his partner, he had been hunkered down in Malmö with his child, who was physically unscathed when the mother was shot dead.

Sadking explained that this wasn't what he meant. He had children, too, and couldn't put his life at risk. Instead, they suggested assaulting the Boxer, or perhaps stabbing him.

The intelligence analysts at the South region saw more and more Encro users mentioning 'war' and referring to their enemies as 'the Boxer's whores'. More than anything, they wanted the Boxer dead, of course. But for that to happen, somebody would have to lure him out of his hiding place in Dubai, and Danni doubted that anybody would sell him out. Or, for that matter, that the Boxer would fall for any kind of ruse.

*

One of the names on the death list was the Boxer's friend, Salle. This heavyset 35-year-old was, allegedly, one of the Boxer's closest associates. Among his enemies, he was scornfully referred to as the Boxer's 'driver' or 'assistant'. However, like many others in the Boxer's closest orbit, he was thought to be mainly involved in drug-related crimes.

On 22 May, just days after Niff and Sadking had discussed visiting Dubai, Salle and his family checked into the Best Western hotel in Ängelholm. He had booked a two-night stay for himself, his wife and their four children. She had chosen this particular hotel because of its spa. After checking into their rooms at around six o'clock in the evening, they sat down in the restaurant next to the reception.

As they sat there, by pure chance, Salle's mortal enemy Danni happened to check into the very same hotel. His reservation had been made less than an hour earlier, and he arrived alone. He checked in under his middle name and headed straight upstairs to his room. Before long, Danni re-emerged from the lift by the reception. With his eyes fixed on Salle's table, he passed by the lounge sofa where one of the children was playing. All of this was captured by the hotel's surveillance cameras.

Salle had his back to him, but his wife recognized Danni immediately. She froze, looked up, and saw Danni approach her husband with his hands inside his hoodie, only to turn and head off as quickly as he came.

Salle's wife tapped him on the arm to alert him to what just happened. He was hunched over his phone, and by the time he looked up, all he could see was the back of the man in black. They both followed him with their eyes as he returned to the lift and disappeared to an upstairs floor.

At first, Salle thought his wife of almost two decades must be mistaken. It was probably just somebody who looked like his enemy. The idea that the two of them would somehow be at the same hotel on the same night seemed too implausi-

D-Day

ble. Despite his wife's anxiety, Salle remained calm, and, as he would later explain to the police, he never saw Danni – or, as he consistently referred to him, 'the rat'.

In normal circumstances, Salle was extremely conscious of his personal security. He chose where to be with great care, particularly when he had his family with him. Not even women and children were safe any more. The murder of Karolin Hakim had proven that.

*

Danni headed back to his room after spotting Salle, and as soon as he was out of sight, he reached out to several contacts on Encrochat. Using his presumed alias, Waterbee, he wrote a series of brief messages to Sadking, the alias of a known criminal from Malmö.

'I just saw Salle in a hotel.'

Danni was excited, and typed quickly on his phone.

'He's there now, now.'

Before Sadking could respond, Danni had written to another friend.

'I know where Salle is now, now.'

'Can we send somebody?'

Then, he wrote to Sadking again.

'He's with his family.'

'Does anyone have a GPS?'

'His car is right outside.'

When Salle had left the restaurant with his family, at 9.14 p.m., Danni wrote to Sadking and others that they needed to plant a GPS tracker on Salle's car.

'I can arrange a shooter if somebody can plant a GPS', Danni wrote to Sadking a few hours later.

The use of GPS trackers has become increasingly common in organized crime. They're easy to get hold of, and their intended use is to help owners locate their cars and boats if they are stolen. However, among criminals, they're often used to locate enemies, so that they can be attacked and shot when they are at their most vulnerable.

This night, though, nobody seemed to have a GPS tracker. The search was already under way for a hitman who would take the job. The intelligence analysts who were trying to follow all these chats had a complicated challenge to contend with. Messages were being sent to numerous users, many of whom weren't even closely connected to one another. Some of them were actually enemies, but on Encrochat they were also potential business partners. It was all a bit like an online auction, with the significant difference that the item being traded was the life of a father of four.

Around this time, the alias Valuedox wrote a message to somebody who went by the name Kitekiller. According to the investigation, Valuedox is a man with roots in North Macedonia, who acted as a broker of various criminal services.

Valuedox wrote that he might have a job, and asked if Kitekiller was ready to take it on. He wanted Kitekiller to plant a GPS tracker under Salle's car.

'I'm ready', he responded, and added that he could be there in half an hour to an hour.

Valuedox wrote that he was still missing 'one thing'. This aroused Kitekiller's curiosity, and he asked if this was a *goish*, i.e., a trap in which somebody lures the victim to a certain location.

Valuedox responded, '*tryckish*'.

This meant that they would be waiting for or surveilling their target from a hideout, much like a police operation. The idea was to wait until the right moment arrived, and then strike. Kitekiller wanted to have a car ready, so that he could travel in the back seat and keep an eye on things.

This individual, who was twenty-one years old at the time, had never even seen Salle in real life, but nonetheless took the job of placing a GPS tracker under the car, because Salle was a sponsor of his friend's enemy, and this put them at cross purposes. Some people might describe Kitekiller as a dedicated PC gamer: he had his own YouTube channel where he posted clips of himself playing Counter Strike. He was an accurate marksman in the game. He did OK in school, but found it difficult to get a job after secondary school, so he 'took the easy way out' and began selling drugs. Soon, he was making good money. This made him greedy, but he was easily persuaded anyway, because he would do 'anything for his friends'.

After Danni left the hotel, he wrote that a guy was heading over there to see if their target was still there. To make sure there wouldn't be any misunderstandings, Danni explained to the alias Haraketamal that he saw Salle and his family at the hotel in person. He mentioned that Salle's wife might have spotted him. Haraketamal sent crying laughing emojis when he heard about Danni running into Salle in such an unlikely fashion. Danni answered 'yes', with four crying emojis.

A few minutes later, Danni was pulled over by a police patrol on the E6 highway, near Torpasjön, about 150 km north of the hotel, headed for Gothenburg. He was driving at 130 km/h on a stretch of motorway where the speed limit was 110, and he was fined 2,400 SEK. He presented his driver's licence when the police asked him for identification. While this was happening, people were making their way to the Best Western hotel in Ängelholm.

*

That night, a number of people had been contacted during the efforts to recruit suitable shooters, and many expressed interest in the job because they wanted to 'give the boys an opportunity to prove themselves'. However, Danni wanted someone reliable. One of his contacts wrote to him that they needed 'somebody who can take out several people if necessary'.

'Yes, we can't miss this opportunity', Danni replied.

By now, the plan to assassinate Salle involved several groups whose interests were aligned. What seems most striking when you read the chats is the callous lack of concern that Salle's children and his wife might end up getting hurt. The only person who seemed to even consider this at the time was Niff. He wrote to Sadking to ask him to 'tell the shooters' that there might be children present, and that nobody else needs to die. The prosecutors who would later be assigned this case would be shocked at how cold-hearted those involved were about the risk of harming innocents.

It became evident that Malmö, and other places discussed in chats the police intercepted, had a far greater population of hit squads and 'lone wolf' operatives who were prepared to take on contract killings than the police had suspected. The explanation for this was that the conflicts needed to be resolved, sometimes by violent means. This had brought about a great demand for people who were prepared to plant GPS trackers on cars or take contract killings from people who didn't want to expose themselves to the risk.

Using the encrypted phones had lulled these criminals into a false sense of security.

Somebody familiar with these events in Malmö described to me how this had produced a generation of young men who appeared to be nothing but harmless loners on the surface. They might take beatings in the streets without daring to resist, but if somebody put a gun in their hands, they were fully prepared to take a life for money.

'That's how they built their self-esteem, by killing. It's a profession to them. Two days later, they might be back on the streets, getting beaten up', he explained.

My contact told me about somebody he knew who actually had a bright future – who had honest employment that paid him 'good money'. Despite that, he still carried out contract killings. The money played a part, of course – a single hit could earn you a few hundred thousand kronor. But the excitement and the respect it brought could often be just as important.

13

The next day, the phone rang, shattering the silence in the Olofsson residence in Malmö. It had been a late night at work on Friday, like so many other weekends in recent months. The phone kept ringing, but Stefan, a police officer, was sound asleep. He wasn't supposed to go in to work until that afternoon.

When the phone rang again, his wife reacted. She saw that the call was coming from the chief of the local police force, Erik Åberg, and answered it. As usual, he had urgent business. The South region police had been working on a special operation codenamed Rimfrost for several months. Erik was heading this operation, and had the overall responsibility for the success of Rimfrost. Colleagues from all over the country had been brought in to assist.

Stefan's wife woke him up, and he held the phone to his ear.

'I need you to come in. We have good intelligence that unknown perpetrators are headed for Ängelholm.'

Stefan sat up, holding the phone, and listened. People were on their way, at this very moment, to plant a tracker on a car. Next, they planned to arrange a new car and a weapon.

'Come in, now', the chief said.

He got going immediately. Stefan put on his clothes, climbed onto his bike and pedalled over to the police station. The whole command staff was heading in: the lead officer

D-Day

from the national task force; the head of the regional task force; the operation's lead officer Erik Åberg; and Patrik Andersson, head of regional intelligence, who also happened to be one of very few who were aware of the Encrochat operation at that point. And, of course, Stefan, who would be leading a team of available police resources in their attempt to prevent the murder.

*

When Stefan was being woken up that morning, a surveillance team in Malmö had already been sent out to the Best Western in Ängelholm. On their way there, by chance, they spotted a familiar car near Glumslöv. It was a red Toyota, which they had observed during previous surveillance assignments targeting criminals around Malmö, and the police knew that a certain young criminal often got rides in this car. That morning, the surveillance team had been informed that intelligence suggested that a murder was being planned.

The police followed the Toyota in an unmarked car, and around lunchtime, it was parked near the hotel in Ängelholm. An unknown individual exited the car and approached the BMW that was parked just outside the hotel entrance. He was skinny, and wore grey sweatpants, a grey hoodie and a black vest. The hood was pulled up over his head, and covered his face, but one of the officers had a good enough line of sight to notice that he had a beard.

This man, who would eventually be identified as Kitekiller, lit a cigarette and made a phone call. As he did this, he put his hand inside his vest and brought out a black, rectangular object that was slightly smaller than a smartphone.

Soon, he walked over and stood right next to the BMW, and stooped down on the driver's side of the car, still holding the object in his hand. A second or so later, he stood back up and walked back to the waiting Toyota empty-handed. He got into the passenger seat, and the driver headed off to the south, back to Malmö.

The surveillance team had no choice but to follow this car, even though they were the only officers on location outside the hotel.

In the meantime, the regional task force had finished their preparations, and left Malmö for Ängelholm at a roaring pace. It was all very stressful. If Salle decided to leave the hotel in his car, the situation would turn critical.

When the task force finally arrived at the Best Western, two hours had already passed since the surveillance team left. The command staff listened anxiously as the reports came in from their task force operatives. They drove around the block without seeing the light-grey BMW, but soon they caught sight of the car they were looking for.

Everybody breathed a sigh of relief. Salle was probably still at the hotel.

In the command staff meeting, Stefan was given clear instructions from the police chief, Erik. He was to prevent any violent crimes, arrest the suspects, and handle any other consequences that might arise. There were quite a few different potential scenarios he might face when he arrived.

The crackling radios in the command centre soon brought new updates from Ängelholm. Civilians were moving about in the area. The police would have to tread lightly to maintain their secrecy; they didn't want to give their presence away to any would-be assassins who might be waiting to make a move on Salle. At the same time, concern was growing over the possibility that what had been planted on what they presumed to be Salle's car might be an explosive device rather than a GPS tracker. This was something that police officers in various parts of Sweden had encountered many times in recent years. Criminal gangs had increased their use of homemade explosives and hand grenades in their attacks on their enemies.

D-Day

'Secure the location', was the order given to the officers present.

One of the task force's cars rolled up alongside the parked BMW.

As it moved along, gently, one of the officers opened his car door, held his phone out underneath the chassis and took a few quick pictures of the object. He saw what it was immediately, but, just to make sure, they sent the pictures on to the command centre, which was liaising with the national bomb squad. They received their answer seven minutes later: it was a GPS tracker.

*

Meanwhile, a surveillance team had positioned themselves outside the hotel. From their location, they were able to observe anybody passing by, and were ready to act immediately if anybody approached the car. Their instructions were to arrest and warn Salle before he or anybody else drove off in the vehicle.

While they waited, more officers arrived on the scene. The police believed that Salle was still inside the hotel, but they didn't want to cause a scene if they could avoid it.

By the time reinforcements arrived in Ängelholm, it was already late in the afternoon. Much like their colleagues, these new surveillance teams had no inside knowledge of the Encrochat operation, and could only marvel at the amazing informers the intelligence officers must have been recruiting lately.

Behind a hedge, officer Richard stood with half a dozen of his colleagues, drinking down a yoghurt he had bought from a nearby shop. On a day like this, you had to eat when you got the chance. He was dressed in jeans and a thin jacket, and his hair was short and grey. He had been a police officer for three decades, and still found the job rewarding, although the violence had grown more extreme over the years.

Along with his colleagues, he was awaiting new instructions from the command team in Malmö.

Discussions went back and forth on how the police ought to confront Salle. The longer the surveillance team was kept waiting, the more intense their frustration grew. Many of them were fatigued after having worked long hours on the Rimfrost operation and had their holiday plans wrecked by the pandemic. They were at the point where they just wanted to get the job over and done with.

Richard had a suggestion for the chiefs: he thought they should let Salle come outside, get in his car and start driving, and then stop him in a 'routine' check. This was usually a rather undramatic event, which both the criminals and their loved ones were used to. The command staff agreed to his proposal, and the surveillance team's members positioned themselves around the hotel.

For a long time, nothing happened.

The streets gradually filled up with people who were heading out to enjoy this mild spring evening. It was Saturday, and the longer they waited, the more they would risk having people get caught up between the police and the criminals in any confrontation that might occur.

As the evening drew closer, the words finally came over the police radio: 'Inform Salle of the threat to his life.'

Rather than spending more time waiting for something to happen, the police decided to be proactive. Although individual members of the team had access to Encrochat, and hadn't seen anything definitive come through, that didn't mean the criminals hadn't made new plans through other channels. Other shooters might be waiting for the moment to strike, whether they meant to do so inside the hotel or when Salle drove away.

Richard and the other officers left their posts and entered the hotel through the main entrance. One of their colleagues, who had been waiting inside the hotel, had already told them that Salle, his wife and their four children were over by the couches in the lobby. The youngest of the children had sketchpads in front of them. The team had barely even walked through the door when Richard and Salle made eye contact. For a microsecond, he saw Salle tense up, but he soon realized that the men approaching him were police officers.

Richard and one of his colleagues identified themselves.

'It has come to my knowledge that there's a serious threat to you and your family. We'd like you to come with us', Richard began, in his usual, casual Malmö accent.

He explained that they could drive the family to a safe location, where they could meet with some other colleagues of his who would be able to offer them more permanent protection.

'Are you a policeman?' one of the children asked, curiously.

'Yes, I'm a policeman, and I want to talk to your Mummy and Daddy', Richard responded, flashing the child a friendly smile.

Next, he crouched down and engaged in small talk for a while.

Salle seemed calm, and, to the police, so did his wife. She seemed almost relieved that they had come to offer their help. If he had been in their place, and had just been told that somebody wanted to kill him, Richard was certain that he would have been far more agitated. He was just thinking to himself that they must be used to this kind of thing when Salle turned to him: 'I saw a couple of guys over by my car earlier today.'

He had obviously noticed the activity outside, but not been able to tell for sure whether it was the police or members of a rival gang.

Once the children's sketch pads and other toys had all been gathered up, the police led the family up to their rooms. As they filled their suitcases with clothes and toys from their two rooms, there were two officers keeping watch by each doorway. The rest were securing the hallway to make sure nobody else could get close.

Richard reported back: 'We've made contact with Salle and explained the situation. The family is onboard.'

This message was received with a degree of surprise, because the police were used to having this kind of criminal refuse any and all help from the police, even when their lives were in danger. This was the only case I came across in all my work for this book where anybody had actually agreed to accept any kind of help from the authorities.

The plan was for the police to drive Salle and his family away in two unmarked cars, and take them to the police station in Helsingborg, about fifteen minutes' drive to the north. That was the nearest place where they could ensure the family's safety.

Meanwhile, the regional task force had started to prepare a trap for the suspected assassins. They had removed the GPS tracker from Salle's car and placed it in a paper bag that they intended to drive to Malmö. Their next move would be to place the tracker in Spillepengen, a desolate outdoor area between the harbour and a suburb called Arlöv. If the hitmen took the bait, they would arrive at an empty car park, where the task force would be lying in wait for them, hidden in the bushes. There, they could capture the hitmen safely, without any danger of bystanders being harmed.

Assuming they *did* take the bait, that is.

As the unmarked car with the GPS tracker headed for Spillepengen, the entire group, including Salle, his wife, the police and the children, took the lift downstairs to check out of the hotel. When they arrived at the police station in Helsingborg, the family was ushered into the passport office, which was closed at this hour. They were instructed not to make any phone calls, and asked to stay where they were. When the security detail arrived, it was already dark outside.

Richard went to see the family one last time and say goodbye.

'Good luck, and take care now.'

D-Day

At this point, he and his team had completed their assignment. They had taken the family to safety. Nobody passed any judgement regarding the circles Salle had chosen to move in, or the crimes he might have committed. Next, the family was driven to a hotel in Ystad, where they spent one night. An offer of protective custody was made, but Salle turned it down, insisting that he had already made other arrangements.

*

Earlier that evening, the police in Malmö had ascertained that the red Toyota carrying the man who planted the GPS tracker on Salle's car had driven into an underground garage near Möllevången. The officers tailing the car waited for the right moment to make their next move. It was eight o'clock by the time the car re-emerged from the garage and headed back to the area where they had seen it drop off the man in the grey hoodie a few hours ago. The officers kept their distance, but were still able to watch the car as it returned, carrying a different passenger now. Tailed by the police the whole time, the Toyota made several brief stops over the next hour. It seemed very likely that they were making deliveries of drugs to a series of different customers.

During this time, the task force had dropped off the GPS tracker at the car park by the outdoor area and prepared its ambush.

However, the people in the red Toyota seemed to have other plans than following the GPS tracker to that remote location. They continued north towards Lund, and made yet another short stop before heading on to Staffanstorp, where they came to a halt outside a school, Anneroskolan.

'The drug trafficking is continuing', the detail reported back.

They also noticed two other cars driving away at the same time as the Toyota. This induced Stefan, Erik, Patrik and the other members of the command staff to decide that it was time to make a move against the subjects. The most important goal had already been achieved: bringing Salle and his family to safety. Because of this, the decision was made to stop these individuals, whom the police suspected might be shooters, and, if possible, book them for other crimes. Hopefully, the officers would find drugs or weapons in one of the cars. As the suspects were under no circumstances to detect anything that might suggest the existence of a more extensive operation, marked police cars were sent out to stop them.

The Toyota was pulled over at Åkarp, but the guy in the grey hoodie was no longer in the car. However, he was found a moment later, in one of the other cars. The officers who stopped that car were equipped for a confrontation with heavily armed suspects, and were prepared to apprehend a dangerous hitman. To their surprise, their target was a 21-year-old who 'looks like a child'. He was immediately moved to a holding cell at the police station in Malmö, on suspicion of a minor drug offence, as the police had found zip-lock bags of cocaine hidden in his underwear. When a pistol was discovered in one of the other cars, which he had spent time in earlier that evening, he also came under suspicion for possession of a firearm.

Once there, he was photographed in the same clothes that the surveillance team had seen him wearing in Ängelholm earlier that day. This allowed the police to connect him to that location. He would also later be connected to the Encrochat alias Kitekiller.

One problem that the police were facing at this time was that they still weren't allowed to reveal the true extent of their suspicions. Only a few officers at the South region were even aware of Encrochat, and the chats weren't yet available to be submitted as evidence. Because of this, several of those involved, including the 21-year-old suspect, were eventually released from custody.

D-Day

The officers involved in the operation still considered it a success. They had prevented the assassination, and Salle and his family were safe. The main suspect, Danni, however, remained at large. Nobody had seen him since he had been pulled over for speeding the night before the operation.

*

A week later, the man behind the alias Sadking, Danni's friend, who had been involved in the assassination plot against the Boxer with him, received messages from the user Ftpftp about an article that had been published in the newspaper the *Sydsvenskan* the previous day. The article mentioned another secret operation the police had carried out, which successfully uncovered a case of extortion from a housing cooperative, a bribery scandal involving the waiting list for rental homes and gang activities in which the Swedish Social Insurance Agency had been defrauded of millions of kronor. One of the people mentioned in the article was Sadking, who was wanted by the police. He was described as a 36-year-old who had claimed to be disabled after a car accident, and received sizeable disability benefits, but was later spotted training in a CrossFit gym in Malmö.

The alias Ftpftp from Stockholm, then, was the same individual who had recently hired the Death Squad's sixteen-year-old hitman from Rinkeby to take out one of his rivals at a bus stop in Viksjö. This showed just how tangled this web of alliances was. Ftpftp had recently hired the Death Squad, long-time allies of the Boxer, to help him out, and then, just a week later, engaged in friendly communications with a close friend of the Boxer's mortal enemy Danni.

14

On 4 June 2020, undercover officers with the Dubai police filmed a man who was coming out of his home to take out the rubbish. He had untidy, dark hair and was wearing black shorts and a black T-shirt. Thanks to this film, he could be identified based on intelligence from Sweden, Spain and elsewhere that had been compiled by Europol.

It was the Boxer.

Encrochat messages allowed Europol to locate him in Dubai. As night fell that evening, the task force struck, and he didn't try to resist arrest.

A source within the criminal underworld explained that he'd known all along that the Boxer was in Dubai, and that while there, he had joined up with the mafia leader Ridouan Taghi, the Angel of Death, who was also in hiding. However, the Boxer was also alone and more vulnerable there, particularly after the Angel of Death was arrested in December and subsequently extradited to the Netherlands. He was declared persona non grata by the government because he had given a false identity when entering the country.

The source didn't know what the Boxer did there during the last few months.

'He probably did fuck all except play computer games. He likes computer games. What else was there for him to do?

The place he was staying in when he was arrested looked completely deserted', they told me.

However, the police were to follow him as he coordinated crimes remotely, from his hideout, on Encrochat.

He used several Encro phones, including one registered to the alias Airwalnut. It's said that the police have a 'gigantic' file that links the Boxer to violent crimes and drug smuggling, including crimes he committed in collaboration with members of the Bredäng network, a faction loyal to the Bandidos.

Meanwhile, Europol had begun to pressure the United Arab Emirates, to have him extradited to Spain. After the Angel of Death was released, there were 'well-established communications' with the oil state in the Persian Gulf, which has no interest in becoming a haven for international criminals.

*

The raid was filmed by the police, and shared with the news media the next day. In the footage, black-clad police officers in balaclavas are seen searching the residence. One of them stands behind the Boxer, holding his head in place so he can be photographed and presented to the world. Next, he is given a turquoise face mask and driven off to the police station. The boxer had entered the country in mid-November 2018, using fake identity documents, after the Spanish police, in cooperation with colleagues from Sweden, had started arresting Los Suecos, who had been wreaking havoc on the Costa del Sol.

The minute Europol's Finnish analyst Hanski received the news, he sent a message to his Swedish colleagues:

'Mekky has been arrested in Dubai.'

The responses, which came immediately, were heart, star and beer glass emojis.

The Boxer's arrest made international news, and discussions followed immediately on Encrochat. In Sweden and in

Spain, his friends were angry and his enemies cheered. The police followed the reactions in the chats:

'The son of a whore has been nicked', one user wrote.

'He looks like a poor little urchin, the bastard', was the reply.

'Yes indeed, the cunt! He's been living like a rat.'

A picture of the arrest was circulated.

'Look at his eyes, do you think he was thinking of us when they took his picture?' Sadking asked a friend.

'Lots of people will be celebrating today', Danni wrote to a friend, with smiley face emojis.

One Encro user wrote that many of Boxer's friends would be going into hiding, now that he'd been caught.

'He was their daddy, they can't make any money without him, and they can't live off of his name any more.'

According to rumours in criminal circles, the Boxer was good for several hundred million kronor of earnings from drug trafficking.

The police continued to gather messages about the Boxer from various users. Danni sent Sadking a link to an article about the Boxer's arrest.

'Great stuff', Sadking replied.

Less than an hour later, Sadking wrote a message in English to somebody. He wanted to know if there was anyone who could carry out a murder in a prison in Málaga.

The person replied that a beating would be fine, but that killing someone was only okay if there was a real war, if people's families were in danger.

'Not for any amount of money', they clarified.

*

The other side of the conflict was also suffering setbacks. In early June, a lorry carrying almost 73 kilos of cannabis that had been smuggled from Spain was stopped as it was

D-Day

about to board the ferry from Rostock to Sweden. The cargo belonged to Danni and Sadking, among others, and was on its way to the Gothenburg area. Intelligence officers in the South region had alerted Customs after monitoring communications on Encrochat. The police officers felt a sense of achievement at finally getting ahead of the game and catching one of Malmö's most influential and evasive criminals, who had been able to hide behind encrypted chats until now.

I've been told that several of the individuals arrested in Malmö in relation to this case were planning to start families at the time. One suspect, who ended up being prosecuted, had just agreed with his girlfriend that their families would meet, and that he would ask her parents for their daughter's hand, as tradition demands.

In the days leading up to the arrest, a bad feeling was growing in his guts, the man told me. He couldn't shake it.

'I feel like something's about to happen', he told his girlfriend.

'Don't say that', she replied, anxiously.

'I'm not saying someone's going to kill me; I just have a feeling that something's up. Something that mustn't happen is going to happen.'

15

It was becoming increasingly obvious that there was something going on. Across the country, murder plots and drug deliveries were being prevented, even though most police officers still weren't aware that Encrochat had been cracked. The same was true of the criminals. So far, users still trusted that the business they were doing was shrouded in darkness.

On 2 June 2020, the police raided the World Exchange bureau in Södermalm, Stockholm. Tucked between cafés and second-hand shops, near Mariatorget, was a small establishment that had been repeatedly mentioned in tip-offs to the police concerning systematic and organized money laundering over the last decade.

When the police gained access to the Encrochat materials, they noticed that there was frequent mention of somebody called 'The Money Changer'. This nickname referred to the individual who ran the exchange office, which was one of many like it that criminal networks used to process their dirty money. On Encrochat, the police could follow the cooperation between several different criminal networks and the World Exchange office.

In a video from the raid, officers wearing gloves can be seen searching through a safe and finding bags full of cash. A Post-it note with notes and nicknames was attached to each bag. Carrying on their search, the police found additional bags holding millions of kronor in cash stashed on top of the ceiling panels. During the raid, they also discovered several notebooks containing records about the accounts of money-laundering customers, which would turn out to be crucial evidence. They contained records of deposits and withdrawals made by criminal customers, including funds used to pay for drugs, as well as exchanges and transfers made to other countries. The aliases in the notebooks could be matched up with the labelled bags.

This marked the beginning of a huge investigative effort. The bags had to be linked to the accounts, and then to individuals appearing in surveillance videos and the Encrochat communications. One major consideration was that the proprietor had been using Encrochat himself. Going by the alias Muteherder, he had been in contact with at least sixteen different criminal networks, including the Death Squad and the Vårby network.

In the summer of 2019, Rio had already launched a secret preliminary investigation into serious money-laundering offences at the bureau. Surveillance operations began, targeting the suspects, and from a building across the road from the exchange office entrance, a camera recorded everyone who came and went. It didn't take long for the team to confirm their suspicions that the staff were helping criminals store, transport and transfer criminal money. The enterprise had been largely unhindered, even though the company was subject to oversight by the Swedish Financial Supervisory Authority, which would eventually be criticized for this lapse in supervision. The surveillance efforts also revealed that representatives of the Bandidos and the Hells Angels had been visiting the exchange office. According to the investigators' calculations, the exchange office, which the police would label a 'criminals' bank', had laundered at least 200 million kronor in the last year alone.

*

One of the people who visited the Money Changer was Rebecca from southern Stockholm, a young girl who had grown up with loved ones who struggled with substance abuse. On 21 April, the surveillance camera captured her entering the World Exchange. An initial check revealed her to be an ostensibly ordinary girl who had worked as a ticket booth attendant in the Stockholm Metro and was studying to become a social worker. However, it would later be discovered from Encrochat messages that she had been working as a mule for a drug dealer from Södertälje, for whom she had handled several hundred thousand kronor. The encrypted chats made it clear that there are more women working in the criminal underworld than the police and the prosecutors had suspected. They work as mules and holders, but are also paid to serve as *goare* or lures, and set traps for intended victims.

In late May, Rebecca and a friend were driving around in the Guldheden neighbourhood, a quiet area in central Gothenburg which has many students among its residents. After a while, they stopped and met up with a man, twenty-six years old at the time, who had a bag that he had brought from his flat. This man was a hockey player, with no previous criminal record. In his teens, he had dreamed of a professional career in hockey, and he even played abroad for a while in Salzburg, Austria. When he injured his back in his late teens, however, he moved back in with his parents.

He spent quite a long time battling depression. Recently, he had been training to become a security guard, and had a job for Volvo that involved leading a drug sniffer dog around the premises. The Gothenburg police have noticed that many people tied to the criminal networks have employment at the auto factory, something a source described to me as 'a big problem'. The Hockey Player also had another job, at his parents' company.

D-Day

In the drug trade, he performed the role of what the police refer to as a holder. His boss had told him on Encrochat that two girls were coming to collect the drugs.

He was sent a picture of a 100-kronor banknote, and told that the women would hand him a note with that serial number to identify themselves. He saw three fingers, with skin-coloured nail extensions, in front of the banknote.

When they met up in the car park a few minutes later, it was just after two o'clock in the afternoon. Rebecca had asked her friend to take a walk, because she didn't want to get her involved. When the Hockey Player approached Rebecca's car, he studied her banknote carefully to make sure the serial number matched. Then, as instructed, he fetched the bag with the drugs inside and placed it on Rebecca's back seat.

After the handover, he contacted his client, whom he addressed as 'Boss'. The Boss was a young man who has been described as a major smuggler, and had previously been involved with the two factions in Biskopsgården. However, he had stayed out of their conflict himself.

'Done', the Hockey Player wrote to the Boss, who asked him if he had found the girls attractive.

'I didn't really look.'

The Hockey player was suspected of having handed over 19 kilos of cocaine to Rebecca and her friend, and receiving 1,000 kronor per kilo as compensation. The drugs were said to come from one of the cartels in South America. Rebecca and her friend drove back east, to Kopparberg, where they delivered 5 kilos of the cocaine to Hamid, the leader of the Örebro Cartel. After this, they headed on to Stockholm. She viewed this job as an opportunity to make some fast money without too much risk, and ended up addicted to the big money it brought her.

*

The day after the drop-off, the Hockey Player asked his employer for a favour. His sister was going to get married, and he sent a message on Encrochat to ask if he could be fronted 10 grammes of cocaine from the goods he was selling.

He promised to pay, and to tell anybody who asked that he had bought it from a friend, so that his family wouldn't learn about the huge stash of drugs he was holding in his rental flat. He promised not to do any of the cocaine himself, and his employer warned him: this was highly pure product, straight from Colombia. The Boss wrote that it was ten years since he had used cocaine himself.

On Encrochat, the Boss wrote that the most recent shipment of cocaine that the Hockey Player had received and was currently holding was 149 kilos. Judging by the chat log, the young holder was not aware of this.

'You're joking, right?' the Hockey Player wrote back.

'No', the Boss replied, with laughing emojis.

Next, he instructed the Hockey Player to be careful with the drugs.

'If you tell me there's a delivery at three o'clock in the morning, that's what will happen', the Hockey Player responded after a while. 'If you tell me seven o'clock in the evening', he continued, 'that's what will happen.'

'Hahhah fucking model soldier', the Boss responded. He had already praised the Hockey Player and told him that he was 'making Swedish history'.

However, the Boss was actually worried at this time. He had begun to sense that the police were surveilling him. They had even started tailing the girl he was seeing, or so he suspected. So, he got in his car, and drove it as fast as he could, all the way to his native country of Kosovo.

*

D-Day

One week after she picked up the drugs in Gothenburg, Rebecca handed over a kilo of compressed cocaine, with the letters GL stamped onto the top of the package, to an individual in Västerås. The police found the cocaine in a cellar storage space. It was inside an orange plastic bag from the Stadium sportswear shop, which had Rebecca's fingerprints on it. After the drop-off, she was stopped on the E18 motorway. In the car, police found 403,000 kronor in cash and a Sky ECC phone, another popular encrypted phone. By now, the police had already identified the Hockey Player through a series of Google and social media searches. They soon realized that he had no previous criminal convictions, and that he started this job to fund his own drug habit. Sifting through the logs of his chats, the police were later able to identify extensive sales of cocaine and amphetamines.

Analyses of the cocaine would later connect the Hockey Player to a Norwegian who had been apprehended after a dramatic attempt to escape from Customs officials. The investigation revealed that the Norwegian had driven from Norway, crossed the border at Svinesund Bridge on the E6 motorway, and then headed south towards Gothenburg. The police suspect that at the end of May, two days after the Hockey Player delivered the cocaine to Rebecca from Stockholm, he was involved in delivering 13 kilos of cocaine to the Norwegian, a young man who had roots in the Balkans.

'Good luck', the man said, and handed over a black gym bag before the two of them went their separate ways.

On 1 June, the Norwegian drove back to Oslo, but took a detour through Årjäng, which is 100 kilometres north-east of the border. Customs officers there became suspicious, and stopped his car at a campsite. At first, the Norwegian was helpful, and helped them remove things from the boot. But when they opened the left back door of the car, they discovered a black gym bag that had been wedged in tight behind the driver's seat. One of the Customs officers pulled the zip open, and found a bunch of square packages, wrapped up in brightly coloured rubber. The Norwegian panicked, and immediately ran away from the Customs officers. During the chase, he managed to lose them, return to his car, and speed off.

However, he was soon captured anyway.

Witnesses had noticed a man attempt to submerge a bag in a lake, and alerted the police. These people fished the bag up as it floated around on the water. It was soon discovered to be full of cocaine, and, moments later, the Norwegian was arrested after entering a courtyard with no escape routes.

In questioning, he would later claim that he had been forced to close his hamburger restaurant in Oslo because of the pandemic, and that somebody had offered him 200,000 Norwegian kronor to transport the drugs. He explained that he needed the money to pay for an engagement.

*

The Norwegian is just one example of the dense web of connections that extends from the Swedish drug market to our neighbouring countries.

One of the insights that Noa gained from the encrypted chats was that the quantity of drugs being smuggled into Sweden was ten times higher than they had previously believed, and could actually reach 150 tonnes each year.

Many former narcotics officers attribute this surge in smuggling to the new jurisprudence and subsequent legislative changes that were introduced during the first half of the 2010s, in conjunction with the so-called 'mephedrone case'. This required courts to take into account whether a particular crime had been committed for profit, the extent of and degree of organization of a drug trafficking operation, the role of the suspect in a drug trafficking operation, and whether any particularly egregious acts had been involved, such as drug-dealing that specifically targeted the young. This led to a significant reduction of the most severe penalties. According to the Swedish National Council for Crime Prevention (Brå), the number of individuals prosecuted for serious drug offences dropped by more than 40 per cent between 2010 and 2013.

'Of course, things were different before the change', explained a former gangster who told me he used to carry a scale with him, so he could make sure the amount of cocaine he was carrying was under the threshold for a serious drug offence. At the time, holding more than 50 grams could get you sent to prison for two years.

'Back then, the narcotics officers were always after us, so it made sense to avoid unnecessary risks', he said.

Today, the threshold for a two-year sentence is 100 grams of cocaine, while possession of a kilo carries a five-year sentence. The threshold for an exceptionally serious drug offence is 5 kilos of cocaine, which carries a six-year prison sentence. From 20 kilos of cocaine and up, the penalty is seven years.

Several experienced police officers believe that the change in legislation meant that criminals no longer feared the harsh penalties that had previously been linked to specific drug quantities.

Now, it's not kilos of drugs that are being smuggled into Sweden, it's shipments of hundreds of kilos, all without any risk of harsher punishment. The demand among Swedes is enormous. This is evident to the police from interactions with the consumers. All this coincided with the disbanding of the specialized narcotics police during the 2015 reorganization of the police force. When loosely connected criminal networks seeking to control the drug trade sprang up around almost every shopping centre, things only worsened, according to several police officers. Competition caused division between former friends, and more drug money in circulation meant that more weapons were brought into play. This eventually led to all the present-day shootings and explosions that are deeply impacting our society and damaging Sweden's international reputation.

Stefan Reimer, Justice of the Supreme Court of Sweden, on the other hand, believes that the new jurisprudence allowed for more 'nuance', so that individuals with leading roles can now be given harsher sentences than their subordinates. A quantity of drugs that would previously have led to a ten-year prison sentence might get somebody seven or eight years today. However, the leaders can still be given the maximum penalties. Mr Reimer also believes that harsher sentences do not have a deterrent effect on drug traffickers.

'I think our drug penalties are still harsh compared to the ones for other types of offences', says the Justice, and makes a comparison to rape, which currently carries a maximum of six years in prison.

The quantities that are brought in have grown so large that Noa's Ted Esplund describes Sweden as a transit country for smugglers. The drugs that pass through are mostly shipped on to Norway, but also to Finland. A certain quantity is sold by mail order, and ends up being sent to much more distant countries, even including Australia. The simple truth is that a parcel from Sweden will attract far less suspicion than one sent from Colombia.

An individual who has now been convicted thanks to evidence from the encrypted chats explained to me that he could sit at home in his flat in Stockholm, selling kilos of cocaine to customers in Norway.

'Sweden is bringing in so much product that we even ship it to Norway. Our area of operations has expanded. I'm making money outside of Stockholm. I sit in my flat, at home with my family, and send encrypted chats to some Norwegians who then travel to Gothenburg by motorbike or in cars to pick up a few kilos of cocaine and then go back', he

D-Day

told me. He ended up receiving a lengthy sentence for drug offences.

*

Another week later, on 8 June, the Hockey Player was arrested, too. He was apprehended in Gothenburg when driving to a post office to mail fifteen envelopes containing speed. He had been under surveillance. The drugs were supposed to be sent to buyers who had placed orders on the dark website Flugsvamp, which some have described as an 'eBay for drugs'.

When the police entered his flat, they were greeted by the powerful, rubbery smell of all the drugs that were stored there. The Hockey Player said that the whole flat 'smelled like a brothel'. In addition to large quantities of amphetamines, LSD and cannabis, 56 kilos of cocaine, stamped with the letters 'GL', were found in the flat. The cocaine seized had a total street value of almost 50 million kronor.

While this happened, the Boss drove to Kosovo. Being unable to contact his holder in Gothenburg was incredibly stressful for him. He wrote to different friends, and managed to convince somebody who worked as a security guard to visit the address and see what had happened. The police were there when the man arrived, but released him after he told them a made-up excuse about dating a woman who lived in the building. In Kosovo, the Boss realized that he had lost 56 kilos of cocaine. He had no idea how the police got wind of the holder. They had already sold so much off, and never had any issues. Apart from the Hockey Player, the Boss was the only person who knew where the cocaine was. He speculated that perhaps a neighbour had noticed the smell and contacted the authorities. He became anxious, and used Encrochat to send what can only be described as a debriefing to several other individuals in the drug trade. To one of his friends, he wrote that he was worried that the police would 'land a helicopter on my head'.

'Yeah, I'm fucking paranoid here too but I'm far away from any evidence that could be linked to me. There isn't anyone who can rat on me, either. But it's such a lot, this isn't going to be just a small investigation, they're going to kick off an insane operation over this', he wrote.

16

Others besides the Boss were beginning to feel paranoid. In recent weeks, a bad feeling had started to set in with Stockholm drug dealer Donvar and several of his friends. An unusual number of people had been caught recently, in strange ways. It seemed as though the police had somehow been able to pick the specific, right moment, that one, rare time in a hundred when friends of theirs – whom they knew to be cautious – happened to be carrying weapons or drugs.

Something wasn't right.

Rumours had already begun to circulate that Encrochat had been cracked. But reports like that had come and gone over the past few years, ever since Encrochat had become one of the favoured means of communication among European criminals. Each of these rumours that some government agency had somehow overcome the 'impenetrable' encryption had ultimately been proven false. It was common knowledge, too, that competing encrypted phone suppliers would use smear campaigns like that to try to increase their own market share.

Donvar's phone continued to receive messages from fellow entrepreneurs who were looking to do business.

A customer asked for a kilo of cocaine.

Donvar wrote to his *stashare*, or holder, in south Stockholm, to tell him to be ready. Then he wrote back to the customer, giving him an address, a time and a password.

Two hours later, his employees – that's what he called them, because he paid them a monthly salary – walked over to a car in the car park outside. As he approached, the driver gave them the password, 'Ferrari'. The drop-off was completed, and the money was collected.

*

When Donvar crawled into bed next to his girlfriend on the evening of 12 June 2020, everything seemed the same as always. Across the world, tens of thousands of Encro users were going to sleep in the belief that their affairs were absolutely safe from prying eyes. That evening, intelligence officer Putte was staying at his mother-in-law's house. Her health had suddenly deteriorated due to her cancer. She didn't have much time left, and he was sitting there with his work computer on his lap, catching up on all the conspiracies to commit violence that were under way in the encrypted chats.

But then, what had been inevitable all along finally happened: Encrochat realized that they had been hacked.

That night, the service sent out a message to its users to inform them that they had been subjected to an 'illegal takeover' by 'government agencies'. They advised their customers to physically dispose of their phones. When this happened, the French authorities had been able to access everything that was written on Encrochat for a full seventy-three days.

In Kosovo, the Boss woke up the next day. Unaware of the warning that had gone out the night before, he sent a message to a friend.

'Hello brother', he wrote.

'Did you see the news? They've cracked this shit', his friend replied in Albanian.

A few minutes later, the Boss sent a short reply: '?'

D-Day

It would be his last Encrochat message.

In Stockholm, Donvar's private phone was ringing like crazy. It was eight o'clock in the morning, and it looked like it would be another hot summer's day in the capital. The caller was a friend of Donvar's, who wanted to warn him before the police came to kick down the door. He explained that Encrochat had alerted him, and was urging him to get rid of his phone immediately.

Donvar got so stressed that he claimed to be 'pooing blood'.

He expected there to be a task force waiting outside his door, but when he peeked outside, there was no one there. He left immediately. All he managed to take was his passport and some money. Out on the street, he zigzagged, to see if there was a surveillance team following him. He went to a meeting point where a friend picked him up. They went to a car park where Donvar smashed his Encro phone to bits with a rock. He gave the shattered pieces to a friend who dumped them 'in the centre of the Earth'.

After that, he drove south, across the Öresund Bridge and on to the Netherlands. It wasn't until he arrived that Donvar realized that he hadn't even brought any spare underwear.

That morning, Putte was sitting on his balcony when he saw that the warning had been sent to the users. On the screen, he saw all the communication cease, practically in real time. It was all over in just a few hours.

Afterwards, he went inside to his wife to tell her that the unusual working hours he'd been having were coming to an end. She hadn't known anything about what he'd been working on, only that it was something important. Now, Putte could relax, and let the regular investigative teams take over. The next day, his mother-in-law passed away.

All over Sweden, and the world, the ripples kept spreading. Phones were destroyed. People sped off in their cars to flee across borders, or to hiding places. Desperate messages were sent through every imaginable means of communication.

Others began to look for countries that didn't have extradition treaties with Sweden.

*

For several weeks, Donvar stayed in hiding abroad, waiting. But nothing happened. Several of his friends in the business had apparently made it, too. Eventually, he went back home. He was even more cautious now, wary of anyone he saw that he didn't recognize. Then, he went back to business, through other encrypted apps this time. His main drug importer was in custody after one of the many busts, but others were standing by, eager to claim a bigger share of the Swedish drug market.

As long as there are customers, the drugs will find a way.

PART 4
FOXTROT
MARCH 2020 – AUGUST 2020

17

The days of Encrochat had come to an end. What had been claimed to be impossible had happened, and for many criminals, the consequences would be devastating.

The work the police were doing would also change drastically after the warning. Their secret operation had been exposed, but they still had a huge log of messages that would prove very useful, to say the least. The police had already identified several highly interesting cases within the materials they had compiled. One of the trails they followed led to a drug network that appeared to be connected to several of the most violent gangs in Sweden. This was the first time the police came across a name that would bother them for a long time to come: the Kurdish Fox.

However, that story actually began earlier in the spring, before Encrochat was cracked.

In late March 2020, a 26-year-old man named Albin checked into the Elite Hotel Stockholm Plaza, which is located a stone's throw from Stureplan. The new guest immediately drew the attention of the staff. His tattoos and beard made him stand out among the business travellers who usually stay at the hotel. He also asked to stay in his room for a whole month, which is unusual.

When the hotel manager asked him what he did for a living, Albin told her that he imported Italian food items, but when he was asked how his business had been affected by the pandemic, he gave a very vague answer.

She sensed that he was lying, or at least that there was something off about him.

The staff's suspicions about the young hotel guest would soon grow. There were a lot of people coming and going to and from his room. He went on long taxi rides outside the city, and would often disappear out for very short walks. Between his outings, he also found the time to do grocery shopping for his grandmother, who lived nearby.

What the hotel staff didn't realize was that Albin's Encro phone was buzzing with messages. A few days after he checked in, someone calling themselves Foxkurdish wrote a short message: 'Älgvägen 62.'

Albin read the message, and soon left for the address, which was in Stockholm. Shortly thereafter, Foxkurdish informed another of his contacts on Encrochat that Albin had arrived.

'He's there.'

The Encro alias that Albin was communicating with maintained a safe distance from any actual drugs. All this person did was organize connections between mules and buyers. He gave the buyers laconic descriptions of the person who would be delivering the drugs.

'Swede.'

'Young.'

'Has a beard.'

After making his delivery at Älgvägen, Albin confirmed that he had received 40,000 kronor at the drop-off, and sent Foxkurdish a picture of a bag containing a bundle of 500-kronor notes and a handwritten note indicating the amount.

And it went on like this. Messages were sent, drugs were delivered, and money was collected. After a week, the hotel staff's suspicions were sufficiently strong for them to decide to take action. The terms signed by the guest at check-in granted certain hotel staff permission to enter his room, so when Albin left the hotel on the morning of 7 April, the staff made their move. The hotel manager was quickly notified. He collected the master key and hurried up to the room. It was messy. The desk was full of coffee mugs, unwashed glasses, and a Pringles tube. Also in the room was a Ralph Lauren bag with two large baggies inside, holding more than 10,000 blue and orange ecstasy pills.

Soon, a team of plain-clothes police officers arrived on the scene, and were shown a picture taken inside the room. While this was going on, Albin returned to the hotel, but immediately turned and left when he spotted the police at the reception. The police reacted quickly, and after a short chase on foot, they arrested Albin.

Next, the officers entered the room, where they found even more drugs, stashed in the safe and other places. About half a kilo of amphetamine, one and a half kilos of cocaine, and more than a million kronor in cash in vacuum-sealed bags. There were also bags labelled with names, which the police suspected identified different people who had paid for drugs. One of the notes read 'Roger', handwritten with an ink pen.

The 26-year-old was carrying a set of keys to his grandmother's flat. In a wardrobe there, they discovered thousands of ecstasy tablets and a small amount of cocaine that she didn't know he had stashed there. Almost 2 kilos of ecstasy were packed up and ready to be sent to somebody in Helsinki.

For the police, this arrest was a success: the case was clear-cut, and a conviction seemed certain. However, at this point, they didn't even know that Foxkurdish existed, let alone that it was his drugs they had just seized. They couldn't get into Albin's encrypted phone, and nobody had any hope that Albin was going to give up his boss.

'No comment, no comment, no comment', was his response to every question.

What the police also didn't know was that the answers they sought were actually available to an initiated few. In France, the contents of a server had been laid bare. All of the different pieces of the puzzle were actually available, waiting for somebody to sort them and figure it out. But at this point, Swedish police still hadn't even been invited to join the operation.

It didn't take many hours for the news of Albin's arrest to reach Foxkurdish. He went into crisis management mode immediately, sending a series of messages from his Encro phone to different contacts. He wrote to the alias Tenstatensta, telling him that he had lost his cocaine and 1.1 million kronor in cash, but also that he was worried that Albin might talk to the police: 'He doesn't know what I look like. But he knows that I'm called the Fox.'

*

When the team of Noa investigators reviewed the chat history from the Elite Hotel raid a month later, after the Swedish team had joined the Encro operation, they could see that the people who had been buying drugs from Foxkurdish in the past were still doing business with him. In real time, they learned of a new drop-off that was about to take place, and this time, they chose to act on the information. Noa investigators were really supposed to prioritize cases where people's lives were at risk, but tips like this one were still sent to trusted police officers.

This was how it happened that Denny, the head of an investigation team in Järva, received a cryptic phone call at around four o'clock in the afternoon on 10 May.

'There is about to be a serious crime committed on Skogstorpsvägen in Sollentuna. It's possible that an Audi RS6a will be involved', the contact told him.

There was no time to waste. Denny's team is always on some assignment or other, and has fewer members than he would like. Now, he had to cobble together an operation in short order, with the scant resources he had.

The RS6 is a popular car among criminals. Its speed makes it difficult for the police to keep up with it in a car chase. However, Denny didn't have the time to plan the operation, or call in reinforcements. This was probably why it was him Noa chose to pass the tip on to. His team wasn't really at the top level of the police hierarchy, but they did deliver – time and time again. And Denny didn't ask any questions about where the information came from – what mattered to him was the opportunity to prevent a crime. He never even considered that he might have found himself on the trail of one of Sweden's biggest drug traffickers.

Shortly after the call came in, several of his detectives were racing towards Sollentuna, where the crime was expected to happen. Two members of the team were driving along a leafy street that led to a car park in a cul-de-sac by a small, terraced housing estate.

When they had parked and got out of the car, the detectives began to walk around in the area, trying to appear like local residents.

They soon spotted an Audi that was parked in the cul-de-sac. There was a person inside, and they sensed that something was going on. As they got closer, the man got out of the car, lit a cigarette and started pacing, back and forth. He kept looking around. This behaviour strengthened the detectives' suspicions.

After a while, the nervous man got back into the car, as if he was waiting for someone, but five minutes later, he got out again and walked across a patch of grass, in the direction of a red Volkswagen that was slowly crawling along the street.

The detectives had a good view of the cul-de-sac from their vantage point, which was on the other side of a road that led to a school. Through a green fence and some bushes, they saw the man who had come from the Audi get into the passenger seat of the car that had just arrived. His name was Mesut, he had dark hair, and he looked like he was in his thirties. His appearance suggested that he had ancestry somewhere in the Middle East. The person in the red car was a white, overweight man in his fifties. His name was Roger, and he worked for Foxkurdish.

'Fifa', Mesut said as he entered the red car.

That was the password he had been told to use to ensure that the seller – i.e., Roger – would know that he was speaking to the right person.

'Is that the stuff?' Mesut asked, nodding towards a white bag. 'Yes', Roger replied, and handed the bag over.

After a quick exchange, Mesut exited the car and headed back to his own vehicle. The moment had come for the detectives to announce their presence. One of them took aim at Mesut, to intercept him before he got to the car. But as soon as the police identified themselves, the man started running. He fled towards the wooded area on the other side of the car park, ditching the white bag and a phone as he went, but he didn't make it more than 50 metres before he was overpowered by the detective.

'What's in the bag?' the officer demanded as he handcuffed the runner.

'Bad stuff, but no weapons', said Mesut, who was handcuffed and laid out on the ground by now. 'I have a debt that I have to pay.'

The detainee claimed that he didn't know who the older man who had just handed him the 'bad stuff' was.

And he probably didn't.

Both of them were couriers, working on behalf of others who needed to move drugs from one place to another. Other people would be responsible for storing the drugs whenever a new shipment arrived.

One holder explained that his role involved measuring out the amount of drugs that was to be sent, to ensure that the customers would be satisfied. He served as the 'eyes on the ground' for his employer, and received a monthly salary for his work. He didn't want to tell me what his salary was, for fear it might reveal his identity, but he told me it was usually somewhere between 20,000 and 50,000 kronor.

'Nobody would take risks for less than 20,000, unless you had some kind of hold on them. It's like working for a regular business', he told me.

To be a holder or a mule, you 'don't need to be aggressive or violent'. Rather, you need 'common sense and some brains'.

The job involves preparing deliveries for customers, then driving the orders out, giving whatever password your boss has told you to, and waiting for the next job. Money drops can be made elsewhere, to minimize the risk of getting caught with both drugs and money. There are 'money changers' who handle the payments – i.e., process the cash. These are mostly university people, the kind of people who aren't actively involved in crime and can keep a low profile. However, they do need to be connected to active criminals, and they do need others to vouch for them.

This person got his job because he was recommended by a friend. What drove him to risk a long sentence was his desire for money. He wanted to buy designer clothes, stay in hotels, and do all the things he hadn't been able to growing up with his mum. So, he started selling cocaine to customers, mostly 'slightly older Swedes, the kind who drink a lot of beer and are Hammarby football supporters'.

'I wanted to reach the highest possible level of the criminal world, and make enough money – at least a few million – before I got out.'

It didn't work out that way.

The police would later conclude that this arrangement was typical of the organization run by the Encro alias Foxkurdish. People served many different roles, and might be completely unaware of each other's existence.

While Mesut was being arrested, Roger – or *gubben*, 'the old man', as he was also known – drove back towards

Sollentuna, and headed south along the E4 motorway, heading for Solvalla. At the racecourse, he was stopped by a uniformed police patrol that Denny had called in. He was calm during the arrest. Unusually calm. The arresting officer asked Denny over the radio if this was really the right guy, because he didn't at all look like a typical drug mule.

'I'm 100 per cent sure that it's the right person and the right car', was Denny's reply.

The role as a mule in the network that Roger belonged to hinged on maintaining an enormous degree of caution. Thanks to the encrypted phones, everyone was confident that their communications couldn't possibly give them away. Roger remained calm and quiet throughout the arrest. This wasn't his first time. It wasn't until later, when he was being questioned at the police station, that he began to answer questions about the drug deal.

'I needed money', he confessed.

Roger is a 53-year-old entrepreneur from Ekerö in the southwest of Stockholm. He was asked how much he had been paid to carry out the drop.

'5,000', he replied.

In this interview, Roger remained cryptic when asked how he had been communicating with his employer.

'Smoke signals, maybe?' he suggested.

The bag he had handed over to Mesut contained 395 grams of heroin, which would give him a prison sentence if he was convicted.

The police took his car keys, and a key bearing the logo of the lock manufacturer ASSA. The key being of this particular make was a good sign. It meant that the police would be able to contact the company and find out whether the key was from a larger locking system used in a specific residential property.

*

That evening, the police raided the home of Mesut, the man in the Audi who had picked up the heroin. He lived in a yellow house in a quiet neighbourhood near Sollentuna. The police didn't have to take many steps inside the house to realize that there was plenty of evidence.

On the stairs down to the cellar, white, filled envelopes were lying around in large piles, waiting to be sent. One of the envelopes was addressed to a Maria in Umeå, another to a Lucas in Södertälje, a third to a Patrik in Avesta, a fourth to a Juhani in the Luleå area, another to an Enrico in Gothenburg. There were also a large number of envelopes that hadn't had any drugs placed inside them yet.

It was no surprise to the police that there were people buying drugs all over the country, in all social classes. When questioned, Mesut explained that he had been given a list of names of customers, and that when he had packed it all, somebody would come and collect the envelopes.

'I was going to be paid 50,000 kronor to do the packing.'

18

As the investigators continued their secret searches of old chats related to the Elite Hotel and the hand-over in Sollentuna, it became more obvious to them how significant Foxkurdish's role really was. He seemed to be the mastermind behind this whole, vast web of mules, holders and dealers that the police had begun to track down.

Denny and his detectives were working in the field like they always did, unaware that their colleagues at Noa were beginning to piece the whole picture together. Just two days after the arrest in Sollentuna, the group managed to trace an address that matched the key they found on Roger's person.

First, the key led them to a warehouse in Uppsala, where they found a consignment note that in turn led them to an industrial estate in Vallentuna, north of Stockholm. Denny and his detectives drove over there immediately. Driving down the road, they passed fields and horse paddocks before taking a right turn and arriving at an industrial estate that was surrounded by a fence. A gate had been left open, and they were able to just drive in. At the site, they located a storage unit that had been rented by a company registered in Roger's name. The storage space was empty, but the team suspected that they had just missed a large shipment of drugs that had already been distributed to the buyers.

*

Over the next few weeks, the detectives staked out the industrial estate, in case other members of the network might be back with a new drug shipment. The detectives also made contact with other businesses that operated within the estate. The people who worked there had noticed a lot of guys leaving the storage unit carrying heavy bags, being picked up and driven off by taxis. The police asked them to get in touch if they saw anything suspicious. All it would take now was patience.

Criminals can be lucky many times, but the police only need to get lucky once.

While Noa was quietly continuing to map out the whole network that orbited the Encro alias Foxkurdish, the detectives were staking out the warehouse at the industrial estate in Vallentuna, waiting for something to happen. Denny knew that Encrochat had been cracked at this point, but he wasn't aware of how extensive the material was, or how significant it would be for his team's work.

At around three o'clock in the afternoon on 3 July, Denny felt his pulse begin to race when his phone rang.

An informant at the industrial estate was calling to let him know that a Dutch lorry and a small white van were parked over by the storage unit. Next door, some people were unloading cardboard boxes. The informant had managed to get a glimpse of some of the white van's licence plate: WXY. Denny's heart was beating even faster. This was probably the same van that had been spotted in connection with the ongoing hunt for other members of the Foxkurdish network. These were people whom the police suspected of buying kilos of drugs from Foxkurdish in order to sell them on to their own contacts.

For Denny personally, this was terrible timing. A relative was visiting, and Denny had promised them a barbecue dinner. But there was nothing he could do about that. Denny called his colleague Erik, who was standing at the meat counter in the supermarket. He was also planning on firing up the grill that night. Once Erik had paid for his meat, he quickly cycled home to deliver the food to his family.

A short while later, Erik and Denny, both still wearing shorts, had arrived at the police station in Solna to collect their firearms and ask their superior to assign them reinforcements. However, everyone was busy working on other cases. There was nobody available. They were determined not to miss this opportunity, so the only option remaining to them was to make their way to the industrial estate on their own.

An hour and a half after receiving the tip-off, the two detectives arrived at the warehouse in Vallentuna. As they approached the shed, they noticed that there were no vehicles or people left at the site. They broke in to execute a search, because they had reason to suspect that a serious crime had been committed. In the storage unit, they saw a car, a pallet jack, and some cardboard boxes that contained hashish. They estimated the weight at about 100 kilos.

Bingo!

Denny stayed behind to comb through the storage room, and Erik went back outside to take a look at the road that passed by the fences and the overgrown shrubs surrounding the industrial estate. He saw a lorry about 300 metres away, which matched the description they'd been given by the informant. He could also see two people who were unloading boxes from the lorry and placing them inside a station wagon.

The white van, however, was nowhere to be seen.

Erik went to fetch Denny, and they carefully drove over to the lorry, which was parked in a dead end. Then, they calmly got out of their unmarked police car, and began to walk towards the men who were doing the loading. Erik was still wearing shorts and a T-shirt, and neither he nor Denny was wearing a bulletproof vest. There simply hadn't been enough time, and besides, it was better if they weren't too easily identified as police.

'Police', they announced, guns drawn.

Erik grabbed the lorry's driver, while Denny ran up to the station wagon, which had its engine running and was ready to go, and apprehended the driver.

In the middle of this arrest, Denny and Erik heard the sound of another car approaching. A white Mercedes pulled up to the scene. Apparently, the driver and his passenger hadn't realized that they were driving straight into an ongoing police operation. When the driver got out, he nodded to the lorry driver, whose arms Erik was restraining behind his back.

Considering the greeting to the driver and the fact that they had driven into a dead end, Denny and Erik felt that it was very likely that these men were also here to pick up some of the drugs that were ready to be quickly unloaded from the lorry.

Erik released the lorry driver, pushing him towards Denny, and showed the men his drawn firearm.

'Police! Get down on the ground! Show us your hands! Show us your hands!'

When Erik saw the surprised faces of the two men who had just arrived, he only just had time to think to himself that he and Denny were outnumbered now. However, the new arrivals did as they were told, and lay down on the ground.

Erik was standing next to them, and Denny was about 20 metres away, covering the other two men.

'Did you bring any handcuffs?' Denny shouted.

'No', replied Erik.

In the rush, Denny was the only one who managed to bring handcuffs, and he only had one pair. When the two men on the ground heard this exchange, they started speaking to each other in a foreign language. Denny shouted to Erik.

'These guys are suspected of having committed exceptionally serious drug offences. We're authorized to shoot them if they try to run!'

The men got the message, and stayed down.

*

While they waited for reinforcements, two lorries came by, and the drivers offered to help the police.

'Block the road with your lorries, to stop any other vehicles from entering the area', the detectives told them.

Eighteen minutes after their request for reinforcements, marked police cars and the regional task force arrived on the scene.

The white van, which was believed to have played a central role, still hadn't been seen. The police were hoping that it would return, and decided to set up postings near to the storage unit. Denny and Erik were still over by the lorry, looking through boxes of furniture for more drugs. After a while, Denny was called over by his colleagues who were standing guard over by the storage unit. They had sighted a large, white van with a licence plate that started 'WXY'.

The driver headed for the storage unit, but turned around instantly when he saw that the unit had been broken into. Denny and Erik came running through the gates to the industrial estate, and just as the van was about to leave, they managed to stop it and arrest the driver.

It was Roger's replacement, a new mule who had been hired by Foxplanet, another alias used by Foxkurdish, to haul a shipment of drugs to customers in the greater Stockholm area. The mule's name was Wilhelm, and the van was registered to his father.

Later that night, when the police were searching Wilhelm's home in Åkersberga, where he lived with his partner and their young daughter, they found similar cardboard boxes, with the same branding as the ones they had found in the storage room. The police suspected that he had already delivered some of the drugs, and had been returning to pick up the next shipment when he was apprehended.

Denny and his family ended up missing their barbecue dinner. And although a few more members of the network were now in police custody, they hadn't managed to get close to the mastermind behind it all: Foxkurdish, or 'The Fox' – a name that would soon be infamous.

19

As July came to an end, the lead investigator Jacob had just returned from his holiday, and had been given a set of chat logs from Encrochat concerning the attempted murder at the bus stop in Viksjö, where a sixteen-year-old who was connected to the Death Squad had been hired as the shooter.

While this investigation was still ongoing, Jacob was summoned to a secret meeting with his superior in Solna. He was asked to lead an effort to identify and dismantle the network that was now firmly believed to be what linked the incidents at the Elite Hotel, the Sollentuna terraced housing estate and the Vallentuna industrial estate.

Within the force, Jacob was known to be somebody who questions both his superiors and their decisions, who's always prepared to present an alternative theory and who's one of the very best officers working in his field. The news that Jacob was going to be involved in another investigation involving encrypted chats was received with mixed feelings. Plenty of crimes had already been committed, and in the North Stockholm police district, which includes Rinkeby, Husby and Tensta, a big backlog of unsolved murders had already piled up. The pressure on the team was immense, and many of its members were already feeling painfully insufficient. Some had even been seen crying in the workplace. For each new case, a team of investigators, analysts and other colleagues had to be scraped together from within the existing organization. As a result, not all commanding officers were happy about having to tie up their precious resources when they were already struggling.

It did happen, though. Since the Fox had ended up on Jacob's desk, he also took over the investigations into Roger and the lorry driver who had been arrested in Vallentuna.

A few days later, Jacob visited the police station in Kungsholmen, to receive more information about his new cases. This office, located a stone's throw from the Stockholm City Hall and the bay of Riddarfjärden, is the headquarters of Noa, and just down the road is Rio, which was formed after the 2018 merger of the three international prosecution teams of the Swedish Prosecution Authority. Along with the other divisions in Malmö and Gothenburg, they were the Prosecution Authority's specialist team for combatting organized crime. They handled everything from genocide and war crimes to extradition cases involving people residing in Sweden who were suspected of crimes in other countries.

Sitting around an oval table in a simply furnished meeting room at Rio, with a flat screen on the wall, were Jacob, the plain-clothes detective Denny, prosecutor Henrik Söderman, and several officers from the Noa intelligence department. The meeting was also attended by Rio's chief prosecutor, Lise Tamm, who became known to the public after comparing the Stockholm suburb of Rinkeby to a war zone. Despite being criticized for this, she refused to back down from her statement, and she was eventually vindicated when the residents of the area themselves described the frequent shootings as a state of war. She had also been in Denmark to follow the trial of the Death Squad, for which several of the Swedish defendants had been extradited to Danish authorities with the assistance of her department. She had come to play an important role in the ongoing collaboration with the French justice system, and helped ensure that chats concerning users from Sweden were passed on to Swedish authorities. A strong sense of trust in each other's competence was important to help speed up the bureaucracy. This was especially true in this case, where the procedure required Swedish prosecutors to send a European Investigation Order for every Encro alias suspected of involvement in a crime, rather than simply being sent all the 'Swedish' Encro messages by default.

'This appears to be a clan-based network', Noa's representative began, and then went on to say that, based on the Fox's Encrochat communications, it was clear that there were many different parties involved in the distribution, as well as in the handling of the money generated by the drug trade. According to the chats, both of the Fox's parents seemed to be involved. There was a clear hierarchy, with the Fox at the top, and his closest relatives just underneath him. The lower levels included the holders who stored the drugs and the bulk buyers who would buy drugs by the kilo, to be sold on with the assistance of mules. Few of the higher-ups in this network ever needed to be around any of the actual drugs, they only ever saw photos of them. The top level was made up of the people that would normally be extremely difficult for the police to reach.

However, in this case, in addition to the Encrochat materials, the police also had forensic evidence in the form of drugs and cash seized at the Elite Hotel.

'Why don't we just use the Elite Hotel bust to take the down the top guys immediately?' Jacob suggested.

In most drug-related cases, the people at the bottom of the pyramid would usually be the only ones that the police could actually target. But in this case, there was solid evidence against Albin, who had been arrested at the Elite Hotel with large amounts of drugs and money. That investigation was actually close to being prosecuted, but the drugs and the Encro phone discovered at the hotel could be used as evidence against the Fox and his closest circle. It was the chats on Albin's Encro phone that had given Noa access to the Fox's many drug deals and contacts.

As the meeting came to an end, Jacob was promised he would be given the resources he needed.

*

The next step was to build the team that would be getting the job done. He requested sixteen people, including a surveillance team, some regular investigators, a financial investigator, and an analyst who would be able to process data from phone towers and large mobile phone dumps. He ended up getting twelve people in all. Among them were two response officers, Thorbjörn and Niklas, who spent most of their time in uniform, patrolling Järfälla by car. They would practically be serving this investigation as trainees, but that was OK. As long as they were willing to work and learn, Jacob would be happy to supervise them.

He summoned his Järfälla colleagues, the team leader Denny and his investigation team and some other team members to a conference room at the Solna police's serious crimes unit. As they sipped their coffee, they were shown a PowerPoint presentation that explained the Encrochat system, and provided with a description of the Fox's network. A pyramid was shown on the screen. The Fox was at the top, and below him were his parents. Below them, a number of major buyers were lined up, and at the bottom, there was a collection of aliases that were presumed to be used by mules and holders.

Denny went through the leads his team had been following recently, and the arrests they had made. Since this drug ring consisted of many individuals, with different roles, the operation was codenamed 'Lego', and the group would eventually name itself Team Foxtrot.

They set three main objectives for their work. The first was to ensure that everyone in the top echelons of the Fox's network was arrested and sentenced to a minimum of one year in prison. The second was to disrupt the network's operations by identifying and arresting the largest possible number of buyers, mules and holders affiliated with the network. They also wanted to secure enough evidence against these individuals to get them sentenced to at least one year in prison. The third objective was to prevent their targets from receiving any welfare payments, and to seize any money and luxury items that could be linked to income from crimes.

To close the meeting, Jacob also presented a vision for the task force's effort, to motivate the team to stay focused: the whole police district would benefit if they could get more criminals off the streets.

Several of those present laughed nervously. They thought to themselves that there were a lot of targets on that pyramid chart. Jacob had been doing this job for a long time, and could see the concern in the eyes of his less experienced police officers. Several of those present were also facing the challenge of instantly learning to do investigative work, something that would normally require formal training. There was no time for that now. Which internal databases to use and what kinds of evidence would hold up in court were things they would have to learn on the job.

Jacob took his snus pouches out, and fed a new one in under his lip. He would have to tackle the nerves in the room head on. He began to speak, calmly and confidently.

'How do you eat a big elephant?' he asked, rhetorically.

Thorbjörn, Niklas and the others looked puzzled.

Denny, the detective, smiled wryly. He had heard this one before.

'You don't swallow it whole. You eat it one bite at a time.'

*

Immediately after their meeting, the investigators began to analyse the materials that had been requested from France by European Investigation Order. These were logs of chats between the Fox's two aliases — Foxkurdish and Foxplanet — and fourteen other people. Their discussions were almost exclusively related to criminal conspiracies.

Denny, who was used to active fieldwork, was surprised by what he saw in these chats. He had known, of course, that a lot of drugs were being smuggled into Sweden, but this was on a scale he had never imagined. And they were only looking into a single person's network.

Jacob decided to use the same approach as for the attempted murder in Viksjö. The team would use details in these communications to identify the people behind all the aliases, and determine which particular offences each of them could be convicted of. The work was time-consuming, but, one after another, they began to be identified.

The more Team Foxtrot learned about the Fox and his operations, the more obvious it became to them that they were dealing with a very serious offender. In fact, his criminal history went way back.

20

In the early summer of 2018, there was a flea market in Fyris Park in Uppsala. It was a mild day, and the big car park behind Ica Maxi by the E55 motorway was bustling with people who were elbowing their way through the aisles between the tables. If you wanted the best bargains, there was no time for niceties like waiting for your turn. Here, books and LPs were piled up next to crockery and clothes that were being sold by the box, for 50 kronor a piece.

A familiar character was standing at the edge of the crowd: the Fox – or Rawa Majid, as he's actually called. He had been away for a few years, but that spring, he had been released from his latest prison term. That summer, he was seen visiting the flea market on several weekends. He was there with his partner and their newborn daughter – only a few months old at the time – who was the youngest of their three children.

This man was well known to the police. Friends and people who had met him described him as a friendly, skilled entrepreneur, who was reliable and good at making contacts. Others portrayed him as someone who was 'prepared to do anything for money'.

During the weekend, he sold children's clothes and toys, but also had other goods for sale in his car. After spending the last few years in prison, he was back outside, and he needed to get his life back on track. This wasn't what his parents had dreamed of when they first came to Sweden to give their newborn son a better future.

The family was from the city of Sulaymaniyah in the autonomous region of Iraqi Kurdistan in north-eastern Iraq. As a young girl, the Fox's mother had joined the Peshmerga, 'those who face death', the armed forces of Iraqi Kurdistan. However, while many of her fellow soldiers met dark fates, she managed to evade Saddam Hussein's regime in 1986, when the long Iran–Iraq war raged.

She fled across the border to Iran on horseback, nine months pregnant. She still remembers how tired, hungry and mentally exhausted she was. In Iran, her son was born, and shortly afterwards, their flight continued to Sweden and Uppsala, where a new life awaited them. It took her six months to learn Swedish.

*

The Fox's parents divorced when he was still very young. He would be their only child. After their bitter divorce, his father moved to Stockholm and remarried. His mother lived with her son, and worked long days and nights in the health service. When she couldn't arrange a babysitter, the Fox had to go with her to her work. His mother's life had already taken a dramatic turn at the time of the divorce, when a relative of hers had named her as guarantor for a loan. She told me she had been deceived, and several setbacks followed from this. She lost her savings, and found herself owing the Swedish Enforcement Agency a lot of money.

The mother told me that they were homeless for a while, and that her son spent a lot of time with his cousins in Kista, two brothers who would later end up becoming criminals.

In secondary school, her son was ambitious, but not exactly a top student. His friends from Linnéskolan remembered that he had been quiet and shy during the first year. He wore simple, worn clothes, and hardly told anybody anything at all about himself or his parents.

But in the second year of secondary school, something happened. It was as though he had become a completely new person. Both his voice and his body language had become much more confident. At this time, he also began to wear clothes from expensive brands, with big logos. To his friends, this transformation seemed strange, but nobody confronted him about it.

In the last year before graduating, he got his driving licence, and would often be seen driving an old red car. Several students at the school were shown what he was hiding in the boot: expensive clothes, gold chains, brand new mobile phones and watches. It was said that he was working with an older man, a known fence from Uppsala, and that they were selling stolen goods together. But beneath all the clothes and jewellery, he was hiding a different product. A schoolmate remembers glimpsing taped-up bags containing something white. Rumours that the Fox was selling drugs began to spread among the students at the school.

After graduation, the Fox made most of his money from sales. It was what he knew. Phones, cars, jewellery, gold, watches, alcohol, clothes. What he was selling didn't matter to him, all he cared about was the profits he earned. He also met a girlfriend early on, who would later become the mother of his children.

During this time, he got into trouble with the law. In August 2006, he was sentenced to three months in prison for theft and receiving stolen goods.

Three years later, he and his partner were caught up in what had been a major drug bust at the time. The police had been staking out a network that was smuggling cocaine in from the Netherlands, flying it in by plane to Skavsta outside

Nyköping. In a raid on the home of the Fox and his partner in Uppsala, the police found several hundred litres of vodka. The couple's garage held more than half a kilo of cocaine, and there were 1.4 kilos of cannabis inside the flat. The Fox would later claim that he had been selling vodka to supplement his income, and in 2010, the Court of Appeal sentenced him to eight years and six months' imprisonment for serious drug offences.

While the Fox was in prison, his partner opened an ice-cream parlour in central Uppsala. The Fox was supposed to be working there when he was released on parole in February 2015, after having served two-thirds of his sentence. According to his lay supervisor, the probation service wasn't going to let him work for his own business. The Fox made other plans, however.

Just a few months after his release, the police searched his flat in Uppsala. A large number of phone cards and more than four kilos of gold jewellery were found in various places. The total value of the stolen goods was about 900,000 kronor. According to the investigation, the items came from robberies carried out in Uppsala and Kista. The Fox claimed that a salesman had come to the ice-cream parlour and sold him the phone cards. He also told the police that the jewellery belonged to a friend of his who had asked for help determining the carats of the gold before selling it. He also ended up being convicted for involvement in the kidnapping and assault of a man who had been extorted for money during that same period.

When the time came to determine which prison he would serve his time in, the Fox submitted a request to the Prison and Probation Service: he wanted to study, and get the right qualifications to apply for university. He ended up in Hällby, a class 1 institution, the highest security level, west of Eskilstuna. There, he soon had his rights to make telephone calls to his mother and his partner revoked when it was alleged that he had actively tried to get them to transfer the calls to others.

*

In March 2018, just a few months before he would be glimpsed at that flea market, the Fox was released after having spent almost a quarter of his young life locked away. During those years, the number of shootings in Sweden had risen sharply, and almost every city had a criminal network of its own that was making most of its money selling drugs. The amounts being smuggled in were no longer a few hundred grams here and there. This all happened at the same time as the new jurisprudence was introduced, opening the door for criminals to handle larger quantities of drugs with less danger of receiving the same harsh penalties as before. For the Fox, this would probably have meant spending a whole year less in prison. By the time the Fox was released, an active mule might be transporting whole kilos of cocaine, cannabis and amphetamines. Demand was very strong, and there were huge amounts of money floating around.

One of the first people to welcome the Fox home after he finished his sentence was his cousin Shad. He is said to have brought him a shiny gift: a gold chain with a fox charm.

They were like brothers growing up, and they both embarked on criminal careers at an early age. A relative of theirs told me that Shad and his older brother had always protected the Fox. Shad's friends and family knew him to be a helpful, playful and funny guy. During a trip to Greece, for example, he allegedly wore a T-shirt with the print 'ABSOLUT SVENSK', 'Absolutely Swedish'. As he grew up, however, he began to gain a reputation for being dangerous. He befriended serious criminals in the Järva area, and became a leading figure in the Headshot Gang, which was close to the Death Squad's leading members from that area.

Now, his two cousins were struck by a profound tragedy that would be of great consequence for the Fox's future. In June 2018, Shad was murdered in what appears to have been a death trap. He was shot dead after arranging to meet a woman who was a relative of a known criminal. Shad was typing messages on his Encro phone when a car reportedly pulled up next to him, and a gunman fired the fatal shots from the passenger seat.

At least that's the story the police were told.

The Fox has stated that he was away on a business trip in Spain when the murder occurred. According to one of his relatives, he didn't attend the memorial service. However, the Fox's mother was there at his cousins' home in Kista, helping with the cooking and serving guests who had travelled from far away to pay their respects. Although the gathered relatives and friends felt both angry and sad about what had happened, many of them weren't too surprised. They knew that Shad had a lot of enemies, and that his position in the criminal world made him a target.

His enemies had allegedly raised 1.5 million kronor to pay for his killing.

While the family was still in mourning, a rumour that would sow division within the family began to spread. Before the murder, Shad had allegedly told a relative that the Fox had been keen for Shad to go to the meeting where he ended up being shot. This raised suspicions against the Fox within the family, although nobody was prepared to jump to any conclusions.

They were family, after all.

However, Shad's relatives would soon receive further information, which would strengthen their belief that the Fox had some involvement in setting his cousin up to be killed.

The relatives are convinced, however, that Shad was 100 per cent loyal to the Fox.

'Shad was his back', one relative told me, suggesting that Shad would protect the Fox at all costs, like a brother. If it hadn't been for his cousin, the Fox would 'not be alive today'.

The Fox has consistently maintained his innocence, and has never been formally accused of any involvement in the shooting. People who work with the Fox have also claimed that he 'would never attack his own cousins'. Whatever the truth may be, Shad's family soon cut all ties to the Fox and his mother. However, they didn't seem to assign any blame to the Fox's father, partly thanks to Shad's mother, who was close to her brother.

Worried for her son's safety, the Fox's mother persuaded him to leave the country. Joined by his wife and their three children, the Fox headed off to live with relatives in the UK and the Netherlands for a while, before moving to his parents' home town of Sulaymaniyah.

In Iraq, the family is connected to people who hold great political influence. This provided the Fox with good opportunities to continue his entrepreneurial endeavours. Without getting the approval of the ruling party, 'you can't do anything', a relative explained to me, and went on to tell me that the Fox was good at making his way into different circles, forming relationships with all the right people. According to this relative of the Fox, these contacts facilitated his investments, helping him avoid having his taxes and accounting scrutinized, which allowed him to invest in a restaurant and obtain a licence to carry a gun, among other things.

All the same, this feud within his family was a heavy blow for the Fox. Shad's relatives made it clear to everyone they knew, both in Sweden and in Iraq, that anyone who had any kind of contact with the Fox should 'forget' Shad's family. In an unsuccessful attempt to seek reconciliation, the Fox sent mediators to Shad's relatives while they were visiting Iraq. Allegedly, he also offered to do favours for them to clear his name and restore their trust, but it was all in vain.

'Despite his youth, he has the experience of ten men. He's as smart as a fox. That's why they call him the Fox', a relative told me.

*

Although the Fox's business was apparently thriving in Iraq, his exile would be temporary. At a record pace, he built the kind of fortune that makes people pay attention. It irked some members of his family to see him live with his partner and children in an enormous flat worth millions of kronor in a newly built 32-floor building in Dania City. This is a modern residential area in eastern Sulaymaniyah, with well-trimmed hedges and generous leisure areas.

After a trip to Dubai in the spring of 2020, when the coronavirus began to spread, international borders were closed. Reportedly, the Fox's partner and children weren't allowed back into Iraq, as they were not Iraqi citizens. Instead, the family flew back home to Sweden and Uppsala.

When the Fox returned to Swedish soil in mid-March, the police had no real cause to question him. Although they did have some intelligence which suggested that the Fox was involved in drug trafficking, they still didn't have any solid suspicions that they could base an arrest on. Besides, they were busy enough with the escalating gang violence.

*

So far, Jacob and Team Foxtrot had a pretty clear idea of how the Fox's career in crime had progressed. However, after the bust at the Elite Hotel and the arrest of the then 26-year-old Albin, their investigation intensified, and it also became increasingly difficult to piece all the events together. Not only had the Fox lost one of his mules, he was also being threatened by Shad's circle and relatives, who still believed that he had been involved in his cousin's murder.

While the Fox had been away, one of Shad's relatives had even gone to the police to tell them everything they knew, based on what they had been told by Shad's friends. They explained how the murder had been a set-up, how several different groups were behind it, and how Shad had been surprised by the shooter in the car. The relative also gave the police the name of the rumoured perpetrator: a notorious criminal known as the Mask.

In response to this account from Shad's relative and other intelligence gathered by the police, the head of the investigation, Patrik Zanders, tried to contact the Fox at this time, by reaching out to people who were known to be connected to him. 'He was a person of interest in our investigation', Zanders confirmed. When we spoke, he had moved on to working for Noa, where he was leading day-to-day operations related to the encrypted chats under Ted Esplund.

One day, he received a call from a man who claimed to be the Fox, but the reception was so bad that it was barely possible to hear what the person on the other end was saying. Zanders wasn't even sure it really was the Fox who was calling. He asked the man to call him back, but he never did. Regarding the Mask, there was never enough evidence to establish 'reasonable suspicion' – a lower degree of suspicion – and, because of this, there has never been sufficient cause to bring him in for questioning. When the Fox returned to Sweden in the spring of 2020, Patrik Zanders never heard anything about it. To prevent the Fox from leaving the country, he would have had to have been arrested *in absentia*, which he wasn't.

The Fox, however, remained a person of interest in the ongoing murder investigation.

Foxtrot

'He's definitely somebody we would have liked to question', Patrik Zanders told me.

However, the police weren't the only ones who were seeking justice for Shad.

21

In the spring of 2020, a plot to avenge Shad's murder was hatched inside the Kumla prison, which is just south of Örebro. The suspicion is that this plan was made by inmates held in a Fenix ward, a designation used for wards in which the country's most dangerous terrorists, murderers and gang leaders, who were also considered escape risks, were held.

The police investigation began when Putte and his colleagues at Noa made a startling realization as they were reading the chats of the alias Mujaheed, whom they had identified as Chihab Lamouri, the leader of the Vårby network. Putte had been keeping tabs on Lamouri after he had settled in Spain.

Lamouri was writing to somebody who called himself Literalbeetle on Encrochat. Based on the chat logs, it seemed that secret information from police investigations was being leaked to criminals, enabling them to adapt the testimonies they gave to the evidence the police had. They were also receiving advice on how to avoid being caught while under surveillance.

'This is a lawyer!', a colleague at Noa shouted.

Putte was sitting nearby, and was genuinely horrified to learn that there were lawyers who were aiding people involved in murders and bombings.

At that point, Putte had to prioritize preventing new murders, and this information was thus passed on to colleagues in the Stockholm region who were later brought into the operation.

This was how the police would eventually learn that the alias Literalbeetle was being used by two successful lawyers at the Devlet law firm in Stockholm. Their names were Ekrem Güngör and Amir Amdouni, and they called themselves 'The King' and 'The Prince' respectively in the chats. On top of the millions they were raking in from the state for their legal work, they were also being paid to leak information to criminals attached to several different networks.

'You help us and we help you, brothers in this life and in the next, inshallah!' This message was sent to the lawyers' Encro phone by the brother of the leader of the Vårby network.

*

In early April 2020, a man who had been sentenced to life in prison for murder and was doing his time in one of Kumla's four Fenix wards, began to open up to the prison officers. He was known as somebody who got into violent altercations with other inmates, but he had remained peaceful recently. Perhaps the conflict resolution training he was participating in had paid off. In any case, he was also being unusually talkative.

Considering the strict code of silence that criminals observe, the things he began to tell different prison officers during his breaks from solitary confinement were very unexpected. He had learned that a fellow inmate at Fenix in Kumla, one of the leaders of the Death Squad, who had confided in him, was planning a hit on the Mask, the man in his thirties who was rumoured to have been involved in Shad's murder and was currently serving a sentence for possession of a firearm at Saltvik prison in Härnösand.

The guard was shocked to hear the next part of the inmate's account. One of the key figures in the murder plot was none other than the Death Squad Leader's lawyer, Ekrem Güngör.

It was difficult to determine the accuracy of this information, but it was too detailed to be dismissed outright. There was a note made in the Prison and Probation Service's internal intelligence system about what the prisoner had said. However, this information wouldn't become truly interesting until later on, when it could be considered in the right context. Another important piece of this puzzle was the testimony that Shad's relative gave the police. When all this information was brought together, the background of the murder plot began to come into view.

Once the police investigation had been under way for a while, they began to form more serious suspicions against Ekrem Güngör, the King, who had already been seen leaking information to criminals. In early April, early on in the Encro operation, the King had been speaking to his client, the leader of the Death Squad. After this meeting, the King wrote an Encrochat message to Leopardmaster, who was another known criminal, saying that the Mask was 'ready'. The police interpreted this as meaning he was to be killed.

This was when the plot to kill the Mask began to be put into action. According to the investigation, in addition to informing him about the plan, the lawyer also instructed this suspect to raise several million kronor from the Mask's enemies to pay for the hit.

One minute after the first message, Leopardmaster began to inform his own contacts about the plan. Just a day later, 1 million kronor had been raised. The money was to be sent via the Money Changer – i.e., the World Exchange office in Södermalm, Stockholm.

The news spread quickly through encrypted chats, both to Swedish suburbs and to people abroad. The Boxer, who was in Dubai at the time, received a message to the alias

Airwalnut, one of several accounts that have been linked to him. He was asked to contribute to the fund, but he had no interest in taking the Mask out. He also claimed to be 'a poor man'.

Others took a greater interest. According to the chat logs, the money appears to have been raised within a few days. For a variety of reasons, the Mask had many enemies who were all eager to dispatch him. Both among the police and on the streets, the Mask was viewed as a calculating and extremely vengeful loner, and he was feared even by criminals with a great capacity for violence. The respect and fear he commanded was largely the result of a story that went around about how he had slept on his best friend's grave after he was shot dead.

The Mask swore vengeance, no matter the cost, and he was a patient man. Two years later, he was wandering around in a residential neighbourhood in Järfälla, searching for the man he believed had killed his friend. After residents had alerted the police about an 'elderly man' who had been behaving strangely in the area, the police reportedly arrived on the scene and a dramatic car chase ensued. When the police finally caught up with the fugitive and dragged him out of his car, they realized that it was actually a young man wearing a lifelike, skin-coloured 'old man' rubber mask. In the car was a loaded rifle with a telescopic sight, and a pistol.

This was how the Mask got his nickname.

Long after Encrochat had been cracked, police investigators learned that the Prison and Probation Service already had intelligence related to a murder plot, which seemed to align with what they had read in the chat logs. Two police officers visited the prison where the informant was serving his life sentence to conduct an interview with him. To their surprise, the prisoner stood by his previous statements, and claimed that the King was involved in even more criminal activities than the ones that investigators had learned of from the chats. During the investigation, it also emerged that even the country's most isolated and dangerous prisoners had little difficulty communicating with the outside world. In this case, they did it by phoning their lawyer, the King, who passed on messages for them. However, even within the walls of the prison, the prisoners could easily communicate with others. Prison officers told the police that inmates could scoop the water out of their toilets and speak freely to each other through the drains.

'This is a big problem in all the prisons', a manager at Fenix told police officers who were investigating the plot to murder the Mask.

Investigators began to search through the massive body of Encrochat messages that Noa had been given access to, to see if there had been any other mention of the Mask during the time when the murder was being planned.

They found several hits. One individual who was involved in discussions about the fate of the Mask was Foxkurdish. This was during the same period when he was cleaning up the mess after his mule Albin had been arrested at the Elite Hotel.

'Bram, did the Mask do something or not?' he asked the alias Modernsky on 19 April.

He soon received a series of replies stating that nothing could yet be confirmed, along with some speculations concerning who had put up the money for the contract on Shad. His friend fingered 24K, a network of individuals from Järfälla and Tensta, which has also been linked to the rap group of the same name. Modernsky also suggested that the Jakobsberg network had been involved. This was the group that had received help from the Death Squad's sixteen-year-old shooter at the bus stop in Viksjö. According to Foxkurdish's friend, the actual reason why Shad had been murdered was a killing that had been committed a year or so earlier, when an individual with close ties to both of these networks had been shot dead. The investigators who were reading the chats had to keep track of countless details, nicknames and violent crimes. Eventually, through the efforts of experienced police officers, some light began to be shed on the long-lasting vendettas that connected all these people. They saw that Foxkurdish's friend had also asked him if anything was going to happen to the Mask when he was released from prison.

'Brother, don't worry and don't talk to anyone', Foxkurdish wrote.

His friend wasn't worried, he just wanted to know about any plans before they happened. He also promised not to talk to anyone.

'Ok brother', Foxkurdish replied, and then sent him a heart.

*

One challenge in carrying out the planned murder was getting access to the Mask. When lawyer Ekrem Güngör started to share information about the contract, the Mask was still behind bars in another Fenix ward, at Saltvik prison. The prisoner who had started to talk to the prison officers told them that somebody had already offered to do the deed. The person in question was the leader of the Södertälje network, Berno Khouri, who was already serving a life sentence and had recently been moved from Kumla to Saltvik. The informant explained that Khouri and the Death Squad Leader had become close friends while they were in the same ward at Kumla, and when Khouri was relocated to Saltvik for some unknown reason, it aligned perfectly with the assassination plot.

Once the money had been raised and the green light had been given, the plan was for the man from the Death Squad to send a letter to Khouri. Since anything they wrote would be read by the correctional officers, the letter was going to contain the following code words: 'The journalist contacted me and wants to interview me.'

The plotters waited anxiously for the mission to be carried out, keeping their eyes open for any news reports about prison slayings. However, the murder of the Mask never happened. Apparently, Khouri and the Mask established a friendly relationship during the months they spent in the same ward. A source told me that Khouri began to sympathize with the Mask.

When the Mask was later released, he wrote to Khouri, wishing him a 'Merry Christmas and a Happy New Year'. Word is that, like many other individuals from the Swedish criminal underworld, the Mask has since made his way to Turkey.

In questioning, Khouri denied any involvement in the murder plot.

'Could you give me a hard copy of the transcripts of these interrogations? I'd like to hang them up in my cell, actually', he said.

The Death Squad Leader kept silent throughout the interrogation, answering no questions. He also declined to make any comment when I contacted him. The evidence from the chats and the testimony of the prison informant wasn't sufficient for either of them to be charged with any crimes. However, the evidence in the Encrochat logs, along with other materials, was sufficient to get both the Prince and the King sentenced to several years of prison in the Court of Appeal. The King was considered to have played a key role in the plot against the Mask, and was convicted of being an accessory to conspiracy to commit murder. The Court of Appeal would later declare that both of these individuals had abused society's trust in them as legal professionals. After sentencing, Ekrem Güngör communicated with *Aftonbladet* through his lawyer, admitting to an ethics breach and 'fully' accepting his exclusion from the Swedish Bar Association. The Prince was also disbarred.

When I asked Khouri about the allegations, he continued to deny them. He told me that they were an attempt to interfere with his ongoing appeal, and that the investigation was based on 'lies, gossip and rumours'.

The prison informant, for his part, suggested that Khouri's claims were tactical, intended to 'maintain a façade'. He went on to assert that every single person involved in the murder plot knew that every word he'd said during the investigation and the trial was '100 per cent true'.

22

A few weeks after the family had arrived in Sweden, in early April 2020, the Fox's partner was visiting Hasse in his home. He was a friend of the family in Kista, who had helped with starting the ice-cream parlour and did their bookkeeping. This particular day, the Fox's partner wanted help applying for a distance-learning nursing course. She showed no signs of stress, and she asked him to give her 20,000 kronor of her ice-cream parlour profits, so she could buy tickets for her family for an upcoming trip.

On the evening after the raid at the Elite Hotel, the Fox wrote to his mother on Encrochat to tell her what had happened.

'They have arrested the Swedish guy. He might mention my name.'

The investigators also noted that the Fox told his mother that his father was holding 4.7 million kronor in cash and five or six watches.

His mother suggested that he leave the country, and sent the Fox's partner an article from Dagens Industri about the last flight between Sweden and the UK, which was scheduled to leave on 9 April, before the borders were to be closed completely because of the pandemic.

At lunchtime on 9 April, the Fox, his partner and their three children flew to Amsterdam. After this, his Encro phone connected to the network near a residential area in The Hague in the Netherlands, just 4 kilometres north of Europol's headquarters.

The Fox had been in Sweden for less than a month, and Team Foxtrot investigators would later interpret the Fox's trip as a panicked attempt to escape before they could follow the tracks all the way back to him.

*

A few days later, the Fox's mother met with Hasse in Kista. The two had once been romantically involved, and had remained friends after that. Hasse was an important source of support for the family. When the Fox had been convicted of a serious drug offence in 2010, Hasse served as his lay supervisor. It hadn't made any difference. The Fox had continued committing crimes, and was eventually convicted again. After that, Hasse began to think a lot less of the Fox.

The mother asked Hasse to meet with the Fox's father to fetch the watches that the Fox hadn't wanted to take along on his journey. Hasse didn't harbour any suspicions, because the Fox's mother had told him that her son bought and sold expensive watches and gold chains, and even ran restaurants in Iraq. However, he didn't want to let the Fox's father into his home, as they weren't on good terms, so he met him downstairs at the entrance, instead. A plastic bag containing several large boxes was handed over.

Hasse went back up to his flat, and left the bag in one of his rooms. The Fox's mother came by later that day. She showed him the contents of the boxes. There were three shiny Rolex watches. One of them, which was made of rose gold, was worth 592,000 kronor. Together, the three of them were worth more than a million.

She wanted Hasse to keep the watches in his flat for her.

This didn't seem like a strange request to him. He had grown accustomed to the family doing these kinds of things. Being immigrants, they were worried about being burgled, and they'd had bad experiences in their interactions with the authorities. Because of this, they would often spread their cash and jewellery around in other people's homes. This time, however, he rejected her request. He knew that the Fox was involved in the sale of luxury items, but these watches represented what he found to be an incredibly vulgar 'Middle Eastern style'. He would later tell me he couldn't stand it.

'Take that shit away. I don't want that kind of stuff in my home', he told the Fox's mother.

23

Based on the chat logs and other investigative materials, Jacob and the other members of Team Foxtrot had begun to suspect that the Fox had fled Sweden. This suspicion was further confirmed after they carried out a raid on his empty flat. Investigators had also come to learn more about the way he did business.

Denny and his team already had their eyes on several individuals who were close to the top of the Fox's pyramid. These people were major buyers of drugs who were in immediate contact with the alleged aliases of the Fox. One of these people called himself Darthvvader. When Team Foxtrot's investigators Thorbjörn and Niklas gained access to the Encrochat messages, they were finally able to draw clear connections between many of the Encro aliases that were working with the Fox in one way or another. Now, all they needed was sufficient resources to make as many arrests as possible, one at a time.

The investigators had no trouble identifying Albin from the Elite Hotel with the alias Buckradio. He was one of the people working for the Fox who had gone out to deliver drugs to customers, including Darthvvader, who had received just over 2 kilos of amphetamine and 2 kilos of MDMA in Haninge, a southern suburb of Stockholm. The total price paid was 92,080 kronor, according to the chats. The police suspected that this highly specific figure was due to the fact that the drugs were sold in euros, which would then be converted into kronor.

Darthvvader was a buyer, but he was also an intermediary for the Fox. The chats reveal that, among other activities, he transported 2 kilos of speed to a user who called himself Efficientbonsai. This alias has been linked to the leader of the Dalen network, which operates in Enskededalen in southern Stockholm. This man, now thirty-nine years old, used a mule of his own to pick up the drugs in Bredäng, another area in the south of Stockholm. The Dalen network leader would later be convicted for having masterminded the kidnapping of the rapper Einár. He had also served an instrumental role in blackmailing Einár for 3 million kronor, threatening to leak humiliating pictures of the rapper in social media posts if he refused to pay. When the blackmail attempt was unsuccessful, plans were made to detonate a bomb at the rapper's home. The leader was also convicted for distributing a total of 113 kilos of cocaine over the entire period that the police were surveilling his communications on Encrochat in 2020. This is a staggering amount, considering that a total of 216 kilos of cocaine were seized by Swedish Customs over that whole year.

In an earlier case, while he had been held in custody on suspicion of assault, his younger brother had been secretly fed confidential information from the investigation by lawyer Ekrem Güngör, and this information is believed to have been used to influence the testimony of one of the men who had been assaulted. His younger brother was arrested in Bulgaria in the spring of 2022, but he was placed under house arrest and managed to escape in somewhat unclear circumstances. He remains at large to this day. The Dalen network's dealings with the Fox's network would eventually undergo some rather dramatic changes, but at this point that was still a long way off.

*

People at the higher levels of the Fox's hierarchy, like Darthvvader, seldom needed to handle drugs themselves. They hired 'workers' to carry out various tasks for them. These could be intermediaries who made connections with buyers from other networks, holders who stored the drugs, or mules who delivered them to customers.

Characteristic of many of the mules in the Fox's network is that they were small-business owners, often of ethnic Swedish origins, sometimes considerably older than their employers, and usually had legal sources of income. In other words, these individuals wouldn't attract much suspicion. One of Darthvvader's mules had a background in the security business. In the chats, Darthvvader was delighted to announce that his mule worked the night shift providing security for the European Centre for Disease Prevention and Control, which has an office in Solna. For the Fox and people in his position, storing their product is a risky and costly business.

'Everyone involved wants to get their product in the hands of their customers as soon as possible', a member of the network explained.

Essentially, they were following the same New Public Management philosophy that had spread from the world of business to the public sector in the 1990s. Just like a public-sector organization or legitimate business, drug dealers want to avoid unnecessary stockpiling, and strive to maintain a 'just-in-time' supply chain.

There was a lot of activity on the Fox's Encrochat accounts. Business was always being done, with sales of cocaine, amphetamines, cannabis, ecstasy, MDMA and heroin being agreed. Supply and demand reigned supreme. Sales were written down in detail, and debts of hundreds of thousands of kronor were paid, sometimes through Bitcoin transactions.

Several members of Team Foxtrot admit that the police are 'to put it nicely, bad at tracing cryptocurrency payments'. It's just too complicated. Few police officers have the technical skills required to follow the trail of payments. In the case of the Fox, sources have claimed that the money from his sales never went to him directly, but was always passed through crypto exchanges.

'They're like financial advisors who deal in nothing but cryptocurrencies, and couldn't care less where the money came from', said one police officer.

All the transactions that the police have actually been able to trace in greater detail have gone through exchangers who were neither Swedish nor located in Sweden. Dead ends, in other words. They couldn't prioritize people like that. One major problem is that the 'police are chasing quick numbers' – i.e., they're content to prosecute the holders and mules. Following the money and going after the people who manage the proceeds of crime takes time, and the police simply aren't good enough at it. According to a report from the police's own internal auditors, they need to get better at tracing money while conducting criminal investigations, and at seizing the proceeds of criminal activity. Several police officers I spoke to agree. However, they told me that there is 'little appetite' within the force for following these kinds of resource-consuming leads.

*

Alongside all the crime-related clues and pieces of gossip, even more clarity was gained as a result of the investigation into Darthvvader. In a bare room inside the police station in Solna, where Jacob's team worked, there were notes pinned to the walls and in shared documents on their computers. The investigators sat behind their screens with white mugs stained with dry coffee dregs, meticulously combing the chat logs.

Encrochat logs revealed that it was Darthvvader who had sent Mesut to pick up the heroin from Roger in Sollentuna on 10 May 2020. The police now also had written proof that it was the Fox's Encro alias that had sent Roger there to sell the heroin.

Again, they were looking at evidence of the direct involvement of the Fox – or his alias, at the very least – in a drug deal.

As the investigators continued to read the chats, they saw how the two drug dealers had panicked when they realized that their mules, who had both just been arrested, weren't answering their phones.

'Brother I'm in trouble', Darthvvader wrote to the Fox's Encro alias.

Darthvvader had driven past the house where Mesut lived, and he was worried that the police might have seen him. He repeated several times that he was in trouble.

'I'm fucked bro', he wrote to the Fox.

'Brother, I'm fucked', was the reply.

The Fox was worried that the police might manage to stop four other shipments he had in the pipeline, or find a stash of product he had that was worth 10 million kronor. Darthvvader, for his part, was mainly focused on Mesut, who had previously been connected to his family through a relationship with his sister.

'Brother this is my brother-in-law he's not even a criminal.'

Darthvvader claimed that Roger probably 'makes ten drops a day' for the Fox, and must have been under surveillance. He wanted to split the loss on the heroin, since he had also lost his own stash. He was shaken, worrying about what his family might say when his brother-in-law was arrested.

'I'm out of the heroin business for good', he wrote, seemingly expecting that they would be coming for him next.

*

The investigators didn't find identifying the person behind the alias Darthvvader particularly difficult. In the car Mesut was driving when he was arrested, the police found mail addressed to a man who was twenty-eight years old at the time. He was registered in Upplands Väsby, but he was really staying with his girlfriend in Solna, next to the Mall of Scandinavia shopping centre.

During the raid on the flat in Solna, police found a drinks trolley with a glass tabletop and gold edges, along with some bottles of whiskey and tequila. This trolley was identical with one that was shown in a photo Darthvvader had sent on Encrochat. His Encro phone and his regular mobile phone could both be tied to crime scenes via phone-tower logs. When the police analysed his personal finances, they discovered that he received a salary from his sisters, who ran an interpreting agency and a media company. This was a family of entrepreneurs, which was said to own properties both in Sweden and in Dubai.

However, the sums that flowed into his accounts didn't match his taxed income. He was also consuming far more luxury goods than he ought to have been able to afford. He regularly shopped at Cartier, Philipp Plein, Dior, Dolce & Gabbana and Royaldesign, and he booked expensive hotel stays abroad.

The police claimed that he was both a major customer and a close friend of the Fox.

Before his arrest, he watched in anguish as the news spread that Encrochat had been cracked, and many of his friends were arrested one after another. However, he still hadn't been woken by any police raids at dawn. He realized that it was only a matter of time before his life of freedom came to an end.

During the summer of 2020, the paranoia among Darthvvader and his contacts intensified. They began to think carefully about who they were seen with, and how they communicated. They began to favour meeting face to face in locations where it would be difficult for a surveillance team to observe them without being detected. They began to view their fellow customers in restaurants with suspicion. Right up until the end, they were hoping that they might have made it, that they had stayed discreet enough when they wrote to each other on Encrochat.

However, Denny and his detectives were keeping a close eye on them.

*

Despite all the arrests of mules and holders, the Fox and those of his allies who had evaded the police continued to do business, apparently unconcerned. Perhaps this was because they knew that nobody would dare to squeal anyway.

However, when August 2020 drew to a close, Team Foxtrot had investigated the Fox's parents, and was getting ready to make a move on the members of his inner circle.

24

On Tuesday 25 August, hard knocks rang out on the door of the rental flat in Uppsala where the Fox's mother lived. The police wore thin, blue gloves as they searched her wardrobe, opened cupboards, and looked inside her flowerpots on the balcony.

'I found something', one of the policemen on the balcony said.

In a bucket, they found bags of banknotes weighed down with heavy dumbbells. They made similar finds all over the flat, in different hiding places. Bundles of banknotes had been stuffed into socks. One of these socks, which was found inside an oven glove in a storage drawer under the cooker, contained 33,400 kronor. There was even more money inside pairs of trousers in the wardrobe, and in two dressing gowns that were hanging behind one of the doors in the bedroom. All in all, it was almost 400,000 kronor. The Fox's mother was receiving welfare support at the time, and only had 4,901 kronor in her bank account.

The somewhat unusual thing about her in particular was that she had her own Encro phone. There are women who work as mules, or handle cash, but they tend to be young, and looking to make some fast money just like the men do. But this was an older woman, a mother.

She went by the alias Inediblepalm, and she had only connected with two Encro users: Foxkurdish and Foxplanet. The investigation would reveal evidence suggesting that the mother and her son had been communicating with each other through Encrochat. He congratulated her on Mother's Day, and sent her two red hearts and a kiss emoji. The mother sent pictures of her grandchildren playing on a nearby skateboard ramp.

She told Foxkurdish to call his son, who was spending the day with her.

Another time, she wrote to Foxkurdish that he should call a Swedish phone number that was registered to the Fox's father. Foxkurdish sent two pictures through Encrochat of him wearing a Rolex watch worth hundreds of thousands of kronor on his wrist, next to stacks of 50-euro notes that were resting on his legs. Next to the banknotes was a large, gold fox pendant.

*

Another person who got caught up in the events on that day in August was a 77-year-old retired economist. He was standing at the counter of the ice-cream parlour, near the Fyrisån river, when three police officers came to arrest him. The ice-cream parlour was owned by the Fox's partner, but it was almost always this pensioner who manned the counter. He said that he worked for free, sometimes with the Fox's mum. He loved it. He got to meet people, and it gave him something to do.

The pensioner had started volunteering at the ice-cream parlour several years earlier. He had been out on his bike, passing by the place, when he saw a woman with long, dark hair carrying chairs and tables all by herself. He offered to help her. After this, he started going back there. He and the Fox's mother formed a relationship, and she soon moved into his flat as a friend. It was only until she found a rental flat of her own.

The pensioner opened the parlour and received the deliveries early in the mornings, and worked until late in the evening. The Fox's mother would usually turn up around lunchtime. The pensioner said it was just like getting a gym membership. He lost lots of weight.

However, in the spring and summer of 2020, things were set in motion that he would eventually come to regret. The Fox's mother asked him for various favours. Strangers would arrive to deliver cash. He was assured that the money came from legitimate businesses. He believed her, and did what she asked him to: he counted out hundreds of thousands of kronor in cash, and then passed the money on to other strangers. One summer's day, he was cycling to a fast-food restaurant with a large amount of cash that he had been instructed to hand over to a man who would be waiting in a car. What he didn't know was that the woman he trusted, the Fox's mother, had received a message from her son telling her that 212,000 kronor were to be given to 'an Arab'.

He was being used as a mule for a drug ring, in the belief that he was just helping a friend.

Apart from these drop-offs, he also agreed to keep hundreds of thousands of kronor in cash in his flat, even though the Fox's mother had a home of her own. He never questioned why she wouldn't want to keep the money at her place. He was arrested, and spent two nights in a cell at the police station. After answering the police's questions, he was released pending trial. In the end, he received a suspended sentence for a serious money-laundering offence. The police officer who questioned him empathized with him.

'You've been used', he was told.

He agreed.

*

While the police were arresting the pensioner and searching the Fox's mother's flat, they also executed a raid at his father's address in Kista in the north-west of Stockholm. The father was eventually convicted of money-laundering offences, for receiving almost 200,000 kronor from Albin, the mule who was arrested at the Elite Hotel. The mule had been told to 'leave the dough with my dad' on Encrochat.

*

The businessman Hasse also had his home raided. When Denny and his team burst into the flat, he was very surprised. Hasse had been a politician for the Swedish conservative party, and had founded several businesses. He had no criminal record. His finances were good, and his views on immigration were well known to his neighbours. He wanted to restrict migration, specifically to prevent 'criminal immigrants' from causing trouble in Sweden.

Still reeling from the shock of being raided by the police, he was taken to the police station in Solna, where an initial interrogation was held. He was still unconcerned, certain that it must all be some kind of misunderstanding. He even found it a bit exciting. 'This'll make a good story to tell the old men at the local pub over a pint', he thought to himself.

After a few hours of waiting, he was questioned by the police. He was asked about several hundred thousand kronor in cash that supposedly came from criminal activities. Hasse had no clue what was going on.

While he was being interrogated, the police were searching his home for secret hiding places. A world map was removed from the wall in his study, and his well-stocked white bookcase was also pulled out. Inside a wooden box, the police found a cardboard box with the Fox's mother's name written on it. The box was filled with cash, which the mother kept in bags and envelopes held together with rubber bands. This was years' worth of tips and cash from the ice-cream parlour, she and Hasse would both claim.

As the police went on to search the balcony, they made a discovery: they found something that Hasse didn't expect them to. Behind a locked metal hatch on the side of the balcony was a plastic bag from the Willy:s supermarket. It contained three watches, worth more than 1 million kronor in total, and a golden charm shaped like a fox.

This was that gaudy Middle Eastern stuff he had refused to let the Fox's mother keep in his home. He would never even think of storing watches like that, on a balcony, as they might be damaged by the humidity. The Fox's mother would later confess to having secretly hidden the bag there, and, after spending three nights in custody, Hasse was released, although he remained a suspect.

*

Arresting the Fox's parents and other family members represented an important step, and at the police station in Solna, Team Foxtrot was pleased to watch their efforts bear fruit. Despite that satisfaction, though, there were mixed feelings. While it was true that they had achieved several of the task force's goals in just a few months, this seemed to have had no impact on the flood of drugs that was arriving on the streets of Sweden. And wherever the drugs went, deadly violence was sure to follow. Big players such as the Fox seemed undisturbed, and were already continuing their activities through new encryption services.

One of the new services that many criminals had migrated to, once the cracking of Encrochat became common knowledge, was called ANOM. Its marketing slogan was 'by criminals, for criminals'. However, as it happened, nothing could be further from the truth.

PART 5
THE HONEY TRAP
SEPTEMBER 2020 – JUNE 2021

25

On 3 September 2020, a week after the raid on the Fox's family members, representatives from the American FBI visited Stockholm. A few days earlier, they had contacted the intelligence department at Noa, to discuss a possible future collaboration on a covert operation. Noa agreed. Their operational manager, Emil Eisersjö, was unable to attend this time, but he sent a team of his staff to the US embassy to get the ball rolling.

One of the participants was Vera, who had been Noa's Europol liaison officer when Encrochat was cracked. She had a long career in the police force behind her, and had plenty of experience combatting serious organized crime. Although she worked on-site at the Europol headquarters, she had been kept out of the Encrochat operation. She was too busy with other operational matters to take part. All the same, she found it frustrating to be physically present and know that there was something big going on without being allowed to take part. For months, she had noticed how her colleagues from France, the Netherlands, the UK and a few other countries were occupying a meeting room on the ground floor. Her frustration came to a head when some French colleagues who believed she had been informed asked her for feedback on what had been done with the intelligence Sweden had been given in the early stages of the operation.

'Have you made any arrests?' they asked.

Sitting there in the office of the Swedish desk at Europol, without a clue what was going on, had made her feel like a fool. After spending almost four years as Sweden's liaison officer at Europol, she knew the representatives from the other countries well, but she had still been excluded by her own colleagues at Noa in Sweden. Towards the middle of May, when Sweden formally joined the operation, she demanded a straight answer from her boss, Emil Eisersjö at Noa.

'You'd better explain to me what the hell is going on!'

She was given the information she needed. Noa was taking part in an operation concerning Encrochat and, along with a handful of other countries, had been granted access to encrypted chats. She had no choice but to get on with all the other duties her position involved, including coordinating surveillance efforts that targeted some of the many Swedish criminals who were operating out of Spain.

*

The FBI representative started the meeting by informing Vera that the US Federal Bureau of Investigation had created ANOM, an encrypted service which thousands of criminals, including ones active in Sweden, had started to use just as they had previously used Encrochat. The operation was like something out of a Hollywood movie.

Vera could hardly believe her ears, and she was soon tasked with managing the Swedish end of this collaboration with the FBI.

She would never have imagined that another encrypted service would be made available to the police like this. Let alone having the service in question be a honey trap created by law enforcement, which desperate criminals would find themselves having to turn to in order to conduct their illicit business.

The Honey Trap

Just as she had been in relation to Encrochat, Lise Tamm at Rio was consulted to ensure the legality of this proposed collaboration. She appointed Henrik Söderman as her contact person again, this time along with an experienced colleague of hers, Ewamari Häggkvist.

And just as in the case of Encrochat, she judged that Sweden could legitimately access intelligence information sourced in the United States, a nation that Sweden had already entered into judicial cooperation with. The principle of free examination and evaluation of evidence applied, and it would be up to the courts to decide whether the chat logs would be admissible evidence. The big difference compared to the Encrochat operation was that ANOM was actually created by the FBI before being distributed to criminal organizations. Would this mean that secret data surveillance was occurring in Swedish territory, with the knowledge of Swedish police and prosecutors? The Rio prosecutors determined that this wouldn't be the case, as the communications from ANOM were passed through a server located outside of Sweden. Although they didn't know exactly where the server was, they knew that it was outside of the country.

Another key question here was whether this constituted entrapment.

'In this case, the criminals in question voluntarily chose to use this particular service to commit crimes, and the service only happened to be controlled by the FBI', said Lise Tamm.

As far as Noa was concerned, this was the green light it needed to go ahead. In addition, at the request of the FBI, the Swedish police was tasked with leading the operation, which would come to be named Trojan Shield within Europol. The first stage of Vera's job would be to set up an organization within Noa that would have the capacity to process the material they would be sent by the FBI.

*

The ANOM sting would also come to be challenged by defence lawyers. 'Be that as it may, refraining from sharing intelligence that might save lives was out of the question', said Linda H. Staaf, then head of intelligence at Noa.

'I would approve it again today', she states firmly.

She doesn't feel that the mere fact that Swedish police knew that the FBI was eavesdropping on Swedish citizens is sufficiently problematic to put the operation's legitimacy in question. With ANOM, as with the Encro operation, the easy way out would have been to turn down intelligence to avoid later criticism. She agrees that this would have been cautious, but she also thinks it would have been immoral. She also insists that, in the event that she'd seen any indication that any of this was somehow illegal, she would have made a different decision.

'We're dealing with serious problems in Sweden. This is a source of useful information that can help us prevent murders and provide us with evidence to convict criminals. I stand behind this operation, I want that to be clear. I chose to go on the offensive, because we had to take action', said Staaf.

*

The idea for ANOM had come about a few years earlier, when the FBI in San Diego began investigating Phantom Secure, a Canada-based provider of encrypted phones. They discovered that the company was only selling their phones to members of criminal organizations, primarily drug traffickers. When the FBI surveyed the user base, they discovered that the people using the company's encrypted devices were South American cartels, European crime syndicates and the Hells Angels motorcycle gang in Australia, and other people of that kind.

In March 2018, criminal charges were brought against the company's CEO and four other executives under the RICO

Act. This is a piece of United States legislation that makes participating in organized crime a criminal act in itself, making it easier to prosecute these organizations' leadership, which issues orders to others to commit crimes. This was the first case of its kind, in which US authorities had targeted the managers of a company that provided technology to criminals that helped them maintain secrecy while committing their crimes.

A similar item of legislation regarding participation in a criminal organization is what French prosecutor Alexandre relied on when authorizing the use of coercive measures against the company Encrochat and its server. The CEO of Phantom Secure pleaded guilty and was sentenced to nine years in prison for providing encrypted phones that criminal networks had used for communication in the course of their international drug trafficking. However, the FBI knew that all they had achieved was a temporary disruption of a communications service vital to the criminal organizations, and that it would only be a matter of time before a replacement made its way to the market. So, when the FBI arrested a previously convicted drug offender in connection with their Phantom investigation, and he agreed to become their informant, they came up with a bold plan. This man had recently invested significant amounts in the development of a new communications platform called ANOM, which he offered to hand over to the authorities in exchange for leniency and a payment of around 100,000 US dollars.

ANOM looks like an ordinary mobile phone, but the usual features for phone calls and messaging don't work. Instead, there is a pre-installed software that's hidden behind an icon that looks and functions just like a regular calculator app on a mobile phone. If a special code is entered into the calculator, this will open ANOM, which can be used to send encrypted messages, pictures, videos and voice messages. The phones also have a 'burner' feature, which can be used to delete messages after a preset amount of time.

A breakthrough in the development of ANOM is said to have been made 'over a beer', when Australian police officers met with colleagues from the FBI. They had collaborated on the Phantom Secure operation, and now they realized that they had a good opportunity to work together to target criminals on their own home turf.

The FBI had their informant, and the Australians were able to provide the technical solutions needed to decrypt and read messages sent through ANOM.

What made the next stage possible was that the informant entered into an agreement with the FBI whereby he was to distribute ANOM phones to three former distributors of Phantom. These, in turn, were directly connected to various international criminal organizations, most of them active in Australia. Gaining the trust of criminals would be a necessary precondition for successfully distributing the phones. However, in this case, there were already existing personal relationships in place and, as the criminals already had trust in the distributors, the new ANOM phones soon found acceptance.

The marketing practically took care of itself, too. The website had a password which the distributors passed on to buyers, all in the name of keeping non-criminals out, which further reinforced the feeling that this was a safe system.

Next, the FBI launched a covert investigation that would eventually become known as Operation Trojan Shield, initiating a collaboration with the Australian Federal Police (AFP) and other agencies to monitor the ongoing communications. A master key was built into the encryption system, which meant that any message could be secretly transmitted and read by the FBI.

To begin with, the AFP received court authorization to monitor about fifty ANOM phones belonging to people with ties to Australia. The test was successful, and provided the police with insight into the activities of two of the country's most notorious criminal networks. The Australian police concluded that ANOM was used exclusively for criminal activities, including weapon crimes and drug trafficking. Their findings concerning the types of conversations that were being had on ANOM was shared with the FBI.

ANOM spread slowly at first, but in the summer of 2019, demand for the phones began to grow even beyond Australia's borders. At this point, the FBI source started distributing the phones to a larger number of criminal actors. The information was still being reviewed by Australian police officers, but the court order they had didn't authorize sharing the content they had gathered with other countries' police forces. To get around this limitation, the FBI enlisted the assistance of a third country, and had the server placed there. The ANOM communications were relayed to the FBI from this server without the data gathered being reviewed by the third nation's authorities. Which country this was hasn't been revealed, but, according to *Vice* magazine, it's a country within the EU. According to my sources at Noa, it wasn't Sweden.

At the end of October 2019, the FBI began to receive messages from the server. At this point, the number of ANOM users was growing gradually, and the FBI was able to access chats, pictures, video clips of drugs and audio messages. This enabled the FBI to identify seventeen key individuals who were acting as administrators, distributors and criminal influencers – in other words, the people who were best positioned to convince other criminals to use ANOM.

That's when Maximilian Rivkin entered the story.

He was born in Malmö, and had previously been sentenced to six years in prison for drug offences. Apart from that, he had kept a low profile in Sweden, and he hadn't received any publicity apart from when he was a witness to the terror attack on Drottninggatan in 2017. At that time, he gave *Svenska Dagbladet* an account of the horrific scenes he had witnessed up close. His next appearance in the media would come two years later on Colombian television, when he was deported from the country after vandalizing a hotel room while high on cocaine and ecstasy.

The hot-tempered Rivkin, who had turned thirty-nine by now, was also registered as a resident in his parents' home country of Serbia. However, it turned out that he was still committing crimes in Sweden. He became one of three main international administrators of ANOM, and was given the rights to decide who could buy an ANOM phone and which account would be deleted when somebody was arrested.

The other two administrators were located in Turkey and Australia.

The most notorious of these two was the Australian drug smuggler Hakan Ayik. Rivkin and Ayik, and two other well-known criminals, were chosen to act as 'influencers' and use their credibility to help spread the FBI's trap. For their efforts, they received compensation for each subscription they sold, at a price of around 15,000 kronor every six months, to be paid in Bitcoin. In addition to remunerations made to the administrators, payments were also deposited into companies that had been set up by the police. Soon, criminals would begin to accuse Rivkin of being an FBI informant.

'Without Rivkin, there would have been no ANOM', one of Rivkin's former associates told me.

*

When criminals all over Europe ended up getting arrested thanks to Encrochat, the ones who managed to evade the authorities began to look for new encrypted communications channels. Maximilian Rivkin was selling phones at discount prices during the autumn of 2020, to build the customer base. He engaged salespeople within Sweden, and coached them on how to market ANOM. They didn't have to be polite. All they needed to do was say that only 'rats and police informants' used Sky ECC, which was the biggest competitor at the time. He encouraged his sellers to offer lower prices in order to dominate the market – which would supposedly guarantee massive profits down the road.

He seemed so convinced of this venture's long-term prospects that he began making his own attempts to convince criminals to start using his super-secure ANOM phones.

'A brand new ANOM phone for 1,500 euros. Insane margins. Plus, we're the first people who have it' – Rivkin wrote this on ANOM himself, according to the police.

In the same conversation, which he had with an individual who belonged to a criminal organization in the south of Stockholm, we can see evidence that the phones had started to spread to various networks in Gothenburg, Farsta, Rinkeby and other places.

'Tensta wanted 10. Some others in Uppsala 10. Our guys 10', the contact wrote back to Rivkin.

'Ok, tell them 5 grand brother', he replied.

All the while, Noa's intelligence officers Vera, Putte, Cattis and Ted were following the spread of the FBI phones. After the successful Encrochat operation, Ted Esplund had joined Noa's intelligence department in Stockholm, where he was coordinating all efforts related to the encryption services within the Swedish Police Authority. Reading the chats, he couldn't help but smile at the screen and thank Rivkin for doing such a good job of spreading ANOM among Swedish criminals. All the time, he had been blissfully unaware of the fact that he was helping the police.

Rivkin's business partner also wrote that the people in Lejonen, 'the Lions', a gang based in Hässelby, also wanted to distribute the phones and get a 'taste' of the profits. They were prepared to purchase hundreds of phones for distribution in Sweden, Norway and Spain.

'Everyone is welcome', Rivkin responded.

The same partner suggested that they start selling ANOM phones in a shop, but Rivkin refused. That wouldn't be safe. While he was keen to set up organizations in different geographical regions, with managers with over-arching responsibility and local support teams, he wanted to limit the operation to in-person sales.

'We move anom like we move kilos', he wrote.

26

One of the networks Rivkin persuaded to use ANOM phones was led by Abdul Haleem, who controlled much of the drug dealing in several areas in southern Stockholm. He was also involved in selling cocaine that had been hidden inside Gouda cheeses, along with members of the Ali Khan family and the Hjällbo network.

Even though so many leading criminals had recently been locked up because of Encrochat, the need to conduct criminal business was pressing. That's why many viewed these new phones, which Rivkin was vouching for, as a blessing.

Abdul Haleem had some business to conduct that he didn't want any outsiders to learn about. He had decided to have his former friend Sascha Viklund killed, once and for all.

*

On an autumn day one year earlier, in October 2019, Sascha had been in Farsta when two cars drove up to him. Several people exited the cars and disarmed him. They shoved him inside one of the cars, in front of several witnesses, and drove him to Vaxholm, which is north-east of Stockholm. It had already turned dark when Sascha found himself standing in a wooded area with a silenced pistol aimed at his face.

'Get down on your knees', somebody shouted at him, and shot him in the behind. 'The next one is going in your head.'

Sascha knew the man who was threatening his life very well. He had squinty eyes, a hoarse voice and a tattoo that reached up towards his neck. It was Abdul Haleem, Sascha's former friend and associate.

The two of them had started committing crimes together several years earlier. Sascha, who had a troubled early life and had spent plenty of time in different residential institutions, was introduced to Abdul by a close friend. This was the beginning of a long partnership, which ended up making both of them the targets of a series of investigations into serious crimes.

Abdul, who was originally from Afghanistan, soon earned a reputation as a vindictive, violent and extremely vengeful person among the older criminals in the southern areas of Stockholm. When he was still a teenager, he was accused of attempting to murder an older criminal who had killed a friend and compatriot of Abdul's during a car chase. He had been involved in several suspected shootings and murders since then, but he had evaded conviction.

After a prison term, Abdul decided to expand his territory. He wanted to gain control of the drug market in certain areas in the south of Stockholm, and launched an offensive.

'Abdul's main weapon was fear', a person who had been close to him told me. The message he sent to his rivals was as clear as day: defy us and die.

There were several other ongoing power struggles in the southern parts of Stockholm, and several murders were committed, most of which remain unsolved. With all these attempts to kill specific targets going on, several bystanders inevitably ended up getting in the way. One high-profile case where this happened was the murder of the 22-year-old trainee teacher Shayan Gaff, who was shot dead with twelve rounds from an automatic weapon in October 2018 as he was leaving a café in Segeltorp with one of his relatives. Shayan hadn't been involved in any criminal activities, and he probably ended up being murdered simply because he happened to look like a rival of the Vårby network.

'God, why me?' were his last words.

'To them, Shayan was the "wrong guy", but to us, this is a trauma. We're left with this grief to get through. The murder has completely changed our lives', a relative of Shayan explained.

Several murders that occurred in Stockholm during this time were thought to be linked to the long-standing conflict between Maykil Yokhanna, who was the target of the Västerås murder plot, and Chihab Lamouri, the leader of the Vårby network.

One of Chihab's close friends was convicted of Shayan Gaff's murder, and was defended in court by the King and the Prince.

Even though they had killed the wrong target, the hunt continued.

Three weeks after Shayan's murder, the actual intended target, a man called Gee, was shot dead with one of his friends in Hallonbergen. A few years earlier, Gee had been in an 'argument' with somebody who was related to Abdul Haleem, and subsequently ended up being banned from Rågsved. I learnt this from a well-informed source who agreed to explain the background of the conflict to me. The incident caused a lot of discord, and criminals began to take sides.

Maykil Yokhanna was said to have sided with Gee. Allegedly, the Vårby network and Abdul's network were both after Gee. It remains unclear who it was who carried out the double murder. One source from the Haleem side noted curtly that they were 'satisfied' after Gee's murder.

*

While Abdul Haleem was looking to build himself a drug empire, his friend and ally Sascha was in a serious motorbike accident. After being discharged from the hospital, he spent some time in a flat Abdul had arranged for him.

During a visit to a beach, Sascha got into a knife fight with a couple who had complained that his younger friends hadn't returned a lifebuoy to its proper place. Abdul was enraged that Sascha had targeted outsiders, who weren't criminals – an act that Abdul felt would tarnish his own reputation. I've also heard that Abdul approaches drug trafficking like a business operation, and that he was annoyed that Sascha was 'using his own supply'.

Abdul felt that he had lost face as a result of all this.

However, accounts differ here, and Sascha's family saw things very differently.

The knife fight ended up getting Sascha a prison sentence, which he began to serve in the autumn of 2018, when he was sent to the Tidaholmsanstalten prison. Another person who was already in that same ward was Maykil Yokhanna, who, as I just mentioned, had chosen to take Gee's side. Soon, there was a rumour going around that Sascha and Maykil had become friends in prison, and that Sascha had 'revealed secrets' to Maykil. When drugs later disappeared from different stashes, Sascha was suspected of having let slip their location. In the days before his release, he was relocated to a detention centre. The transfer was made under heavy security, because of the existing threat against him. This only seemed even more suspicious. Was he cooperating with the police?

Allegedly, this was why Sascha would later be taken into the woods in Vaxholm one day in autumn, squatting down with a gun to his face, and feeling his heart pound against his ribs.

'What information did you give Maykil?' one of the men asked him.

Sascha received a punch to the face.

'I didn't tell him anything', Sascha allegedly replied firmly.

They went through his phone, reading his messages and inspecting the phone numbers he had been in calls with. Nothing of interest was found. Sascha's family told me that cooperating with the police was something he would never do.

The plan had been to shoot him dead and then bury him right there at the site. That's why they had brought shovels. However, after more than thirty minutes of beatings and interrogations, an unfamiliar car approached the group. Everybody panicked, and Sascha saw his chance. He stood up and ran as fast as he could into the forest. He had been shot, he was limping, and he was wearing a thicker sole on one foot to compensate for his bone length discrepancy, which he had had since his motorbike accident. Several people chased after him, and shot at him, but the bullets missed him. Sascha disappeared into the forest, and eventually arrived at a road where he managed to get a car to stop.

People in the southern Stockholm area began to say he had more lives than a cat after this event.

However, this wouldn't be Abdul Haleem's last attempt.

*

A mutual friend, who was respected by both of them, allegedly tried to mediate between Sascha and Abdul.

'Could you put all this behind you? Could you forgive him, and give him another chance?' the mediator is said to have asked Abdul.

Reportedly, the response was that 'That chance is gone for him now.'

People who had been close to Abdul knew that there were three principles he had followed unerringly ever since his childhood in Afghanistan, and that he expected his allies and rivals to observe as well: respect, loyalty and fear.

Respect came from being fair to others, not putting them down. But if somebody threatened or harmed a member of the group, they had to be made aware that there would be serious consequences. They had to know that vengeance would come, and that they would pay with their lives. Anybody who had dealings with him knew this about him.

'We won't give up until we've accomplished our objective. This is the fear that we want others to feel inside', one person with insight into the network's internal organization told me.

Loyalty is a bond that money can't buy. You mustn't betray it, or show jealousy. And you must protect each other. You have to prove that 'I'm prepared take a sentence for you, or take a bullet for you, and to be there for your family if you're not here tomorrow.' If somebody wanted to have a family and leave their life of crime, the decision would be respected. Joining another group, however, was unacceptable.

It's said that the principles Abdul Haleem lives by are the same ones that have kept his community, the Tajiks, strong in the face of threats from Soviet forces and the Taliban. He applied those values in the streets, and provoked the fear he needed in order to control and beat down anybody who tried to offer even the slightest resistance. This was the path he chose publicly, but privately Abdul tried to lead a normal life with a flat and a partner who had studied to become a doctor.

He tried to separate these two worlds as best he could, but it was difficult to do in practice. As the couple walked around in Rågsved together, the police saw teenage boys standing up and shaking his hand or adjusting their clothes. As the police saw it, Abdul was the leader and the shot caller, and the fact that he himself didn't need to carry a firearm was evidence of this. He had plenty of subordinates to do that for him, who were prepared to act on his behalf.

Sascha's relatives, on the other hand, claimed that he would never have asked for a 'second chance' – he had too much pride for that. Asking for something would have been beneath him. Abdul wasn't his leader, they were equals, they insisted. Abdul was the brains, and Sascha was the brawn. They were in business together, in the criminal world. That's all it was.

'Sascha was a genuine doer. But he would never have followed anyone else. Sascha wasn't anybody's bitch', one of his sisters told me.

Sascha's relatives are convinced that Abdul must have been motivated by a fear of Sascha – not because of what he knew, but because he was afraid of what Sascha was capable of doing if he were to become Abdul's enemy. The Haleem side doesn't share this view, insisting instead that Sascha was never a threat. If he had been a threat, 'Wouldn't he at least have tried to get revenge?'

*

In early December 2019, snow covered the ground in Bjurhovda in eastern Västerås. Allegedly, Sascha was there to meet with Maykil. Their relationship, according to close associates, was strictly business.

Sascha felt safer in Västerås, but he was extremely cautious when he was in town to buy drugs. He was wearing his bulletproof vest, which had been reinforced with plates that could withstand automatic weapons. He hadn't quite been himself since the failed assassination attempt.

Although it was only half past three in the afternoon, it was already dark. An eleven-year-old girl was at home, waiting for her mum, when she suddenly heard loud noises that cut right through the walls of the house. Moments later, she heard a man's voice calling for help. Just then, her mum came home from work. As she pulled into the driveway, she heard the same, desperate voice. She rushed over, and saw a young man covered in blood, with an open wound in his mouth. It was Sascha. The mother called emergency services, and helped the young man make his way towards her home. Suddenly, she realized that he couldn't come in. Her daughter couldn't see him like that, with a gaping hole in his mouth. They walked into the garage instead, where the man sat down on the stairs. He seemed to be making sure he had a quick escape route to the cellar. The emergency services call-taker told the woman to lay him on his side, and try to stop the bleeding.

Sascha was airlifted to the Karolinska University Hospital with life-threatening injuries. Miraculously, however, he survived this attack as well.

27

A few months later, in May 2020, a police officer went to Sascha's mother's house to find him. The police had 'information' they wanted to share. When Sascha called the police back later, he was told that they had learnt of a serious threat against him. This wasn't exactly news to Sascha, who had also been placed under police surveillance during the ongoing Rimfrost operation. Although Sascha's conversation with the police was entirely respectful, he had nothing to say to them. He did ask them questions, though.

'What information do you have about why he's coming after me?'

This was something the police didn't go into, but they did note that Sascha had been keeping a low profile since those violent crimes were committed against him.

Sascha had chosen to live as a criminal, and this meant that cooperating with the police was out of the question. He wouldn't do that even to save his own life. He also didn't want any help from the police, or their protection.

'I'm not a rat', Sascha told them, and hung up.

*

That summer, he was skinny and gaunt, physically scarred and literally wounded. He was staying with his mother temporarily, and the two of them were slowly salvaging their relationship after not having spoken to one another for years because of his lifestyle choices.

Both his mother and his siblings felt that he was changed, more mature. Before, he had been ready to die at any moment, but now, he wanted to live. He had a girlfriend he loved. He had bought her a chihuahua, and he was talking about having children. But he was weighed down by his past.

When his mother went off to work in a school canteen, he stood behind the curtains of her kitchen window, in her second-floor flat in southern Stockholm. He stared at cars he didn't recognize, wrote down registration numbers on a calendar that had been stuck to the fridge behind him with magnets. Could it be one of Abdul Haleem's boys, out looking for him?

They knew where his family lived.

Sascha was worried for his nieces and nephews, and if they offered him a lift, he refused to get in the car with them. He didn't want to put them in any danger. In early June, Abdul Haleem wrote to a friend on Encrochat, and mentioned the assassination attempts.

'That bastard from Stockholm who I shot last year survived.'

However, Abdul's plans to eliminate Sascha weren't even paused when Encrochat sent the warning to their users in mid-June. Abdul believed he was safe, because he hadn't been arrested yet even though he had been using Encrochat. Like many others, he ditched his phone that summer, and bought an ANOM instead.

Some younger boys had put Abdul Haleem in touch with twenty-year-old Kevin, who had ties to a network in Årsta, which is also in the southern parts of Stockholm. They bought weapons and drugs from Haleem's network, and Kevin was looking to make an impression, so that his elders would reward him 'with money or other favours'. Now, somebody who kills a rival for the gang can't necessarily expect to be given a large sum of money, but an inside source assured me that shooters know that they'll be 'generously rewarded'. That's just how it works.

'If you're a soldier, you get well taken care of', the source explained.

It turned out that Kevin knew of a way to get to Sascha. He was friends with a guy called Toj, who had in turn been close to Sascha since they were in prison together.

'Kevin was asked to recruit Toj to lure Sascha out from hiding. Kevin's mission was to execute Sascha, to do the job', the source continued.

Toj became Kevin's *goare*, according to the investigation. A source with inside knowledge told me that Toj was prepared to sell his friend Sascha out 'for 200,000 kronor and two guns'.

Toj himself claimed to be innocent. 'Those chats have been deliberately misinterpreted, and the information you've been given isn't correct', he told me.

But my source on the inside claimed that Toj *did* know what was going on, and the Court of Appeal would later arrive at the same conclusion. The source said that the sum he was paid was 'just pennies' to the people involved. The network could sell drugs for more money than that in just a single day.

'Do you know how much money we were making?' the source asked me when we met in one of the southern suburbs of Stockholm.

Thinking back on it brought a grin to his face. He described how they used to hang out in a restaurant in Huddinge, which had been full of students from Södertörn University and 'ordinary Swedes', many of whom worked at the nearby Karolinska Hospital.

'The students loved weed', he told me.

It was the drug of choice on weekdays, while cocaine was in demand for the weekends. They also bought Concerta, a drug used to treat ADHD.

'They took those pills to help them concentrate.' My source gave me a serious look.

'You have to understand, Diamant. It isn't kids from the hood who buy our drugs. It's regular citizens. They're the ones who provide most of the money. They are our biggest customers.'

When I asked him if it was these students and other people who bought drugs who were providing the gang with the funds they used to buy weapons and fight their wars, his answer came immediately.

'Yes. They claim that we're a menace to society, but they don't even know what their own kids are getting up to.'

*

As summer turned into autumn, Abdul Haleem's allies were trying very hard to locate Sascha, or 'the Swede', as he was also known. On ANOM, Abdul wrote the following to Kevin.

'We're going to bust his door down and go in with Kalashnikovs, I'm so mad.'

But Sascha was keeping out of sight, and Abdul was growing increasingly impatient. On Tuesday 15 September, he wrote to Kevin again.

'Brother, can you take him out today?'

'I'll pop him the moment I see him', Kevin replied from his ANOM phone.

Sascha had become very cautious after all the attempts on his life. The guy who never used to be afraid of anybody had changed. Sascha knew Abdul, and he knew how vindictive he was, particularly when he felt it was a matter of honour. Sascha's only way out of this was death. That was the only thing that would satisfy Abdul.

Sascha's relatives claim that Abdul knew very well where Sascha's family lived, but that he didn't dare to go there and 'bust the door down with a Kalashnikov', because it might put one of the other family members in the line of fire.

If Abdul had harmed one of Sascha's sisters or their children, that would have been a 'death sentence for his own mum and dad and his own sisters and brothers', Sascha's mother Carina told me, and went on: 'Sascha would have chewed them all up. He would have tortured them.'

'That was the difference between Sascha and Abdul. Sascha wasn't a talker – he shut up and went to work. I think that's why Abdul never dared to go after Sascha himself', one of Sascha's sisters told me.

Sascha was suspicious of everything and everyone. He could count his trusted friends on the fingers of one hand, and he counted Toj among them. On the evening of 16 September, the two of them were planning how they would celebrate Toj's birthday.

'So when can you come out and play then?' Sascha asked.

He wouldn't receive an answer until just after eleven o'clock that night.

'Want to meet in Södermalm?'

'Haha, if you want', Sascha replied.

Sascha and Toj agreed to meet at Södra station in Södermalm, Stockholm. Before leaving the flat and heading into town, Sascha told his older sister that he was going to meet Toj. His sister called a taxi for him and lent him a few thousand kronor so he could buy himself a warmer jacket and stay at a hotel for a night.

When Sascha met up with Toj, he was with Kevin. The plan was to take Sascha across Årstabron Bridge, which is 800 metres long, and then take the left turn after the bridge, which leads down to a football pitch.

'The idea was to execute him there', a source told me.

Reportedly, there was an armed 'helper' by the football pitch, waiting for Sascha to show up. But Sascha sensed that something wasn't right, and when Kevin joined them, his alarm bells began to ring.

The investigation has shown that Sascha had his hoodie pulled up, and that he was caught off guard when the first shot hit his cheek from close range as they walked along the pedestrian and bicycle lane of Årstabron. He wasn't wearing body armour, and he tried to escape back towards Södermalm, but was shot three times in the back before he collapsed. Next, he took a fatal close-range shot to the temple from the converted starter pistol that was used as the murder weapon.

After the murder, Kevin wrote to his boss Abdul Haleem to tell him that the mission had been accomplished, with three red hearts and this message: 'The Swede is gone now.'

He soon received a reply from Abdul:

'You're the best, my dear brother.'

Abdul told him he didn't want to write any more in the chat, but he couldn't help himself.

'I'm with you until death.'

'You too, my brother', Kevin replied.

After several failed attempts, Abdul's persistent plotting against Sascha had finally succeeded. Like so many times before, an old friendship had turned into a rivalry, and ended in bloodshed.

28

The morning after Sascha's murder, his family gathered at his mother Carina's house. She had called her children and told them to come over to her place immediately. They were told that Sascha had died, and that afternoon, his relatives got into several cars to travel to a memorial site by the bridge to light candles.

Close to the main square in Årsta, Sascha's sister, whom he had visited the night before, saw Toj standing by a pedestrian crossing. They made eye contact and he waved to her. The sister walked over to Toj to talk to him. When she got closer, she saw that his pupils were dilated, and noticed foaming at the corners of his mouth. He seemed very intoxicated. The other members of the family didn't realize who the guy the sister was talking to was.

'Shit, I'm so shocked', Toj told her, according to the investigation report. He had been meaning to call the sister after he heard about the murder, he says, but he didn't have his phone.

'Where's your phone? Where's all your stuff?' she asked.

'I don't know, I don't know', he replied, and went on to tell her that it was his birthday yesterday and that he met with Sascha.

'Yes, I know, he told me', the sister answered.

What Toj said next, however, made the sister and the mother react. According to him, there had been five of them hanging out the night before. Toj, his girlfriend and her best friend, a fourth friend, and Sascha. They were supposed to get a taxi to Årsta, but there hadn't been room in the taxi for Sascha. So, they decided that he would make his way there himself, and meet the others at a football pitch. Toj said that, after a while, he had seen blue police lights, and realized what had happened.

Sascha's relatives thought that there wouldn't be many taxi drivers out there who would let four people get in their car during the pandemic, particularly not if they had to take a passenger in the front seat. This meant that, reasonably, two of the group would have had to get their own taxi together. His story didn't add up.

'How did you know it was Sascha who was lying on the bridge?'

When she asked the question, Toj turned to Sascha's mother, knelt down, and started crying. He told her that somebody had shot at him, too, just a week earlier.

'Do you think it was me? Do you think it was me?' he asked.

'No, I don't think it was you. I don't know anything about this, but you must understand that I have to ask how it happened, because your story isn't adding up', the sister replied.

Carina found the whole situation bizarre. She stood there, her face frozen solid, without shedding a tear. Anyone who knew her was aware that she could come across as cold, and didn't display a lot of emotion, at least not openly. This was true even now, when her son had been shot dead. Her hard exterior could sometimes obscure her intense love of her eleven children, regardless of the choices they had made in life. She had done everything in her power to ensure that her children would have better lives than her own.

'Let's go', another member of the family shouted.

Finally, the mother thought to herself, feeling relieved.

When they got into the cars to drive over to the memorial site, Toj ran over to the car of one of the sisters, the one Sascha had been with the night before.

'I'll call you, I'm going to go and buy a phone now.'

During the conversation, Sascha's mother Carina had been listening attentively. Toj's obvious anxiety immediately convinced her that he must have been involved in the murder somehow. Her son, whose leg was badly injured, would never have agreed to being the one who couldn't go in the taxi. He would have thrown someone else out to get a seat.

*

In an interview, the police learned from Sascha's relatives that he had met Toj just before the murder. They also learned that Sascha's former friend Abdul Haleem had been trying to kill him. But allegations like that are only leads, not solid evidence that somebody was involved.

Early in the investigation, the prosecutor Lisa dos Santos was granted authorization to wiretap both Toj and Kevin. However, this didn't yield any useful evidence, as both suspects knew better than to discuss crimes on their ordinary phones. But they were both arrested by the police a few weeks later. The prosecutor had CCTV footage of them at Södra station, which isn't far from the bridge where Sascha was murdered. The prosecution also had witness statements in which the descriptions given of the perpetrators closely matched how Kevin and Toj were dressed on the night of the murder.

Based on investigative leads and the information that Abdul had already instigated two attempts on Sascha's life, Abdul was also named as a suspect.

*

Several months later, in the spring that followed the murder, the trial date was approaching. Prosecutor Lisa dos Santos had received analysis results from the National Forensic Centre that further strengthened her suspicions. Gunshot residue that could be tied to the bullet casings at the crime scene had been found on Kevin's black down jacket. Since data and mobile phone scans had also been performed, without finding much of interest, Lisa dos Santos was preparing to press charges towards the end of May.

She felt that she had sufficient evidence to get Kevin and Toj convicted, but that she couldn't prove Abdul Haleem's involvement. Because of this, she had dropped the case against him. However, she didn't know about ANOM. At this point, the operation was still a closely kept secret.

Just when she was about to set a trial date, Lisa dos Santos received a peculiar phone call. The person calling her was Marie Lind Thomsen, senior prosecutor for Rio.

'Leave both of your mobile phones outside of your office', the Rio director instructed her.

Lisa's immediate response was fear. Was she in trouble somehow? Not that she had committed a crime or anything, but she thought maybe somebody had made a complaint regarding something related to her job. She placed her phones on a table outside the office, closed the door, and answered a Skype call. However, the conversation wasn't about anything related to Lisa personally. It concerned her investigation into the Årstabron murder. Lind Thomsen asked if Lisa was looking into suspects called Kevin and Abdul Haleem. She responded that she was, but that she had dropped the charges against Haleem. Next, another name was mentioned, one that hadn't yet appeared in her investigation. This was a member of Haleem's criminal network, who would later turn out to have been in contact with Maximilian Rivkin to discuss violent crimes and other matters.

Lisa was still very confused. What information did Rio have about her case?

The Rio director briefed her on the top-secret operation, Trojan Shield, which was still ongoing. Basically, the FBI was running a sting, and had intercepted chats involving Lisa's suspects. She was told that the messages came from an encrypted service called ANOM. However, the operation wasn't going to be revealed until 7 June, so Lisa would have to wait a little longer before pressing charges. She was also instructed not to share any information about the operation, even with colleagues.

Lisa was hopeful, but didn't want to get her expectations up too much. She had heard chatter from the police about exciting text messages before, but the language used in them had been too coded for anybody to understand what was actually being said.

Keep cool, she thought to herself.

A few days later, she was summoned to the police station in Kungsholmen. The lead investigator ushered her into a windowless room, and presented her with a stack of papers containing excerpts from chat logs.

Noa had prepared drafts of ID analyses, which indicated that Kevin, Abdul Haleem and a third unknown party had used ANOM phones to plot the murder of Sascha. For example, Kevin had sent a picture of a hand holding a sub-machine gun in what looked like the entrance to a building next door to his home, while Abdul Haleem had been identified in part through messages where he'd sent pictures of his cat. As far as the investigators could tell, Toj didn't use ANOM, but he could be linked to the crime through witness statements from the bridge and the fact that he was mentioned in the chats. He was also the last person Sascha met with.

Lisa felt a great sense of relief over receiving more evidence of what had happened. In murder cases like this one, it's difficult to get anybody but the actual shooters convicted.

Now, she would be able to reopen the case against the person who ordered the hit, and even prosecute him. The most striking thing, however, was how unfiltered the conversation was. The murder was discussed without the use of any code words. It was all in the open, direct and ruthless.

*

The Court of Appeal convicted Abdul Haleem of soliciting to murder, and Toj of murder. Both of them received life sentences. Kevin, on the other hand, was sentenced to fourteen years in prison for murder, because he had only been twenty years old when Sascha was killed. Ahead of the trial in the Court of Appeal, chat logs from Sky ECC were added to the evidence.

Toj insisted that he would never act as a lure in a murder plot against anyone. The claims against him were 'bullshit' — doing that would go against all of his values.

He explained to me in a letter that he ran over to Sascha after the shooting. At that point, he and Sascha were the only people who were still on the bridge.

'I saw that there was a bullet hole in his head, and I panicked and ran away', he wrote.

He said he regretted not staying at the scene.

'I feel like I abandoned him. That's why I'm so ashamed', he went on.

Toj, who was sentenced to life, wrote that he hadn't realized what was actually going on until he read the ANOM chats. Next, he was going to do whatever it took to get an appeal and prove his innocence. The other two who were convicted for the murder have decided not to comment on their cases.

29

On 26 September 2020, irritation was running high in the ANOM chat called 'Firman', the Firm. A member of the chat, who goes by the name Soko, hadn't replied to any messages for the last two days. It turned out that his phone had been switched off, because he had been to a spa with his wife.

'She beats him up once a month', joked a user called Microsoft, whose ANOM alias was 7ed648.

This code, combined with the nickname, instilled false confidence in the users, making them believe they were unidentifiable. However, in reality, everything was proceeding as the FBI had planned it. Microsoft was one of the FBI's international influencers, Maximilian Rivkin, the former Malmö resident who had been distributing ANOM phones to criminals.

When Soko saw the message about his wife, he laughed and replied: 'I've got it rough!'

Rivkin wrote to him again.

'Just don't drink any champagne from strange women's shoes, and you won't get in trouble.' The message was followed by a smiley face emoji.

Unbeknownst to them, however, this was the very day that Noa had got their system up and running and started to receive updates from the FBI. From their server, data was being forwarded to colleagues all over the world who were taking part in this huge operation.

Vera, the Noa officer in charge of their intelligence work, was beginning to get an organization in place for prevention of serious crimes in Sweden. Noa received batches of messages from the FBI three times a week, and before the Swedish police could access the chats, agents with the FBI had to open each individual conversation for them. That was what the law required.

It was frustrating. It wasn't until later, when Noa had managed to identify some aliases, that they were able to tell the FBI which ones to prioritize for faster processing. The most obvious choice was Rivkin, who had a hand in 'almost everything'.

The police soon noticed a significant difference between the ANOM chats and Encrochat. The FBI's phones were mostly used for drug-smuggling operations, but, as they expected, murder plots were also being made. This is evident from the chats of the thin-skinned Rivkin.

The police were surprised to discover what Rivkin was hiding at a farm near Olshammar, a small industrial town with just over 200 inhabitants in the municipality of Askersund. In the cellar of the house, Rivkin was running a secret amphetamine lab with two other people.

One of these was Rikard, a man in his fifties from the Stockholm area who had received several serious drug convictions in recent years. He was of average build, with steely eyes and cropped hair, with specks of grey at the temples. A prosecutor described him as an 'extremely ambitious, astute and intelligent person, who could have made a very good entrepreneur if he had decided to run a legitimate business'. This was how police officers and prosecutors described many of the leading players in the drug business. They were good administrators, who could lead a team and manage complicated logistical operations both within the country and abroad.

Rikard had been released from his last prison term six months earlier, just before the authorities had started to get access to many criminals' encrypted phones. He seemed to have arranged new employment quickly. Later on, Noa would realize that Rikard had very rapidly become a far more significant player on the Swedish drug market than anybody had imagined.

Since Rikard, Rivkin and their third partner, a friend of Rivkin's parents, were spread out across Sweden, they used ANOM to run their operations remotely. They used their group chat, Firman, to discuss money, accounting, their amphetamine oil supply, amphetamine manufacture, customer contacts and sales.

Several Polish citizens had been hired to carry out the actual manufacture, and their group was named Köket, 'the Kitchen'. This team was also responsible for shipping the speed to mules, who received instructions from Firman regarding how and when to drop drugs off to customers.

Noa soon realized that they had major plans for their manufacturing operation. They wanted to produce a tonne of speed every month, and would be able to do that as long as they could get sufficient amounts of amphetamine oil.

After following the chats in this group for a few weeks, Noa learned the details of their next drug deal. It was to take place in two days, in the car park of the Marieberg shopping centre in Örebro. A map with an address was shared on ANOM. Local detectives in Bergslagen were called in, but weren't told where the intelligence was coming from. They followed a white Mitsubishi Pajero from Olshammar to the car park outside the Jula DIY shop at the shopping centre. The detectives filmed Piotr, the driver, unloading three white parcels from his car and placing them in a shopping trolley, before proceeding to walk around the car park and fiddle with his phone. After a while, he nodded to a man, Lennart, who stepped out of his Saab. Piotr made a quick trip back to his car before returning with the parcels and loading them into the boot when Lennart had walked away from the car.

Piotr moved three jerry cans from the Saab over to his trolley. He loaded the cans into his own car, and then the two mules went their separate ways. Piotr went back to Olshammar, and Lennart headed for Eskilstuna. Both of them were being followed by plain-clothes police.

That evening, Lennart was pulled over while driving towards an exit. In the car were vacuum-packed parcels containing almost 60 kilos of amphetamine, which would have had a street value of many millions of kronor after being cut. When the mule failed to answer messages, anxiety began to spread among the people who arranged the deal.

'We've probably lost him', one of the people involved wrote in the group chat Firman.

Later that evening, the Bergslagen regional task force made their approach on the house in Olshammar. It was difficult to enter the small community in a stealthy fashion. However, as the police officers had been informed that there were chemicals in the house, they were wearing gas masks and protective gloves. There was an ambulance ready nearby, and the emergency services were on standby in case something went wrong.

The police stormed the house from several entrances at once, to improve their chances of apprehending the amphetamine cooks before they had time to destroy any evidence.

'Police! Police!', they shouted.

A man on the ground floor was quickly subdued. The whole raid was captured on film by the task force's body cameras.

'Lie down!', they shouted at him, and pushed him down with his face to the floor. While this was happening, three other members of the task force were making their way down to the cellar.

'Keep still! Lie down! Get down on the floor! Down on the floor!', they shouted, aiming their SIG Sauer pistols at another worker they encountered downstairs.

The man, who was wearing blue shorts and a dark T-shirt, complied with the officers' instructions. A few seconds later, one of the police officers shouted: 'The cellar is secured. The cellar is secured.'

Just as the police were entering the house, somebody managed to send Rikard a panicked message that the police were there.

'Everything is fucked. Everything', Rikard wrote to the others. He shared a screenshot of the message informing him that the lab was being raided by the police.

The text read, 'Micie polis in laboratorium.'

'What? Cops in lab?'

'Yes. Kurwa!!!', the person who raised the alarm continued. The answer came quickly.

'Fuuuuuuck.'

*

The mule Piotr was one of the men arrested. In the car that he had driven to Jula's car park a few hours earlier, the police found three containers holding a total of 50 litres of amphetamine oil, which he had unloaded from Lennart's car.

The house had an upstairs floor with several sleeping places, where the workers rested when they weren't mixing chemicals to synthesize the white amphetamine powder.

In two storerooms in the cellar, protective clothing, pH measuring devices, filters for breathing masks, vacuum bags and sealing devices for the bags were found. Other parts of the house held stores of three of the chemicals needed for the manufacture: methanol, sulphuric acid and caffeine. The actual amphetamine lab itself was located in an old laundry room that had been fitted with extra vents in the ceiling. The windows were sealed with Styrofoam to shield the lab from view.

Noa was soon receiving new conversations from the FBI. The panic after the raids was apparent. The founder of Firman, who had produced and sold over 400 kilos of amphetamine, worth around 9 million kronor, in just over four months, didn't understand how the police could have known about the lab.

'It doesn't make sense!' wrote Rivkin's old friend, who had known him since childhood.

The decision to execute the raid was made by Vera and her team at Noa, because they wanted to put a quick stop to the production. They had judged that the main perpetrators wouldn't be able to figure out that it was ANOM that had given them away. One of the reasonings was that, since they were selling ANOM phones themselves, they would be confident that they were safe to use. Indeed, they suspected that one of the workers had been careless and attracted attention from somebody in the small community nearby, instead.

'So Rivkin carried on chatting through ANOM, making plans for new criminal schemes', explained Örebro police officer Ted Esplund, who had become the national project lead for the encryption-related operations at this time.

The discussions on ANOM continued even after the lab was shut down. The police decided not to arrest Rikard yet, because they didn't want to alert anybody to the fact that they were getting evidence from ANOM. Unaware of the fact that the police were reading everything he wrote on ANOM, he continued selling drugs on the Flugsvamp 3.0 dark web platform. He would later be accused of having served as the manager of the operation, along with a group of men and women who were spread out across various locations. Payments for the drugs were made in cryptocurrency, and the shipments were made by mail, to avoid detection.

30

In the middle of October 2020, a freighter ship, the *Manil Maersk*, left the port of Casablanca for Skandiahamnen in Gothenburg. The ship was holding a hidden cargo.

Meanwhile, apart from having access to Noa's intelligence officers, Vera had now also been given access to personnel within the Swedish Customs. The idea was that their cooperation would make them more effective at countering the constant attempts of smugglers who were trying to find ways to get drugs into Sweden. During the Encro investigation, there hadn't been any Customs officials involved in the operational work. Vera realized, however, that the Customs officials had other tools and channels they could use to respond to smuggling operations before they could cross the border. Working together would help them all to do better jobs. This decision would prove to be a wise one.

At 03.12 in the morning of 1 November, a man from Gothenburg who was wanted by the police, and was presently in Morocco, sent a message through ANOM. The recipient was the person who was waiting for the shipment.

'Are you awake?'

'Yes.'

The next message from Morocco took about two minutes to come in.

The instruction was to be ready any time now.

'I'm always ready', was the response.

The investigative team had a new person of interest: a contractor who carried out bathroom renovations and other plumbing work in the Kungälv area. He was the intended recipient of the shipment. In early November 2020, Noa saw that a shipment of three containers of stone tiles from Morocco was being shipped to the businessman. The details weren't entirely clear initially, but soon almost the entire operation had been laid bare on ANOM. They even posted information on what the cargo actually contained: marble slabs filled with hashish.

We have to get this information to somebody somehow, Vera thought to herself. She knew that it was impossible for Customs to inspect every single container that was delivered to the Skandiahamnen harbour in Gothenburg. However, she gave Customs a tip that was specific enough to allow their staff to carry out a targeted check. The Customs officials and the police launched a surveillance operation targeting both the harbour and the businessman, checking in with Vera to make sure they were on the right track. Vera's instructions were cryptic, but convincing enough to make her colleague believe that she must have found an incredible human source. Vera felt a bit uncomfortable to be fudging the truth like this, but she had no choice. This was absolutely necessary to keep the ANOM operation secret.

She had to take measures to eliminate even the potential for leaks from colleagues.

Despite her caution, information was beginning to surface that risked unravelling the whole surveillance operation in the harbour. The reason for this was a message on ANOM, which had been written by the main suspect, who was orchestrating the smuggling activity. He was a 33-year-old man from Gothenburg, who was believed to have a leading position in the criminal Bergsjön network.

'It's all sorted, I have a cop on the inside who tells me everything', he wrote.

The Noa investigators were chilled to read that chat. However, officers who had been following communications on Encrochat had read similar claims before, including from members of that specific network in Gothenburg.

'We haven't been able to find a single name yet', a source who worked on the encrypted chats in the west of Sweden told me.

Several of the people I've asked about whether there really were corrupt police officers involved claim that, while it was sometimes discussed in the chats, it was the kind of thing criminals liked to boast about to their contacts to boost their credibility. Noa has also actively searched for terms like 'leaks', 'dirty cop', 'bribe' and so on. According to Ted Esplund at Noa, none of their past efforts to investigate these chats further has yielded any evidence that conclusively supports the idea that anybody was actively, deliberately leaking operational information to criminals. A handful of the mentions of insiders in the encrypted chats had been sent on to the Special Investigations Department, an independent department within the Police Authority that investigates suspected offences committed by police officers, police cadets, judges and prosecutors.

The case with the marble tiles was said to be the most 'tangible' piece of evidence suggesting any inside information was being leaked. The suspicion this raised was that a police officer in the Gothenburg area might have revealed to an outsider that the harbour was under surveillance, and that this information had somehow reached the 33-year-old from Gothenburg who was running the smuggling ring.

In the chats, however, the smuggler seemed confident that the cargo would get through the port controls without further scrutiny, despite the ongoing police operation. He had no idea that Noa and the Customs officers knew exactly which containers to examine.

The suspicions against the officer that Noa developed after their discovery in the ANOM chats would eventually result in the conviction of a police officer working in the West region in early 2022. The officer was prosecuted for carrying out three unauthorized searches of police records.

*

One of the containers that was opened contained ten wooden pallets wrapped in plastic, labelled 'Marbre Taza', a light variety of marble. Nothing in the container stood out, and the huge mobile scanner they used hadn't found anything out of the ordinary, either. But when Customs officials inspected the tiles from the side, they noticed that they varied in thickness. One of the thicker stones was taken out and tapped with a sledgehammer. The stone broke easily, exposing the contents: bricks of hashish, in brown vacuum-wrap, and labelled with the stickers 'Special Police' and 'Los Pollos Hermanos'. The latter was a fictional fast-food chain in the TV series *Breaking Bad*.

Under normal circumstances, the drugs would have been replaced with something else so that the police could follow the shipment without allowing any real drugs through Customs. However, that approach was suitable for findings along the lines of a few kilos of cocaine. In this case, they would have had to crack open all of the marble and replaced it. So, instead, the Customs officials removed the broken tile, and rigged the containers with cameras and microphones in preparation for the delivery. After this, the port officials were authorized to notify the consignee that the cargo had been processed and was ready to be collected.

On 12 November, the marble tiles were to be sent on to the plumbing contractor in Kungälv. However, the very same day, the delivery address was changed to a removals firm in Kinna. The police had eyes and ears on the entrepreneur and his wife as the three containers were unloaded with a forklift and a palletizer.

'I thought this stuff would be quick to unload, but it bloody well isn't', the man said as he was unloading the pallets of marble.

'What is all this?' his wife asked.

'Stone tiling.'

'Why the hell did you bring in a delivery of all this shit?'

He explained that the tiles were only going to be stored there temporarily, before being transported on to a customer.

'Who the hell wants this much stone?' his wife wondered.

*

That whole weekend, the entrepreneur stayed in the warehouse, even sleeping there. On Sunday 15 November, the surveillance team watched him walk out carrying a rubbish bag, and drive about 10 kilometres to the north, to Fritsla. There he entered a private spa owned by the smuggler, the same 33-year-old Gothenburg man who was thought to have a leading role in the Bergsjön network, and who had claimed to have a police officer on his payroll. Shortly after the man with the rubbish bag arrived, the spa owner's girlfriend drove up in a Mercedes. A little while later, a man in a Volvo joined them. After spending some time inside together, the man who came in the Volvo got out and drove off in the Mercedes.

After a few moments, the man in the car was pulled over. When the car's interior was searched, the police found a special compartment under the passenger seat which contained hashish with the same labelling as the stuff that Customs had found in the container. That day, police and Customs officers raided several addresses. Inside the spa, a black bin bag was found, containing empty salad boxes and the remains of a shattered stone tile. At the warehouse in Kinna, an encrypted phone was found, but it was remotely erased soon after being seized. The original recipient, the entrepreneur from Kungälv, was also arrested. There turned out to be 1.2 tonnes of hashish hidden among the stone tiling, making this one of the largest drug seizures ever in Sweden. The total street value was estimated at just over 120 million kronor.

When the raid was under way, there was cheering in the office where Vera worked. The ANOM operation had started to bear fruit. However, despite the size of the seizure, the police and Customs kept completely silent about the operation. This frustrated the other people who had been involved in the deal. Vera saw them write to each other, wondering why there wasn't so much as a line of news in the papers about it when such a huge shipment of drugs had been seized.

Despite the cracking of Encrochat still being a recent event, nobody seemed to even suspect that ANOM might actually be controlled by the police. They seemed to figure it was just bad luck.

Vera and her colleagues knew that they still had an arrest to make: the man from Gothenburg who owned and ran the spa. According to chats, he was in charge of the smuggling operation, and the one who was handling communications with the wanted individual in Morocco. The previous year, he had been released on probation after serving a term in prison for various offences, including drug trafficking. In the ANOM chats, his stress and shock were showing.

'This has me sick, fuck.'

In the chat, he confirmed that, apart from the spa, he might also be linked to the warehouse where the marble tiles had just been found. Soon, he began making plans to flee the country.

Noa decided not to take him into custody immediately; they wanted to gather even more evidence first.

31

While the ANOM operation was under way in the winter of 2020, the legal system was just beginning to try cases involving evidence sourced from Encrochat. One of the first of these cases was the attempted murder at the bus stop in Viksjö, where a young man connected to the Death Squad had been recruited to carry out the hit.

The taciturn sixteen-year-old sat in the defendant's chair in Attunda District Court in Sollentuna. This was the boy who had been ordered to kill Peter, somebody who was a complete stranger to him.

In the chats, they had called him a 'true soldier'.

The lead investigator on the case was Jacob, the same officer who was leading the hunt for the Fox. Based on the chats the French police had provided, he and his investigators had been able to quickly identify the three men who had given this teenager the order to commit the murder.

The defence lawyers raised several different challenges against the evidence from Encrochat in both the District Court and the Court of Appeal, but the trials nonetheless resulted in convictions. The lawyers argued that the chat logs hadn't been collected in a manner compatible with Swedish law, and that no reliable conclusions could be drawn from them, in part because they weren't presented in sequence. The Encro phone's burner feature might also have been used to delete messages, which meant that the evidence was potentially compromised, the defence team argued. The Court noted that the chats 'must be interpreted with a degree of caution', but went on to state that the information obtained was nonetheless relevant to the case and should be considered when a verdict was passed.

This would be the first of a series of convictions in which encrypted messages were used as evidence, targeting a grand total of 400 suspects.

*

I met one of the people who had been sentenced based on Encro evidence in a Class 1 prison. Behind a glass wall, a man of almost 2 metres, with a trimmed beard and a fade haircut, sat down across from me. He had lost weight after spending a long time in a holding cell and then an even longer time in the prison. There were a few years of prison left for him to serve for his exceptionally serious drug offence. In front of him on the table was a legal book with a red cover, *Beviskraft: Metod för bevisvärdering i brottmål* – 'Strength of Evidence: A Method for Evaluating Evidence in Criminal Trials'. In this text, Christian Dahlman, a professor of law at Lund University, discusses famous Swedish court cases including the trials of Thomas Quick and the murder of Lisa Holm. The man, who was in his early twenties, had underlined various sentences related to the principle of the free examination of evidence, which was the justification used for allowing the encrypted chats to be used as evidence in Swedish courts, regardless of how they ended up in the possession of the police.

'It wasn't done right', he insisted.

His light T-shirt clung tightly to his body. He told me he tried to get regular exercise with the other inmates on his ward. They all got along very well. Many of them were familiar with the cases involving the encrypted chats, and they were studying up on the legal aspects of the cases together. Other convicts I've been in contact with share this feeling of having been treated unfairly by the authorities. They haven't even been told how the French got hold of the evidence in the first place, as the French claimed keeping it secret was a matter of national security. Many of the people I've been in contact with have accused the authorities of deliberately using other countries – France and the United States, in this case – as proxies to authorize illegal coercive measures against Swedish citizens. They've described what happened to them as a 'judicial scandal'.

'What about the rule of law?' an alleged gang leader asked me in a letter.

'Don't criminals have human rights, aren't we entitled to a fair trial?' wrote another person, a leading member of a notorious criminal network.

Many felt that their judges and jurors had been influenced by political discourse, which was full of calls for harsher measures. One of the letter writers believed that he hadn't been sentenced by a Swedish court so much as by Swedish politicians.

'I'm a political prisoner', he told me after being convicted for an exceptionally serious drug offence.

He says that this abuse of his rights never caused any debate because so many people were 'very proud of all the Encro sentences'.

Lawyer Thomas Olsson represented several of the defendants who were convicted based on evidence gathered from encrypted chats, and he is one of the most vocal critics of the practice. According to Olsson, more and more foreign courts were beginning to appreciate the legal complexities involved in the use of the encrypted materials, and that various aspects of the evidence had been challenged in several European countries. In the defence lawyer's opinion, the Swedish courts' decision to admit this particular evidence on the basis of the principle of freedom of evidence was too hasty.

'They used it like some kind of universally applicable disclaimer', Olsson told me.

*

Several of those convicted have made the claim that Swedish officials have withheld relevant information about the encrypted chat operations, specifically the one targeting Encrochat. One name that was mentioned over and over is Solveig Wollstad. One thing that has attracted particular criticism is the fact that she was originally called to testify during an organized crime trial in Gothenburg, but her participation was later cancelled.

According to Wollstad and the Swedish Prosecution Authority, the reason for the cancellation was diplomatic immunity, as she was representing the nation of Sweden at Eurojust. Furthermore, the questions that were going to be asked concerned matters under the purview of the Swedish Secrecy Act.

Wollstad emphasized that she didn't personally decide not to testify, and that she was only acting in accordance with the laws and decisions she was obliged to observe. She clarified that the courts had made the decision that the hearing couldn't proceed, based on these considerations. She also wanted to be clear that, as a Eurojust prosecutor, it was 'out of the question' for her to make her own decisions about what was admissible as evidence, how to organize European cooperation, or how the French police operated.

'If Swedish prosecutors had asked the French to use coercive measures, that would have required the authorization of a Swedish court', she explained, and continued: 'In this case, however, the French decided to share surplus intelligence.'

The since-retired chief prosecutor said that she had no idea how France had gained access to the chats, as the methods used were protected by French secrecy legislation.

'I have met people, mostly men, who claim to know. But I don't believe anyone actually does know.'

*

During my meeting with the convicted drug offender at the prison, he showed me a printed document that has given him and others held in Swedish prisons hope that they might be able to get their cases heard by the Supreme Court. In Germany, a regional court asked for clarification from the Court of Justice of the European Union regarding how the Encrochat materials ended up in the hands of the German authorities. If the Court of Justice of the European Union were to rule that the transfer of Encro data had constituted a breach of EU law, this might potentially influence how national courts viewed these kinds of evidence in the future. Since many cases involving Encro evidence have already been decided, the only remaining option is to try to get the case reviewed by the Supreme Court. Some experts argue, however, that this wouldn't make any difference to cases that have already been decided, as a 'change in legislation is not sufficient reason for an appeal'.

As it stands, experts have repeatedly responded to questions concerning the evidential value of encrypted chats by referring to the principles of free examination and evaluation of evidence.

'The Court of Justice of the European Union doesn't have the authority to change the fundamentals of Swedish evidence law. That is a national matter', Stefan Reimer, Justice of the Supreme Court – who has so far denied all appeals related to the encryption cases – explained to me.

However, Ester Herlin-Karnell, a professor of EU law at the University of Gothenburg who specializes in EU criminal law, believes that the Swedish views regarding the handling and gathering of certain kinds of evidence could actually be affected in the long term if legislative changes are introduced at the EU level. She's eagerly awaiting the response to the German court's inquiry, and hoping it will offer some clarification on whether evidence from the Encrochat operation was shared illegally. She would have preferred if the Swedish courts had requested such a preliminary ruling from the Court of Justice. However, as she noted to me, they haven't done that in this case, 'nor in plenty of other cases'.

Defence attorney Thomas Olsson told me that he and several of his colleagues have made extensive efforts to understand the 'legal and factual issues surrounding the matter of the encrypted phones'. They felt that they presented strong arguments in challenging the courts' approach to the encrypted chats, but that they had been 'met with ignorance'.

In conclusion, he accused the Supreme Court of 'always arriving late to the game'. Nonetheless, he still had hopes for his appeals, even though he realized that it was unlikely that the many Swedish verdicts based on encrypted evidence would ever be overturned.

'The Supreme Court has painted itself into a corner. What the hell are they going to do now? They can't just turn around now and say, "We can't have this, we'll have to retry the Vårby case." That's just never going to happen', he said, laughing.

32

Team Foxtrot, which was unaware of the Trojan Shield operation, had continued their investigation of the Fox's network. During the autumn and winter of 2020, under Jacob's leadership, they made several major seizures and arrests of key individuals. However, for every loose end the investigators tied up, two new ones seemed to appear. And none of their leads seemed to be getting the police any closer to the Fox himself.

Team Foxtrot could only look on as he continued to bring in drugs as usual, although he had to change his methods. They suspected that the Fox's network had started to co-opt the names of real businesses and created similar email addresses, which they used to conceal drugs among goods ordered from abroad. Using these faked business email addresses, accounts were registered with the shipping company Shiplink, which picked up orders for customers and then delivered them to the provided addresses. Each shipment had a waybill bearing the fake company name and a phone number to the person who was receiving it.

If somebody called the number, a member of the Fox's network would answer.

When Denny's team raided various addresses, they found several waybills that became leads to new criminal suspects. One of these was discovered in a storage space in Södermalm, where 50 kilos of cannabis were found in early February 2021.

They managed to find out that the phone number on the waybill had been topped up in a shop in the south of Stockholm. When the police got hold of the CCTV footage from the shop, they realized that a bald, spectacled man in his forties was the one who had made the transfer.

They were able to identify the man quickly, and soon gained authorization to put a wiretap on him. A background check revealed that he was a divorcee with a single child, and that he worked as a coach for a handball team. Police theorized that he had taken over the role as the Fox's first point of contact in Sweden after his predecessors had been arrested by Denny and his detectives. Now, it was the Coach who was tasked with receiving and passing on the drugs that were being smuggled in from the Netherlands.

*

In the early spring, an assessment meeting was attended by directors from the region, northern Stockholm and Noa. Jacob reported on the hard work that Team Foxtrot had been putting in, and tried to convince several senior directors that the Fox was a major smuggler and ought to be treated as a priority target by Noa as well. Those present were informed of addresses in the Netherlands and Spain where the Fox was suspected of obtaining his synthetic drugs and cannabis. An international operation could cut off his supply and do serious damage to his network, Jacob argued.

He didn't know about the ongoing, FBI-led ANOM operation, and that it was competing with his team for Noa's resources.

After 'difficult deliberations', the directors informed Jacob that the investigation of the Fox wouldn't be handled by Noa, but would be managed at the regional level. The head

The Honey Trap

of Noa's intelligence department at the time, Emil Eisersjö, was one of the directors who didn't recommend making the Fox a priority target. The Fox wasn't particularly violent and 'we had a lot of other stuff on our plate', he told me, adding that there were other targets who were causing greater harm, and 'who we saw we might be able to catch through ANOM'.

Jacob, Denny, Niklas and the other team members, who had spent the last ten months trying to track down the Fox, were annoyed that their request was ignored.

Soon, it became obvious to them that the region was returning responsibility for the Fox investigation to the North Stockholm police district. There, Jacob and his colleagues were told that their operation would be closed down as soon as the Coach had been arrested.

*

Meanwhile, investigations into the Coach, who was still being watched by Noa's surveillance team, began to get more interesting. They saw him sitting alone in his car in a car park in Nacka when he received a phone call from Shiplink. Thanks to the bug they had planted in the car, the investigators could tell that there was some kind of trouble involving a shipment that had been sent from Amsterdam to Södertälje. It was stuck in Landskrona.

The reason for the delay was that Shiplink had called the phone number for the recipient indicated on the shipment – i.e., the number for one of the prepaid phones – and hadn't got an answer. Shiplink had gone on to search for the company that was registered as the buyer of the shipment, and called them. The people at the company in question had stated that they hadn't booked any shipments through Shiplink, and they apparently had no idea that their company's name was being used as a cover by drug traffickers.

When Nobody's Listening

The Coach explained that it was all a misunderstanding, and made an agreement with Shiplink to pay the invoice immediately, so that the shipment could be sent on to an industrial estate in Södertälje.

Since analysing the wiretap feed to determine what had actually been said during the Coach's phone call took a day or two, Denny and his team didn't find out immediately that there was a shipment of drugs heading to Södertälje. It's the same old story, Denny thought. It frustrated him to always feel that the police were constantly one step behind. Of course, he realized that his team of eight detectives couldn't follow up on every single lead. Hunting for the Fox was a project that was beginning to engage the detectives on a personal level. They would stay after working hours to map out different relationships, check new posts in social media accounts, and go out to take a look at potential stash sites and homes. They had caught his scent, and chasing all the 'little foxes' was becoming an obsession, as there was always the promise that the next one might lead them to the Fox himself.

On a Sunday off, Denny and a colleague arrived at the industrial estate in Södertälje. The place was quiet and peaceful. They could see that the locking bolt on the storage unit's large, black doors had just been replaced. There were iron filings on the ground, and a cardboard box and a bag of keys to the newly installed lock had been discarded to the right of the door.

The Coach had sent a mule to collect the drugs. However, Denny and his colleagues strongly suspected that they were on the right track, and that they'd discovered the location of one of the Fox's network's many drug stashes. Later, another waybill for a delivery sent to the Södertälje depot would be found to be connected to the Coach.

Excited, they began to research different methods for tracing any taxi rides that had been booked to and from the industrial estate. Fortunately, the place wasn't a common destination for taxis, which meant that the number of rides involved could reasonably be expected to be small. Denny's suspicions were soon confirmed. He learned that taxis had travelled there from central Stockholm on two occasions in recent days. After the most recent visit, a return trip had been made four hours later. The bookings suggested that the suspected holder was staying in a flat at the Forenom Aparthotel on Johannesgatan, close to Stureplan.

They soon managed to get the name of the passenger.

Denny and his colleague tried a long shot: as they drove towards Stockholm, they called the hotel to ask who had been staying there that week.

'Could you repeat the name?' Denny's colleague asked over the phone.

'Rodrigo.'

This name matched the individual who had made the taxi booking to the storage space in Södertälje. They were making progress.

Despite all the arrests and major drug seizures, lethal shootings remained a huge problem in the area they were working in. Preventing gangland slayings was a greater priority than seizing drugs. Because of this, two days later, the team was out looking for suspects believed to have committed one of those killings. However, they didn't discover anything of interest, and just as their shift was coming to an end, Denny's colleague decided to call the taxi company again to see if Rodrigo had booked any more rides.

The answer was a huge surprise:

'He booked a taxi to Märsta a few minutes ago.'

This wasn't really a job for Denny and his detectives but, nonetheless, he decided – after gaining the approval of Jacob and another director, who didn't actually have any authority over Denny's team – to send half the team to Märsta.

Denny quickly contacted his detectives through the police radio.

Martina, a colleague who had just arrived at the newly opened police station in Rinkeby, and whose evening shift wasn't really supposed to begin for another half an hour, was ordered to head for Märsta, accompanied by another plainclothes officer. Martina and her colleague quickly changed their clothes, got into their unmarked police car, and drove there as fast as they could.

To win some time, Denny instructed other members of the team to join them as soon as possible.

Denny decided to raid the apartment hotel on Johannesgatan, where they knew Rodrigo was staying, and sent two officers over. There was nobody in the room, but there were a lot of drugs. They found 13 kilos of cocaine hidden in a kitchen cupboard and in a textile bag under the bed. The drugs were wrapped in plastic, and stamped with either the letters 'CD' or a picture of a cobra. Apart from the cocaine, the police also seized a large amount of cash and 9 kilos of MDMA that had been sealed up in foil bags. Rodrigo's bank ID device, which was marked with his name, was inside a bag that had been left on the kitchen countertop. He was a young man from Hässelby in north-west Stockholm. Now, however, he was nowhere to be seen. Most likely, he was in a taxi heading to a meet with a buyer in Märsta.

Two of Denny's detectives were instructed to remain in the room and wait for Rodrigo to return. As this was going on, Martina and her colleague were just arriving in the area in Märsta that had been given as the destination when the taxi ride was booked. It was dark, and the detectives weren't too sure who it was they were looking for. Right in front of them was Bokloster Villahotell, a white, two-storey building with a car park out front. Around the corner was an apartment hotel that was part of the same chain that operated the one on Johannesgatan.

After searching the area on foot, the two detectives split up. Martina got into the car to keep watch, while her colleague went over to the aparthotel. She noticed a car that had been parked for a while with the engine in neutral. There was a man sitting in the driver's seat, while his friend was standing outside in the cold. He was smoking, and seemed nervous. Martina reported this over the radio, and hit the 'push to talk' button to allow her colleague to follow what she was doing.

'There's a car I want to check', she said. She tried to glimpse the licence plate from where she was sitting, but couldn't make it out.

Just then, she saw a man of massive build come walking from the entrance to Bokloster Villahotell. He was wearing an unbuttoned jacket, and walked over to the car briskly and got into the back seat.

'Someone's coming.'

Martina knew from experience that this had all the hallmarks of a drug drop-off. The product would be handed over and inspected, and then the money would change hands. She thought to herself that that specific interaction was what she was witnessing.

'I'm going to check the car', she said, and quickly exited her vehicle.

Walking fast, with her hand on her holster, she approached the car in the glare of the streetlights. She had no idea that her radio had malfunctioned, as it sometimes did. This time, it had done so at the worst possible moment. Her colleague had no idea what she was about to do.

To make sure the driver wouldn't have time to think and decide to drive off, she pulled the car door open, and announced her presence with an authoritative voice: 'Police!'

The young man in the back seat opened the car door and made a move towards his jacket. Martina thought he might be reaching for a gun. Instead, however, he lunged out of the car and pushed her out of his way. She grabbed hold of his jacket, and tried to get him to the ground. He resisted, and struggled to break free. Since Martina was holding his jacket with both hands, she was unable to radio her colleague for help. She wasn't going to let go of the suspect, but she was also very aware that there were still two unknown individuals inside the car. Because of this, she tried to turn around so that she wouldn't have her back to them if they decided to jump her. Suddenly, the car drove off, and the wrestling match she was in continued for what felt like several minutes. When the car disappeared, the man Martina was grappling turned more desperate. She realized that he had raised his arm and began to pull back. His fist landed right across her nose. She remained standing, and held her grip tight, while the searing pain she began to feel brought even more adrenaline into her bloodstream.

Her colleague was just returning, and saw Martina receive a punch to the face.

'Officer in trouble', he shouted over the radio, and then ran over as fast as he could and tackled the man. The suspect did everything he could to resist, but the officers soon managed to wrestle him to the ground together and handcuff him. It wasn't until two more officers arrived on the scene that they were finally able to get him fully under control.

The arrested suspect was called Jerker, and during the arrest he had tried to discard two bags of white powder. Inside his hotel room, he had more packages of cocaine, wrapped in red plastic and stamped with the letters 'CD', the same marking that was on the drugs seized at the apartment hotel in the city. The total amount seized was 1 kilo, which the court would later determine that Rodrigo had brought there by taxi just before the police arrived. He had already left the scene when they got there, however. The two men in the car were Jerker's own customers – his plan had been to move the cocaine on quickly.

While the police gathered evidence in Märsta, the two plain-clothes officers who had stayed in the hotel room in the city were waiting for Rodrigo to return. He didn't know that the police were also keeping an eye on this stash site. Time passed, and the detectives' families began to send them messages asking them when they'd be home. They didn't have any good answers to give. At eleven o'clock that evening, the officers heard a key in the lock, and saw the door swing open. The moment Rodrigo entered the room, the detectives shouted 'Police!', and brought him to the floor. It was over before he had a chance to react.

*

When Denny and his team arrived at the station after the arrests of Rodrigo and Jerker, they had made quite an impressive seizure for one night's work: 14 kilos of cocaine and 9 kilos of MDMA. Denny had expected his team to be welcomed back with a cake and lots of high fives. Drugs worth many millions had been taken off the streets. Instead, however, several of the officers involved were reprimanded by their commanding officers.

'You have to learn to stick to the rules', Denny was told.

When Jacob spoke to his boss, he tried to make him see that authorizing the operation had been the right decision. But Jacob was criticized for giving Denny bad guidance and encouraging him to drop everything else to focus on the drug case. According to him, what had annoyed the brass was that they hadn't followed the proper chain of command, and that Denny's detectives were supposed to be keeping an eye on people involved in Järva's ongoing gang conflicts, which were expected to intensify after another fatal shooting.

Denny has worked as a paramedic, and has been the first responder on the scene after several shootings. During the conflict between Shottaz and the Death Squad, he had tried in vain to save the lives of Izzy, the first victim of the conflict, and the Malmö-based Atto, who police suspected was shot in Tensta by members of the Shottaz side. The latter, as it happened, was also one of the Boxer's closest friends.

Several of the people involved believed that the mission in Järva could be handled just as well by half the force on that particular evening. Emotions quickly boiled over, and the people who were there could hear how upset Jacob was. After that phone call, a rift began to develop between Jacob and the local police leadership.

Jacob and Denny still maintain that they made the right call. Ultimately, what the brass said didn't matter. They were both firmly convinced that taking down the Fox's network was an absolute priority. All they wanted was to do what they did best. This was the final straw for Jacob. His dissatisfaction with police leadership, particularly at his workplace in Solna, had been growing for several years by this point. It frustrated him that the commanding officers didn't seem to realize that it was the drugs that were fuelling the deadly violence that was plaguing society in the first place. The money that the drug use generated inspired greed, and debts, conflicts and revenge cycles inevitably followed.

'How could I know that there were 14 kilos of cocaine in a hotel room and not do anything about it? That would make me a sell-out, not a policeman', Denny reasoned.

The director with whom Jacob had been on the phone insisted that it had been Jacob's responsibility to consider the big picture, and everything else that was going on at the time. He explained that his irritation was a response to 'a failure to cooperate', but also expressed his appreciation for the drive and commitment that his officers had shown during the operation.

However, the argument, along with the clear message from Noa that the Fox was not a priority, made Jacob feel that he'd had enough, and that it was time he moved on. Before he did that, though, he wanted to wrap up some ongoing investiga-

The Honey Trap

tions being handled by Team Foxtrot. Hopefully, they would be able to take another bite of the elephant.

*

Wiretapping the Coach had provided Team Foxtrot with new leads on various members of the Fox's network.

After Rodrigo's arrest and the discovery of the stash in Södertälje, the Coach was on the phone a lot, trying to find new storage spaces that he could have his drugs delivered to. He found one in Lillvreta, outside Uppsala, but the police were quick to act, installing hidden cameras and surveillance teams to watch over the site. By this point, the Coach had new mules to receive the drugs and move them on from the stash site.

When another shipping company arrived with a shipment, the police raided the storage unit and arrested the Coach's workers. They found about 100 blue cardboard boxes, containing 850 kilos of tahini, a sesame paste that's used to season food. However, hidden among the tahini were plastic packages containing 89 kilos of amphetamine, almost 9 kilos of cocaine and 7 kilos of 'crystal'. The latter was a new drug that had recently gained popularity among the young party crowd in Uppsala and other towns.

The wiretap operation against the Coach was still revealing unexpected leads even after everybody he was working with had started getting caught. The Coach was trying to convince an ex-criminal to kidnap two children from a wealthy family to hold them to ransom. This was a family the Coach knew through school and his sports team. The police suspected that he might be desperate over being in debt – after all, he had recently had millions of kronors' worth of drugs seized.

Jacob's team would eventually learn even more, thanks to the bug in his car. In late March, they heard him speak on the phone with somebody, and sound very different from how he usually did. They were intrigued, and wondered what was going on.

Soon, they realized that the person he was speaking to was a police officer.

A while before he received the delivery in Lillvreta, the Coach had actually contacted the police himself. Jacob and his investigators hadn't known about this. Despite the risks it involved to his own safety, he had offered to become an informant, and told the police that he had information to share about drug shipments that were coming to Sweden. He also specifically offered to provide information about his boss: the Fox. The Coach explained how the Fox was running his operations remotely from abroad, and that he had a relative in Uppsala who 'hid things' for him and handled his money.

The police handler gave the Coach a phone so that they could keep in contact safely. The Coach was instructed not to commit any crimes or instruct anybody else to do so. He was to do nothing but listen and pass on what he learnt to the police.

Team Foxtrot already knew about the Lillvreta deal he provided information about. They suspected that the Coach was doing what he was doing because he had realized that he was very likely to get caught, like all the others had been before him. One by one, the Fox's henchmen had been arrested.

The Coach earned a monthly salary from the handball club he worked for. He was a popular figure among the people close to the team, but many of them never realized he was in debt to the sum of more than half a million kronor. Every month, the Enforcement Authority was seizing 9,117 kronor of his wages.

The police suspected that he had started working for the Fox when a friend who knew about his debt had asked him if he wanted to earn some extra money. They needed somebody who didn't have a criminal record, who spoke good Swedish and could make and take calls from a shipping company. He was arrested in late March, outside a school, and would later be sentenced to eight years in prison. Taking the Coach off the board represented another step forward for Jacob and his team of investigators at the police station in Solna, whatever Noa might feel about their priorities.

33

Denny's phone rang. A colleague who worked in police intelligence had contacted him to let him know that a serious crime was likely to be committed at noon in the south car park at the Bro commuter train station in Upplands-Bro municipality, about 40 kilometres north-west of Stockholm. Denny had no idea that this tip came from ANOM, but he trusted his colleague. He sent Erik and a group of other detectives to the named location.

At lunchtime, on a cold winter's day early in the year, the team was sent to what they thought would be just one of many investigative efforts that were under way at the time. They noticed a man in his thirties, dressed in black, walking from the car park towards a small industrial estate near the train station. There weren't a lot of people about, so it was quite easy to get a good look at what was happening. Erik, who was more than 100 metres away, was on the lookout for the man in black, waiting for him to return so he could give the order to the team to apprehend and search him. Just then, a pick-up truck with a crane arrived and came to a stop close to the station, with the engine running. Almost ten minutes later, the man in black returned with a bag he hadn't been carrying when they last saw him. He walked over to the driver of the pick-up and spoke to him for a few seconds, before proceeding to toss the bag onto the bed of the vehicle.

From his vantage point, Erik watched the pick-up drive off, and gave the order to a colleague to stop it some distance down the road. Ten kilos of highly diluted amphetamine were found inside the bag.

Meanwhile, the younger man was walking towards the train station. He seemed shocked when plain-clothes detectives approached him on the platform to arrest him. He was soon identified to be Oliver, from Årsta in Stockholm.

After the arrest, Erik and one of his colleagues went back to the industrial estate. Inside the lot, they found about ten garages and a motorcycle club's clubhouse. There was a shovel in front of one of the garage doors. This raised Erik's suspicions. He walked over and tried to peer through a cracked Plexiglass window, but couldn't make anything out.

He knocked on the door.

Nobody seemed to react inside.

The shovel was moved aside, and the door slid open. The first thing Erik saw was a Glock pistol on top of a cabinet. They closed the door behind them and conducted a search of the premises, while one of the detectives remained outside to keep watch. Judging by the two mattresses on the floor, covered with sheets, it seemed likely that somebody might come. Inside the safe, they found another pistol and some ammunition, and there were about 15 kilos of amphetamine and several hundred thousand kronor in cash hidden in different boxes.

'Someone's coming', their colleague outside suddenly announced in their earpieces.

Erik drew his firearm. Outside, he saw a man with unseasonably thin clothing and a swastika tattoo on his stomach. He was peering in through the broken Plexiglass, but, apparently, nothing he saw raised any suspicions. He soon opened the door and walked inside, and was immediately overpowered by the police. The man was identified as Teemu, a Finnish citizen, and a leader of a criminal network in his native country. He had just left the sauna at the motorcycle club next door. Shortly thereafter, a woman arrived at the building, and was also arrested.

*

When Oliver from Årsta had been arrested by the plainclothes officers, he had been using his mobile phone. The police took him by surprise, and managed to seize his phone before he could engage the lock mode. This wasn't just any phone – it was an encrypted Sky ECC phone. One of the detectives immediately brought the phone to the police station in Kungsholmen, and handed it in to the technicians to have a data dump performed.

It took a week or so for the technicians to extract the data in the phone and provide Team Foxtrot with the messages it contained. Apparently, Oliver had picked the drugs up on behalf of somebody who called himself SAS. However, there was no evidence on the phone that they could use to identify the person using the alias. The investigators were disappointed that this was all they gained from a successful seizure of an unlocked Sky ECC phone. However, at that point, the seizure alone was sufficient cause to arrest everybody who had been apprehended at the industrial estate, without having to declare the existence of any other suspects. The police didn't want to have to divulge the fact that they had accessed the contents of that Sky ECC phone during the upcoming custody hearings, or in front of one of the suspects' lawyers.

Jacob had actually suggested that Thorbjörn should see if he could find any other leads in the Encrochat materials. There were still tens of thousands of chat messages they hadn't had time to go through yet, and this was just one of several ongoing investigations they were pursuing alongside their efforts targeting the Coach and the other members of the Fox's network. However, Thorbjörn refused to give up, and went back to read through the messages on Oliver's Sky phone one last time. There was a sentence that he found interesting, where the person who called himself SAS had asked Oliver a rather unusual question.

'Can you catsit for Spex 20–28 December, brother?'

The tone and contents of the message suggested that Oliver and SAS were close friends. Thorbjörn decided to try to identify the suspect he was looking for by searching through Oliver's ordinary phone one more time. For six hours, he combed through the data, with The Hellacopters blaring in his headphones. Finally, he found a message from a woman who mentioned a cat called Spex. It was clear from the conversation that Oliver had volunteered to catsit for her. There was also a picture of Spex in one of Oliver's messages to the woman.

'What are the odds that there are two different cats called Spex?' Thorbjörn wondered to himself.

He looked up the number the woman had sent her message from. It was registered to the same name that had been mentioned in the message to Oliver. Thorbjörn wanted to make sure that the same person was still using the number, however, so he tried calling the phone from an anonymous line. After a few tries, he got an answer.

'Hello', a woman said, and introduced herself by name.

'Sorry, I have the wrong number', Thorbjörn said, and hung up.

He had the confirmation he wanted. A search in the records revealed that she had previously cohabited with a man called Lars, and that the address had been mentioned in intelligence related to drug-trafficking suspicions.

Thorbjörn shared his discovery with Jacob, who was already being pressured to wrap up all his open cases and move on to other tasks. Despite this, he was assigned detectives that would be available the next weekend. All Thorbjörn had to do now was tell the team about the leads he had discovered and tell them who they were looking for.

He prepared a PowerPoint presentation that he showed to eleven detectives. The first slide featured a picture of an orange and white toy aeroplane underneath the heading 'Operation SAS'. The next slide described the mission: 'Locate Spex the cat, and arrest his owner!'

The detectives laughed.

'We have two days to get this done. We'll spend Friday on surveillance. On Saturday, we strike', Thorbjörn informed the team.

After this meeting, the detectives were divided into two teams. One of them would be staking out the woman's home, and give the others updates on her whereabouts and activities on WhatsApp. 'There's no need to disturb her by knocking on her door at this point', said Jacob. Meanwhile, the other team would be outside Lars's flat, and keep everybody updated on any activity there. He changed, looking out the window as he got ready to go out.

'Stay alert', one detective wrote to the group.

The police needed sufficient suspicion that a criminal offence had been committed to search Lars, but the police can usually find some reason or other to carry out a search. To facilitate this, the detectives had deliberately chosen to take positions close to his home. For example, if an individual was suspected of being under the influence of drugs, the police were entitled to search that person's home, as they could reasonably suspect that there might be drugs there. And, unsurprisingly, when Lars left the flat and got inside his car, he was quickly stopped by the police. In court, the police officer who apprehended him would state that the reason he had stopped Lars was that he had driven the wrong way down a one-way street.

While the police were questioning him, a mobile phone he had placed between the front seats of his car began to ring. It was a Sky ECC phone. Lars's mouth was dry, and he seemed nervous. The officers suspected that he might be under the influence of drugs, and decided to carry out a search in his home.

Inside the flat, they found large amounts of cash and several mobile phones, but they didn't find any drugs. When the police searched through one of his private phones, they found photographs, including one of a cat.

'Is that your cat?' one of the officers asked him.

'No. That's Spex, my ex-girlfriend's cat', Lars replied.

Thorbjörn and the other officers gave each other a look. At this point, they felt that they had sufficient cause to make an arrest, but Jacob wanted to wait, for strategic reasons. It was the weekend, which meant that they would have to hand the arrest over to the on-call prosecutor, who wouldn't be familiar with the case.

Lars wasn't actually brought in until two weeks later. Since he had moved out of his ex-girlfriend's place during the previous summer, the investigators didn't believe that she was involved in any criminal activity.

A few days after Lars's arrest, Thorbjörn visited the ex-girlfriend to conduct an interview. They sat in her kitchen. She told him that she had lived with Lars until they broke up in the summer of 2020, after he began to act 'weird' and 'cold' to her. Lars's odd phone, which didn't have a normal display, had troubled her. Eventually, she had issued an ultimatum to her boyfriend.

'That phone is leaving my flat, and it's up to you if you're going with it or not.'

After that, he had hidden the phone from her.

Soon, Thorbjörn transitioned to a series of questions about her cat.

'Did any friends ever look after Spex for you?'

'Yes, Lars had a friend, Oliver, who helped out.'

She told Thorbjörn that Oliver had looked after the cat a few times. The ex-girlfriend was puzzled by this line of questioning, and eventually, she turned to Spex, who was in the kitchen, and asked the cat: 'What have you been up to? All these questions are about you.'

Thorbjörn explained that the cat had been mentioned in an ongoing investigation.

He took several pictures of Spex, including one of the cat standing on a marble table, next to a vase with a gold-coloured rim. They had found a similar picture on Lars's private phone. More details would eventually emerge that tied Lars to the Sky ECC alias SAS.

Once the investigators had figured out who had been communicating with whom in relation to this specific drop-off, they began to see that there were even more people involved. They still had a lot of work to do, but they didn't have much time left before Team Foxtrot was going to be disbanded.

*

The investigators' suspicions that Lars and one of his close friends had been in direct contact with the Fox would soon be strengthened. In mid-March 2021, it was announced that the Sky ECC encryption service had also been cracked. Once again, French authorities were involved. This time, they had initiated the operation in collaboration with colleagues from Belgium and the Netherlands, two countries that had become Europe's most popular destinations for cocaine traffickers.

Sky ECC had kept their server in the same server room in Roubaix that Encrochat had used. Because of this, the case had ended up on the desk of the same young prosecutor, Alexandre from Lille. He approved covert coercive measures, and then passed the case on to the national Police Authority in Paris, because he was still too busy working on Encrochat.

This time, no other countries had been invited to join the operation, even though Sky ECC had been serving 170,000 users worldwide, and processing 3 million messages every day. This meant that, even though there were several thousand Sky ECC users who had ties to Sweden, the Swedish police had never been able to follow these communications in real time.

Many members of the international justice community would wonder why this intelligence had never been offered to police in other countries. It would remain a source of irritation with colleagues all over the world for a long time, as many felt that they had been denied a good opportunity to prevent serious crimes.

*

Later, when the chats from ANOM and Sky ECC began to be released, Swedish police would receive additional information that helped them piece together the course of events in several of their ongoing investigations.

One of the cases that was clarified in this manner concerned the identities of the others who had been involved in the drop-off that had occurred at the train station in Bro. It seems that the whole affair was the result of a complaint from a dissatisfied customer. Apparently, Teemu, the Finnish man with the swastika, had bought a bad batch of speed, and wanted his money back. An important behind-the-scenes role had been played in the deal by an individual who went by the name of Smeden, 'the Blacksmith'. He drove a Tesla, had young children, and lived in a detached house in southern Stockholm. After Teemu's complaint, the Blacksmith quickly found a new buyer on ANOM. This was a friend of his from the construction sector, who was known for his cheerful mood.

The Blacksmith had asked his friend Lars to organize the drop-off, and Oliver was recruited to assist for a fee of 7,000 kronor.

'You're meeting the Finn in the usual spot', Oliver was told.

The password he was to provide was 'Frodo'.

What made the Blacksmith particularly interesting to Team Foxtrot was his familiar tone in the chat messages he wrote to another Sky ECC user, who the police strongly suspected to be the Fox. They discussed some firearms that the Fox wanted to acquire, but the Blacksmith asked the Fox for favours, too.

Could he receive 5,000 euros?

He could do that.

The Blacksmith went on to ask, 'where do I leave the dough?'

'Uppsala', the person suspected to be the Fox replied.

'At the ice-cream parlour?' the Blacksmith asked, and made a joke, asking if complementary ice cream was included.

'Yeah brother, hahaha', the Fox wrote back.

The Blacksmith told him that the password used for the drop-off would be 'lurken', 'the scoundrel', and asked who would be there to receive the money when he sent Lars over with it.

'No code, my mum', the Fox replied, and sent over the address of the ice-cream parlour in Uppsala where his mother usually manned the counter.

Just a few days later, the police carried out their raid against the Fox's parents, and against the retired man who volunteered at the parlour. Large sums of cash were found, and tied to the Fox's criminal enterprises. Inside an envelope, the police found 5,000 euros, which had both Lars's and Teemu's fingerprints on them.

As we've covered, Denny was tipped off about this deal when it was in the making, and the intelligence would prove to have been sourced from ANOM. All along, unbeknownst to the police, Noa had been keeping tabs on everyone involved.

The mysterious customer – the friend who had been happy to buy the Blacksmith's bad speed, and sent a mule called Kent to pick it up – had also been identified.

His name was Robin. He claimed to have a background in the French Foreign Legion, an elite military unit, and was the CEO of a construction company, a job that provided him with a taxable income of over half a million kronor a year. Team Foxtrot was aware of him, as he had been questioned after Kent went to pick up the speed in the company's pick-up truck. He had no idea what his employee had been doing up in Bro, but suggested that maybe he had been 'picking up some tools'.

'We had suspicions about him from an early stage, but we had no evidence against him', Niklas of Team Foxtrot told me.

Robin was questioned after the raid on the industrial estate, but only in his capacity as the employer of Kent, who had been caught with the 10 kilos of amphetamine.

Noa, on the other hand, had other reasons to be keeping a close watch on the former Legionnaire Robin. He would eventually be convicted of buying speed from Maximilian Rivkin, the ANOM influencer who was very well known to the police. In a chat, the latter had offered Robin the drugs and begun to negotiate the price.

'It's the cleanest stuff I've sent out in 2 years', the ANOM account linked to Rivkin wrote.

Rivkin also appeared to be collaborating with a friend of Abdul Haleem, who would also be suspected of involvement in the murder of Sascha on the Årstabron Bridge. The officers at Noa who were monitoring the chats, and had all the information from all the encrypted chat services, realized that many of the criminal networks in Sweden were in business with one another in some way or other. One of the many people who were involved in these investigations confirmed this picture in conversation with me.

'This is all much bigger than you can imagine. We're talking cartels.'

34

The night-time air of 7 June 2021 was still cool when the officers from the National Task Force, who were wearing camouflage gear and hiding in the woods, surrounded a two-storey house in Haninge in southern Stockholm. In recent months, after Sky ECC had been closed down, thousands of new users had migrated to ANOM. ANOM, however, would also come to an end before long. This was the day when the ANOM operation was to be brought to a close, through a series of synchronized efforts in all corners of the world.

The task force operatives relayed the licence plate numbers of several vehicles that had been parked outside the house. The target for this operation was Robin, the 32-year-old CEO of a construction company and former Foreign Legionnaire who had become suspected of drug trafficking based on evidence from ANOM.

There was concern among the officers that Robin, who had mentioned his military background in the chats, might have access to weapons. Because of this, extra reinforcements had been brought in. The task force was waiting for the go-ahead, and was ready to react if the suspect they were watching should suddenly become suspicious and try to escape. If that happened, they would move to apprehend him.

If he behaved normally, on the other hand, the plan was for the operation to continue for another twenty-four hours, after which point police in sixteen different countries would make simultaneous strikes against serious criminals who had used ANOM.

While this was happening, Vera, who was in charge of the Swedish participation in the ANOM operation, was cooking herself dinner in her small flat in The Hague, which was not far from her workplace at Europol. She had spent the last few weeks here, in daily meetings with her counterparts in other countries. This had been the most exciting time of her professional career. It was thanks to her that the FBI had agreed to cooperate with Europol. She had helped the American Feds write their application to Europol to get approval for their cooperative operational plan. Unlike the Encrochat operation, which Sweden had been invited to join a month after it began, Sweden had played a central role in this operation as a major European partner of the FBI. This time, Sweden had invited other countries to join the operation.

Vera was proud of her own work, and the achievements of the Police Authority, which had proven itself to be very effective by winning a lot of convictions based on the Encrochat evidence.

ANOM would be another opportunity for the Swedish police to show everyone what they were capable of. Vera recalled how difficult it had been in the past to get countries like Spain and the Netherlands to cooperate on seizures of tens of kilograms of cocaine. Her foreign colleagues hadn't been too impressed. After all, they were used to dealing with tonnes of drugs, being brought in constantly on cargo ships from South America. It was difficult for them to understand that 10 kilos of cocaine represented significant amounts of money to criminals in Sweden who were habitually involved in deadly shootings. The Swedish gun violence problem was unique in comparison with the situations in many other European countries.

Since the very beginning of the operation, in September 2020, the FBI had made it clear to everyone involved that the ANOM operation had a predetermined end date: 7 June 2021. The authorization to gather data in the country where the ANOM server was located was set to expire on that date.

Keeping an international operation secret for that long was quite a challenge.

As May came to an end, the sense of urgency at Europol was becoming increasingly palpable. After spending a few weeks in Stockholm to visit her family, Vera had returned, and was once again monitoring the communications of criminals who were beginning to sound stressed. More and more were writing that ANOM was also 'leaking'. When Sky ECC was cracked, the tension had intensified even more among the criminals, who were already under pressure. Fortunately, the criminals who were administrating the service silenced the critics, and continued to emphasize that ANOM was the most secure platform in the world.

Vera thought that the worst-case scenario would be if the criminals panicked and began to discard their phones. Because of this, she urged all of her contacts in Sweden to maintain 'information packs' that were ready to be used at short notice. These packs were to contain all the evidence needed to establish grounds to arrest the highest-priority targets among the Swedish ANOM users. This list included about seventy high-profile criminal suspects.

She worked long hours at Europol, and spent her evenings in her small flat, which didn't have an oven. She enjoyed this unglamorous life, which gave her opportunities to meet like-minded people from other countries, who were just as passionate about their work as she was. Since The Hague had been locked down for the pandemic, she ate simple meals in the evenings, frying fish and vegetables on her little stovetop, and watched *Say Yes to the Dress*, a reality show about the difficulties involved in choosing a wedding dress.

*

After many months of intensive efforts, the day that everybody had been waiting for had arrived. Vera had slept for about two or three hours when she woke up at two in the morning. This was when ANOM was going to be shut down. An hour later, she was at Europol, where a group of excited colleagues had gathered. They were all relieved to finally be striking against their targets. Vera filled up on espresso, and kept a store of snus and Coca-Cola Zero ready next to her keyboard. She didn't have time to eat any food.

In Sweden, her colleagues were ready to strike at four in the morning. All over the country, police officers were preparing to go after different targets. Many of the officers who had been called in had only been told to be at a specific place at this particular time. They had no idea where the intelligence they were acting on had come from. They were used to the secrecy after the Encrochat operation.

Team Foxtrot, which had been disbanded after making a series of arrests that spring in the course of their hunt for the Fox, had been given no choice but to settle for never reaching the person at the top of the network. Now, though, the activity in the police force was picking up again. All over the country, police officers with different, specific skill sets were being called in to join a big operation, although few of them were told what it was all about.

One of the seventy or so priority targets on Noa's list of people who were to be arrested as part of operation Trojan Shield was the ex-Legionnaire, Robin.

The officers who were most familiar with him were those who had been part of Team Foxtrot. The team had come close to catching him earlier in the year, when Denny's detectives

The Honey Trap

had arrested several mules at the industrial estate in Bro after a transaction involving 10 kilos of amphetamine. The ANOM chats revealed that the mule who had picked up the drugs had been sent to the location by Robin.

Thorbjörn from Team Foxtrot had been asked by his colleague Niklas to lead two surveillance teams in the search of Robin's house, which was planned to take place as soon as the task force had arrested Robin.

He was wearing thermal underwear to keep the cold out when he met with one of the surveillance teams in Järfälla at half past three in the morning. They drove to an address in Haninge where they met up with the second surveillance team. They all paused some distance from the house, and waited.

At six o'clock, officers from the National Task Force moved towards Robin's house from the rear, where the wooded area offered them better cover for their approach. One team headed for the two large glass doors on the ground floor, while another team moved towards a similar entrance on the first floor. Within seconds, they had smashed the glass and begun to secure every room of the house. They had to move quickly to apprehend their target and secure any electronic equipment. Robin heard the window shatter and lunged out of bed in his underwear. He ran upstairs, towards his partner and their daughter, who was nearly three months old, but he was almost immediately apprehended. Other police officers walked into the room where the woman and her child were. She was composed. Her partner had been arrested before. However, what made this time different was that he would be going away for a long time – he would eventually be sentenced to seven years' imprisonment.

*

As the morning continued, Vera received a steady stream of updates, and provided her boss, Linda H. Staaf, with a summary of events to help her prepare for the press conference that would be held in The Hague the next day. All in all, 155 people were arrested in the Swedish operation. This was a higher number than the 70 initial targets, and it included 5 people who were taken into custody in Spain. Weapons, money, drugs and jewellery had all been seized.

Since Vera had forgotten to eat lunch, she kept herself going by eating the biscuits her colleagues had brought to the Trojan Shield offices at Europol.

Almost everything went as planned, with just a few exceptions. Several of the suspects were away from home, or had already made their way abroad. One of the ones who had already escaped was the spa owner from the Bergsjön network who had smuggled in 1.2 tonnes of hashish in marble tiles. However, he was soon arrested in Greece after having been refused entry to Turkey while travelling with his brother's passport.

'I'd like to exercise my right to remain silent, and will not be making a statement', he would say when he was shown the chat logs from ANOM.

*

As these events unfolded, Linda H. Staaf checked in with the team at Noa who were coordinating all the many efforts. Among the people arrested was the then 72-year-old Kjell Johansson, the former leader of Grodmansligan, 'the Frogman Gang', who had been one of Sweden's most infamous criminals for decades.

In the late 1980s, he had become a notorious figure after being apprehended in scuba gear during an attempt to swim ashore with 20 kilos of amphetamine. Now, he was arrested on suspicion of an exceptionally serious drug offence, which involved packing and mailing drugs to customers who had ordered them through the dark web. Rikard, who had run the speed lab with Rivkin, and was still considered a key figure in the operation, was arrested as part of the same investigation.

When the task force came to arrest Rikard, he had been with his family, preparing to celebrate his son's sixth birthday the next day.

However, the ANOM influencer Maximilian Rivkin remained out of reach to the FBI and the Swedish police, and was not taken down in their coordinated raids. In recent months, apart from the extensive drug operations he managed, the police had been able to follow his involvement in a murder plot against a man in the central Stockholm area, who was known as the Arab. Rivkin wrote that the Arab owed him 6 or 7 million kronor, and that he wanted him to be finished off in a violent fashion.

'Mexican style.'

When his ANOM customers were being arrested, he was safe in Turkey, a country he had described as a 'gangsters' paradise' in the chats.

Despite the successes of this FBI-led operation, the US federal agency remained unable to take action against ANOM users in the USA. The FBI wasn't allowed to access the communications of the small number of users within the country, as this would have constituted an illegal surveillance operation against US citizens. Rivkin and the sixteen other key administrators, all foreign nationals, were on their wanted list, however.

On the day of the operation, Staaf had booked an afternoon flight to Schiphol Airport outside Amsterdam, from where she was going to travel on to The Hague to attend a press conference there, which had been planned in great detail. After an operation that had taken several years to carry out, it was important to announce the successful arrest of more than 800 criminal suspects to the world.

The intelligence director had prepared her speech; her main concern at the moment was making sure she didn't contract

Covid. If she were to begin to develop symptoms, she would miss her opportunity to highlight the efforts of the Swedish police, who had brought one of their biggest operations ever to a successful conclusion. She took two Covid tests that day, to make absolutely sure she wasn't infected. The second test was taken at the latest possible moment before the flight. When the tests came back negative, she was able to relax, and boarded the plane. At ten o'clock the next morning, she took her face mask off and entered the stage.

'Good morning! In the early hours of yesterday morning, the Swedish police carried out one of its most extensive raid operations ever', she began.

In front of journalists from all over the world, Staaf spoke of the people who had been arrested in Sweden, and how the information from the encrypted chats that operation Trojan Shield had provided had helped the police prevent more than ten murder plots on Swedish soil. She said that the police expected to make further arrests in addition to the ones made during the recent raids. She concluded her speech with a phrase that made her a household name overnight:

'We're never going to give up.'

PART 6
THE FOX HUNT

SEPTEMBER 2021 – DECEMBER 2022

PART 5

35

After the summer of 2021, when the ANOM operation came to an end, the investigation into the Fox was picked up again. One thing that had changed since before was the escalating violence.

In September, a hand grenade was thrown through the window of a flat in Rotebro, nearly killing a babysitter and two toddlers who had been sleeping on the floor inside. The grenade detonated next to them, but the shrapnel flew towards the ceiling. Around that same time, homes in Upplands Väsby and Vallentuna were shot at, a hand grenade was thrown into a stairwell in Valsta, and a car with children inside was fired upon. The police received a tip that somebody was preparing to fire a rocket launcher at a flat, but this particular individual was shot at himself from inside the flat before he could pull the trigger.

This violence was an effect of the 60 kilos or so of drugs that the Fox is said to have lost, and it wouldn't stop until all debts had been cleared. He wasn't in Sweden himself, but the suspicion was that he was issuing orders to his allies within the country from Iraqi Kurdistan. These events occurred in the vicinity of investigators who had been members of Team Foxtrot, the task force that had targeted the Fox's drug distribution network. That autumn, two of those investigators, Niklas and Thorbjörn, were back at their usual workplace, the police station in Järfälla. Along with two other colleagues, they were carrying on the investigations they had worked on in the spring, as well as following up on operation Trojan Shield, which had led to the National Task Force's arrest of the former Foreign Legionnaire Robin at his house in southern Stockholm.

They felt a gnawing feeling inside almost every day, whenever they saw the effects of the violence they suspected was being orchestrated by the Fox and his allies. Like many of his colleagues, Niklas believed that going after the street-level pawns wasn't good enough, especially not in a case in which the evidence always seemed to lead back to the same person: the Fox.

The thing that finally made it impossible for Niklas to keep his silence was when some colleagues in Värmland contacted him to tell him that they had recorded the Fox in the course of a wiretap operation against an inmate at Kumla prison. These conversations had given them reason to believe that lives were at risk. Something had to be done, there was no denying it.

On 6 October 2021, Niklas sent an email to his immediate superior in Järfälla and the top brass in the North Stockholm police district. He wanted to summon them to an 'emergency meeting', and emphasized that there had been a whole series of recent violent crimes that were connected to the Fox. Niklas wanted them to make a decision about how they would act on the information he had just received from Värmland, before anybody's life was put in danger.

He was disappointed to read the response from the head of the local police district in Järfälla. There was to be no emergency meeting at this point, but the director would be back at the station after the weekend, and he would have spoken to the other commanding officers by then as they were away on a business trip together.

Four days later, Niklas received their decision: because of the investigative burden the North Stockholm police district was facing, they had to prioritize domestic violence offences and crimes targeting particularly vulnerable victims. At the time, the manager also wanted to wait to see what would be uncovered by the Sky ECC materials that they had requested. The batch they were soon be sent contained 800,000 messages from about 100 different accounts, which were thought to be connected to the Fox and his network in various ways. The data was from the time after Encrochat had shut down.

Niklas and other officers believed that it was wrong to weigh crimes against each other that way, and felt that the police needed to allocate staff to investigations of both kinds of crimes.

After the summer, the Swedish Police Authority appointed a coordinator to assist colleagues in various parts of the country to use evidence gathered from three encrypted chat services: Encrochat, ANOM and Sky ECC. In the North Stockholm police district, this task was given to Christoffer Bohman, a police officer who had lengthy experience of gang-related investigations and was highly respected within the force. He quickly learnt of the 'frustration' of the investigators who had received the cold shoulder from Noa last spring, when they were told that the Fox wasn't a sufficiently dangerous target.

Since nobody seemed to have a particularly good grasp of the overall situation, he brought a group of nine intelligence officers and investigators together, with Niklas, Jacob and Denny among them, to update him on the case.

'What I'm seeing is an organizer who's presently in Kurdistan, who holds significant influence, particularly when it comes to the influx of drugs into Stockholm, and who is quick to resort to violence against anybody who gets in his way', said Christoffer Bohman.

On 18 October 2021, he emailed the same commanding officers whom Niklas had alerted. However, he sent them a five-page 'operation plan', which detailed the danger posed by the Fox's network, which was referred to as 'Foxtrot' in the document.

The Fox's network was described as an ethnically Kurdish family-based criminal network, or clan, which primarily engaged in smuggling operations moving large volumes of drugs from Spain and the Netherlands to Sweden and other Nordic countries. The organization's leader was the Fox, who was running things from Kurdistan with the assistance of relatives and contacts in Spain and the Netherlands, and underlings who were mostly concentrated in and around Stockholm and Uppsala. According to police intelligence, the network was estimated to be bringing in about 150 kilos of drugs to Mälardalen every week. The Fox's private fortune was estimated at around 100 million kronor. This estimation was based on a note of New Year's resolutions for 2020 that Team Foxtrot had found in one of the Fox's Encro phones: 'I'm going to have 100 million kronor, that's my motto.'

The police had already frozen the assets in a Bitcoin account they had been able to connect to the Fox, but they suspected that there were probably many others like it out there. They had also learned from the Fox's chats that his ambition was to become the biggest cocaine dealer in Europe.

In the operation plan, Bohman also wrote that the Fox was seeking to take over the drug market in Stockholm, an assessment that was supported by a series of attempts that had been made to rob rival drug sellers. The network operated under a system of specialized roles, in which some individuals booked legal shipments of palletized goods in which the drugs were hidden, and other individuals received the drugs or distributed them to other parts of Sweden. Other people were responsible for debt collecting, acts of violence and collecting payments. All in all, there were already twenty ongoing investigations that were linked to his network.

Since the Fox was still in Iraq at this time, and hadn't yet – as far as the Swedish authorities knew – been granted citizenship there, because he had been born in Iran during his mother's flight to Sweden, it was believed that an extradition could potentially be arranged, and there had already been communications with the Ministry of Foreign Affairs regarding this matter. However, they also knew that the Fox was well connected with political figures in his parents' native country, and that this was bound to complicate things. Other sources also confirmed this, and claimed that his lifestyle became a source of aggravation for other influential people living in the city.

Since Noa had recently made the assessment that the Fox wasn't a particularly dangerous target, the report emphasized the shootings, explosions and drug-trafficking activities that could be attributed, in various ways, to the Fox and his allies in the Bro and Märsta networks. The idea was to communicate clearly to leadership that the Fox and his organization were highly capable of violence and had already shown great indifference to the risk of harming bystanders, including women and children.

In the same report, the Fox was also said to have created a kill list of his worst rivals. On top of this, the danger that violence might be used against police officers and municipal officials was underlined. Unless his network was weakened, the more experienced police officers believed that he would be successful in claiming a greater share of the Stockholm drug market, and orchestrate even more acts of violence and slayings in Stockholm. Given sufficient time, he was also likely to move his criminal proceeds to legal investments, an outcome that would make him 'hard to stop'.

The senior leadership at the police district was also provided with other alarming information. It was reported that the Fox's network had – not *may have* but *had* – insiders within the police, Customs and social security authorities, and that the rule of law could potentially be undermined from within if the network was permitted to grow larger. I have been unable to clarify which specific intelligence this information was based on.

A series of measures was proposed, including 'working up a suspicion' that the Fox was involved in conspiracy to murder, as this would make getting him extradited from Iraq more likely.

Other suggestions included gathering the various ongoing investigations under a joint prosecution and investigation team based in the North Stockholm police district. Information was to be pooled to identify commonalities, and the case would have a dedicated task force, which would be authorized to use covert coercive measures and given the resources needed to take swift action against key players and seize their weapons, explosives and assets.

In conclusion, a list was given of police functions that the investigative team was deemed to need access to in order to be successful. An investigative lead, a surveillance lead, an administrator, detectives, analysts, financial analysts, intelligence officers, and an operational coordinator to act as a link between them were all requested. Twelve team members would be required to fulfil all these roles.

*

A few weeks later, their efforts were rewarded: Team Foxtrot was being revived, although the scale of the operation wouldn't even come close to what they had proposed. Instead, Niklas, the investigator who had been part of the operation from the beginning, and six others, including one colleague who would soon go on parental leave, would lead the efforts against the Fox and his network, which their report had shown to be a violent one.

Several people involved felt that they had been mistreated and 'tossed aside'. They argued that this case had exposed serious leadership problems within the police, and a preference among senior leadership for 'door-kicking and raids' over long-term strategies for taking down the leaders and enablers within the criminal networks. Christoffer Bohman agreed with this analysis. He had extensive experience of both operational and strategic work, and noted that one challenge the Police Authority faced was its prevailing culture, which emphasized and prioritized urgent cases to an extent that harmed its ability to look 'beyond the next hill'. Long-term strategies weren't given sufficient attention. The result was that they ended up spending too much time and effort just putting out fires. This was a view that several of his experienced colleagues shared.

All four commanding officers who received Niklas's request for an emergency meeting and the operation plan have told me they acted in a timely fashion, and provided reasonable resources in relation to the risk assessments that were made at the time and the other priorities they had to consider. One important consideration was that they believed the team would have limited prospects at best for getting the Fox to court, as he was abroad. Anders Rissel, chief of police in the North Stockholm police district, told me that he would have made 'the same assessment today, even though I have access to some facts that I didn't have then'.

Lisa Granqvist, head of the serious crime section in the same police district, believed that the team's warnings had been taken seriously, and that they had been granted access to specialists and permission to 'work in coordination, without disturbances', privileges that even murder investigations were never offered.

The leadership stated that a lot of efforts had been made to get the Fox extradited to Sweden, but that they had been unsuccessful, and that this wasn't because the Police Authority had failed in its duties. Granqvist offered some reflections on whether a different decision, such as assigning more resources, would really have had any effect on the outcome.

'Would the violence have escalated sooner? Or would the escalation have been prevented altogether? Would all these things have happened anyway? Or would we maybe have been dealing with some other problem? What I'm trying to point out is that it's difficult to measure the impact of things that didn't happen, or the specific consequences of granting resources to this case instead of other ones.'

Although Team Foxtrot had been reassembled, their main target, the Fox, was out of their reach. And when Iraqi police raided a number of addresses at the request of their Swedish colleagues, he had already left the country. He was also about to take a major step, which would bring him closer to truly becoming the dangerous leader that the experienced officers had been warning their commanders about.

36

In early March 2022, a man was found shot dead in a car outside the Bandidos clubhouse in Haninge in southern Stockholm. However, the murdered man had no connections to the biker gang. He had simply been attending a party held in a function room next door to the clubhouse.

A mere two weeks later, plans were being made for another attack on the Bandidos. The police discovered this from voice messages stored on a seized phone, in which a person calling himself Animal, who was suspected of being the Fox, instructed the recipient to use a *kalle*, or Kalashnikov. However, this murder plot was cancelled, because the police had a surveillance team working outside the biker gang's clubhouse.

Two weeks later, another attack was carried out, and another innocent bystander was killed.

Just before lunch on 28 March, a masked man entered the Delta gym in Vasastan, an area in the Stockholm city centre. The gym was busy at that time of day, with plenty of visitors who had taken the chance to get a workout in during their lunch break. The man walked over to the strength-training machines, where he had spotted his target: a Bandidos member who worked as a personal trainer at the gym, competed in bodybuilding and had tens of thousands of followers on Instagram, where he shared workout videos and pictures of himself in the biker gang's branded clothes. Apart from that, he had maintained a low profile, at least in terms of criminal activities.

Just as the shooter was about to fire, another visitor to the gym realized what was about to happen and tried to prevent the attack. The man who intervened was Fredrik, fifty-four, a father of three. He had worked as a barman at Riche, and had no connection to the Bandidos member besides going to the same gym. In the commotion that ensued, the shooter turned and shot the man who had intervened. The bullets hit him in the head, and he died. Meanwhile, the Bandidos member and the other gym-goers ran away, and soon the shooter did the same.

That day, several media outlets reported on the shooting, which had been carried out among a crowd of witnesses. The sad truth was that the first three months of the year had already seen eighteen fatal shootings, a record-breaking number. It was becoming clear that conflicts among criminals were bringing harm to people who were in no way involved in them. People were ending up getting shot just for going to the same gym as a target, or happening to be outside an MC clubhouse.

Later that evening, I spoke to several police sources about the shooting, and received an update on the Bandidos and their ongoing conflicts. One of these sources told me things were 'incredibly tense'. I asked my sources who they thought might have ordered the shooting at the gym, as the Bandidos were involved in several conflicts at the time. My question was really more of an attempt to gain better insight into what was going on in existing conflicts I was already aware of. But then I got a text message with an answer that I hadn't expected: a fox emoji.

'The Fox? Why?' I replied immediately.

The Fox's network was extremely difficult to get a handle on, as there were so many people operating at various levels of it who didn't have any obvious connections to anybody on the level above them. But his name – or, rather, his nickname – seemed to pop up constantly, in the most unexpected contexts.

A sixteen-year-old boy would later be sentenced to 2 years and 11 months in juvenile detention for the Delta gym slaying. He was connected to a network in Upplands-Bro, and the suspicion was that he had been hired to carry out the hit. In this investigation, too, there was mention of a Turkish phone number and somebody who had been using the alias Animal, the same username that had previously been linked to the Fox.

According to police sources, both of these murders, which had actually been directed against the Bandidos, were linked to a conflict between the motorcycle gang and three criminal networks that had aligned themselves with each other to make a joint move on the drug market: the Fox's network; Bro, from northern Stockholm; and Zero, from Jordbro in southern Stockholm.

The police believed that this conflict had been sparked after two police raids were carried out in Lidingö and Älvsjö in February 2022. In those raids, more than 300 kilos of drugs were seized in total. A 23-year-old woman who had been arrested in conjunction with the raid was later convicted. The police had seen instructions she had received on Signal from the alias Animal.

In the criminal underworld, it was rumoured that the Fox's beef with the Bandidos had started when a drug deal 'went wrong'. It wasn't even over that much money, just a few hundred thousand kronor. However, as the story went, both parties had stubbornly blamed the other side. The killings outside the clubhouse and inside the Delta gym were meant to convince the Bandidos to provide the reparations that the Fox and his allies were demanding.

'It was all a show of force', a source with insight into the conflict told me.

The same source also explained that escalations of this kind could also be caused if 'somebody who had been pushed around grew a pair and wanted to get back on somebody', or a girl was 'spreading her legs all over the place' and triggered a fit of jealousy in somebody. This time, apparently, a mediator was able to bring about a reconciliation. Since the two attacks, the man who was targeted at the gym has left the Bandidos.

Since December 2022, the Fox has been arrested *in absentia* on suspicion of conspiracy to commit murder, for his involvement in the mid-March plan. The two murders that were actually committed were connected to the same conflict as that conspiracy, but the Fox has not been named as a formal suspect in relation to them.

'He can be bad to bad people, definitely', a source with knowledge of the Fox's activities told me.

*

I had already begun to research the Fox's background before the murder in Vasastan. He had been given some mention in the national media, including when his parents were prosecuted. However, I hadn't written a single line or made any mention of him in my work. I had been focusing on the deadly shootings.

At that time, Noa was no longer treating him as a priority target.

The police officers I spoke to gave me a big stack of printouts, which included some of the verdicts that had been handed down. They wanted me to see that the Fox had been involved in all of the cases. There were too many names and details for me to take in, and, besides, they wouldn't let me record our conversation either. All I was permitted to do was take notes on my phone.

Just over six months later, I started to interview police officers, the people who had been involved in the cases, and anybody else who could help me get a clearer picture of what had happened. My attempts to understand how all these events were connected became an obsession. Soon, all of the different people, addresses, stash houses, cities, waybills and encrypted messages were beginning to form an enormous web, with the Fox at its centre.

That was also when I learned that there was a group who hadn't given up on catching the Fox, and that they called themselves Team Foxtrot.

When we met, the team consisted of a handful of investigators and analysts who had wallpapered their offices with pictures of foxes and toys that symbolized their various investigations, which had already produced forty or so convictions. At that point in time, apart from Encrochat, the investigators had also been given access to chat logs from ANOM and Sky ECC.

Information gained through conventional policing methods was supplemented by this mass of communications between criminals from three different encrypted platforms. By the summer of 2021, when the ANOM operation was revealed, they had a backlog of millions of messages to read. It wasn't just Noa's intelligence officers who were working on the material, local police investigators had also been granted access to the Acus Table platform, a computer program that can handle large amounts of data.

One investigator explained how the software gave him access to databases of chats from Encrochat, Sky ECC and ANOM.

It was an inexhaustible source of vital intelligence. Sky ECC alone consisted of more than 35 million unique messages that were connected to Sweden, while there were almost 4 million in Encrochat and almost 2 million in ANOM. At the time of writing, Swedish police still have 'several years of work' to go before they'll have read through all the Sky ECC material – that is, if they ever do. To address this problem of scale, AI software has been used to search for keywords indicating discussions about serious crimes in the chats and audio files that have been sent.

The program makes it easier to read the messages, and, with a single click, an investigator can also see which phone masts the phones were connecting to when different drug deals were agreed. Investigators have already tied enough drug-related offences to the Fox to seek a maximum sentence, so they don't really need any more of those.

'We're looking for violent crimes, bombings, attempted murders and murders', one of them told me.

*

The two murders in March and April 2022 would also finally convince the Police Authority to begin allocating more resources to their hunt for the Fox. One measure they took was to move a handful of investigators from the conference room in Solna to the regional investigation department in Kungsholmen, where Noa is also based. More colleagues would join the investigation there.

They also got back their old boss, Jacob. Before long, he would be observing a development that nobody could ever have predicted.

37

Since the Fox left the country in April 2020, he had been living in his parents' home town of Sulaymaniyah, Iraq. This was what several sources had told the team. Because of this, the Swedish police had been exerting pressure on the Iraqi authorities in various ways.

Efforts to convince Iraq to aid Sweden in hunting the Fox had also been made by top-level politicians. During a visit to Iraq, the foreign minister at the time, Social Democrat Ann Linde, reportedly made mention of the arrest order against the Fox, and announced that she wanted him extradited to Sweden. Ministers don't usually mention names like that – a request of that type would normally be communicated by an ambassador, for example. The fact that she did mention this particular case suggests that she took it very seriously, according to an informed source. When I contacted Ann Linde, she told me that she had no comment to make regarding the matter.

Police in the region would eventually raid several addresses, including the Fox's home. Several sources have told me that the family was living in a large flat in one of the 32-storey buildings in Dania City, one of the more upmarket neighbourhoods in Sulaymaniyah. However, he had already left, as had his family.

A few weeks later, Team Foxtrot's investigators received a long-awaited package that was covered with Iraqi stamps.

Thorbjörn, the investigator, was eager to open the package. He put on his blue examination gloves and a face mask, and took out two dozen mobile phones and almost as many wireless routers and laid them out on a table that he had covered with brown construction paper.

'A hair!'

That was all Thorbjörn found. The rest of the material was sent to the IT forensics team, a department that many hold to be severely understaffed, so that they could look for evidence and new clues to where the Fox might be hiding. However, the police didn't have to look for too long, because he was about to reveal his location to them himself.

*

For Ali, a park worker, 14 April 2022 began just like any other day. Today, he was going to be working at a playground outside the walls of a large, detached house with a private swimming pool in İçmeler, an affluent neighbourhood in the tourist resort of Marmaris in south-west Turkey.

While Ali was clearing the pine needles and withered palm leaves away from the stone slabs with his leaf blower, he spotted a small, black Philipp Plein bag on a bench in the park. The specific location was popular with parents, as it gave them a good view of the playground and the slide. Behind the benches were two large, newly built houses with a shared private pool, on the other side of a wall. The owner was hardly ever there, but kept an eye on his property through the many surveillance cameras he had installed.

Ali immediately realized that somebody must have forgotten their bag. He opened it, to see if there was anything inside that might help him find the owner. The moment he saw what was inside, however, he shivered, immediately closed it, and looked around nervously.

The Fox Hunt

Ali called his boss, who hurried over on his scooter. The bag contained 12,400 US dollars in neat bundles of hundred-dollar notes. There was also 2,400 Turkish lira, along with 3 credit cards and a receipt. Park workers often found clothes, phones and bags that had been left behind on the beach and in the parks, most often by tourists. The items would usually find their way to their rightful owners through the municipality or the local police. However, nobody had ever found a bag like this one.

The bag also contained clues to the identity of its owner. The same name was on a credit card: Miran Othaman. He must be a tourist, they thought to themselves, and called the police.

Turkish state media would later report that the police had examined CCTV footage from the park and managed to identify the man who had left the bag. His name was indeed Miran Othaman, and he was an Iraqi. When the police contacted him and told him where to go to collect the bag, he went to the police station, where he introduced himself as an entrepreneur.

He wanted to give Ali a $400 finder's fee, and asked the police for the park worker's phone number, but he was given the number to his boss Hüseyin instead.

'I received a call and gave him my address. After a while, four people in a dark Audi came here and handed me 400 dollars', the park manager explained.

He asked to take a photo of the men, who were speaking English.

'No, we don't like to be in photos', he was told.

That evening, the local police began a deeper investigation into the individual who had come to pick up the bag. According to reports in Turkish state media, the police had begun to suspect that something wasn't right while they were talking to the man. When his ID was examined more closely, they discovered that Miran Othaman also had another name.

He was a Swedish citizen of Iraqi origin who was suspected of having committed countless drug offences in Sweden and was red-listed by Interpol.

It was the Fox.

He had walked right into a police station voluntarily.

This prompted the police to search a house in the İçmeler neighbourhood where the Fox was living. Inside the house, they found two firearms and ammunition, which further strengthened their suspicions against the Fox, and would ultimately lead to his arrest.

In questioning, he claimed to have left the bag on a bench in the park when he was taking a rest during a walk along the beach. Several media outlets published a video of the police walking him down a flight of stairs. In the footage, he was wearing a face mask, white trainers and a black tracksuit with red stripes at the shoulders. There were two police officers, each of them holding one of his arms. His hands were in shackles.

In the Turkish media, the park worker Ali received praise from the police and the mayor for assisting in the capture of an internationally wanted 'drug lord'.

*

In Sweden, links to articles in Turkish media were sent around among the members of Team Foxtrot. Their group chat was littered with smiling face emojis as they expressed their relief that he had finally been caught. When I read the articles, I believed that the hunt for the Fox had finally come to an end, and wondered what was going to happen to him now.

The Fox had already been arrested *in absentia* in Sweden for exceptionally serious drug-trafficking and drug-smuggling offences. According to the police, the total quantity of drugs involved was close to 1 tonne, of which the majority was cannabis, amphetamine and cocaine, as well as tens of thousands of ecstasy tablets.

Team Foxtrot helped prosecutor Henrik Söderman compile a long list of all the crimes the Fox was suspected of having committed. Next, he rushed to send this documentation over to Turkey through the Ministry of Foreign Affairs, in the hope that this would secure an extradition of the Fox. Henrik and Team Foxtrot did recognize, however, that there was almost no chance of that.

The Fox's arrest coincided with major political events that made Turkey far less likely to extradite anybody to Sweden. In mid-May 2022, the government of Sweden, with the support of a broad parliamentary majority, decided to apply for NATO membership.

38

'I'd love to talk. We've been sentenced on false grounds', the Fox's mother told me when she called me from an anonymous number one day. Her son's arrest had just become a major news story in Turkey and Sweden.

I had written a letter to her, explaining that I would like to talk to her about the offences she had been convicted of. This was when her case was being heard by the Court of Appeal, and she maintained her innocence throughout the proceedings. She agreed to meet, and told me she would give me a very different picture from the one that the judicial system had presented of her and her son.

A few weeks later, we met at Ikea in Uppsala. She stood outside in the car park, waving, so that we would be able to find each other. We bought coffee, and sat down in one of the outer parts of the restaurant where tired parents of young children eat meatballs with sauce, mashed potatoes and lingonberry jam while they take a break from their kitchen planning.

'I may not be a saint, but I am a good person', the mother told me.

That was how our conversation began. Slowly, she fed me fragments of her own story, the family's background, and other details that helped me understand how her son had ended up being labelled one of Sweden's biggest drug smugglers. She was smartly dressed. A knitted, tight-fitting jumper and jeans. Subtle make-up. She was friendly and charming, just as several people I had spoken to had described her.

'I don't know what my son gets up to. Does your own mum know that you're sitting here with me now?' she said, smiling.

'No, she doesn't', I admitted.

She found the claims about her son difficult to believe.

'He's a wonderful father. He changes their nappies, buys food for them, and spends time with them. When I'm there with them, he relaxes', she said.

She was keen to demonstrate to me that she was also a kind, caring person. She told me she often helped hand out food to homeless people, something that was important to her as she had been homeless once herself. She was obviously looking to counterbalance the image of her son as a charming, manipulative individual that had been presented by the police officers who were working on his case. She made a point of telling me that, whatever people were saying about her and her son, she was very good friends with several police officers.

'Look at this', she said, and showed me a thread of friendly chats on Messenger with an individual she claimed was a police officer.

During our conversation, she also asked me questions.

'Are you a Muslim?'

'Well, since I was born into a Muslim family in Kosovo, I suppose I am, but I'm not particularly devout. Most people in Kosovo are secular', I replied.

She explained that she wasn't too fond of Islam as a faith, nor of men who felt entitled to tell women what to do or how to dress. She wasn't going to let a man run her life for her. She grew up in a Muslim family, but now she proudly wore a large cross around her neck.

'I love God. I love Jesus!' she told me.

She had left the Islamic faith, and she didn't care what her relatives in Iraq might have to say about that. She went back there as often as possible. Her sister, who was ill, was still living there, and in recent years, her son, his partner and their three children had also been there.

The Fox's mother was easy to talk to, and was surprisingly open with me about her life as a young Peshmerga soldier, and all the struggles she'd had to deal with in her life. First, it was persecution under Saddam Hussein's regime, then it was having to adjust to Swedish society, divorcing her husband and, most recently, debt and homelessness. She had done whatever she could to support herself and her son. In more recent years, she had been selling *Situation Stockholm*, a magazine that homeless people sell in the streets. She was one of their best vendors, and had sold thousands of magazines. It was an extra source of income for her, on top of her welfare payments, and she claimed to be earning a lot of money from it, in the area of 60,000 or 80,000 kronor a month. She claimed that the cash the police had found in her flat was money she had saved from the magazine sales, and that she was going to use it to pay off a debt of just over 400,000 kronor that she owed to the Swedish Enforcement Authority. She didn't want to deposit the money in a bank account, because she didn't trust the banks. This was why she had hidden the money in all those different places, including inside socks. She didn't want any burglars who might break into her home to find it.

The cash and the Rolex watches that were found at Hasse's home, however, definitely came from criminal activities. The court had stated that this was beyond any doubt. The Fox's mother was thought to have played 'a central, essential role' in these activities, and one piece of evidence that was taken to support this was the fact that she had been using an encrypted Encro phone.

She, on the other hand, has always claimed to be innocent of any crimes.

When I asked her about all the charges against her son, all the convictions of people in his orbit that the prosecutor had lined up like trophies, she grimaced in embarrassment.

'A drug smuggler? What can I say? He's not the criminal they make him out to be.'

But in the next breath, she spoke with caution.

'I don't know everything about him.'

Again, she emphasized what a wonderful father her son was to his three children. She loved her grandchildren, and was worried about them.

'Of course, it makes me feel terrible. I cry almost every day.'

We agreed to meet again, as she wants us to have time to go over her case properly. The next time, she asks to bring her close friend Hasse along. He too, she claims, has been incorrectly convicted of being involved in the Fox's business.

*

A few weeks later, Hasse was showing me around in his flat in Kista, where the raid took place during the hunt for the Fox. It was just the two of us, as the Fox's mother never showed up. He was wearing a neat, blue cardigan with a blue shirt underneath. His home was tidy, and everything seemed to be in its own specific place. Traces remained of the police's search of the premises. There were visible scratches on the floor from when the bookcase had been dragged away from the wall. Worse than the property damage, though, was the anger he felt over having been branded a criminal. The district court had found him guilty of serious money-laundering charges over the cash he had allegedly held for the Fox's mother. The court ruled that he had not been aware of the Rolex watches and the gold fox pendant in the bag on the balcony, finding his and the Fox's mother's accounts to be credible.

He had been handed a suspended sentence, which meant that he wouldn't have to spend any time in prison. However, the mere fact that he had been associated with crime was a serious indignity. He had never imagined that this would be how he spent his retirement. He had always tried to do what was right.

'It's awful', Hasse said angrily, and raised his voice.

We walked into his study, where he had a neatly arranged row of binders containing the accounting for the ice-cream parlour, going all the way back to 2014. He had been there from the beginning. On his computer, he showed me a long Excel sheet with recorded personal expenses that reached many years back into the past. Everything was recorded. With just a few keystrokes, he could find out how much he spent on wine in a year, or bananas, milk or salt. He liked to feel in control of things.

It was difficult for me to understand how he had ended up in this situation, being charged as an accomplice in a major drug case. However, he was quick to point out to me that the 'so-called Kurdish Fox' was nothing like the drug lord that articles, police officers and prosecutors described.

'He's more of a wannabe criminal, with gold chains and cars and all that.'

I found the confidence in his voice striking. Considering all the various convictions, and especially considering the fact that he himself had been fingered as an accomplice, it surprised me to hear him rush to the Fox's defence without any hesitation. He did this consistently, in all our conversations. I thought to myself that most people would probably have felt angry over getting caught up in somebody else's criminal activities like this.

Hasse explained to me that he had an engineering degree, and had made a career in sales. He had done well for himself financially. He told me that he didn't have any debts, and didn't need money. Hasse loathed anything to do with crime. He felt that Sweden had been going in the wrong direction, straight to hell. That was why he had become a supporter of the Sweden Democrats. He felt that criminal immigrants ought to be deported, because they were ruining society for all the law-abiding citizens. He found being associated with an immigrant who had been accused of extensive drug smuggling 'most uncomfortable'.

*

The story of how the lives of Hasse and the Fox came to intersect began in the mid-2000s. He had met the Fox's mother at a gym in Kista, where she had been working as a spinning instructor. They entered into a relationship, and lived together for a while. It was during those years that the Fox had begun to commit increasingly serious crimes. After his drug conviction in the Court of Appeal in 2010, when he was sentenced to eight and a half years in prison for a serious drug offence, Hasse became his lay supervisor and tried to get the Fox to cease his criminal activities. It was while the Fox was in prison that Hasse had helped the Fox's partner open up the ice-cream parlour, where the Fox was supposed to be working after his release.

According to Hasse, the sentence was a miscarriage of justice, and the Fox had been wrongly convicted. He didn't deny that the Fox had been involved in illegal business, that he was probably a fence and had been involved in money laundering, but he told me that there was no way he had been involved in any violent crimes or drug-related offences. The Fox was a naive young man who kept letting others get him into trouble. His biggest problem was the company he kept, Hasse believed. Hasse was so convinced that the Fox was innocent that he went to great efforts to clear his name. He spent 'at least 500 hours' writing an appeal for him.

He showed me the presentation on his computer in the study. I listened to him for half an hour. It was clear to me from Hasse's commitment that he genuinely believed he was doing important work.

He was convinced that the Fox could have gone down a completely different path if it hadn't been for that wrongful conviction. Unexpectedly, he suggests a title for my book: 'Making a Criminal Mastermind'.

*

Hasse got in touch with me after the Court of Appeal passed judgment on his case in mid-September 2022. He was angry, because the court had once again found him guilty of a serious money-laundering offence. The Fox's mother had also been sentenced, and had been handed a harsher sentence this time: she was to be imprisoned for a year and a half.

He felt that the Court of Appeal hadn't listened to his explanations at all, and that his lawyer had actually messed his case up for him. If he couldn't rectify all this in court, he was determined to try to rectify it in the media. He thanked me for my interest, but made it very clear that the story he would tell me might not be what I was expecting.

'The story here could very well be that the person at the centre of all this is far more innocent than you might believe', he said.

'Do you mean the Fox?' I asked.

'Yes.'

'I'd be happy to meet with him', I said.

'I'll help you meet everybody involved.'

'How?'

'I'll make sure to arrange it. He's a pathetic little coward. He'll do as I say.'

'Do you really think he will?'

'You can bank on it.'

Next, Hasse went on to tell me that the Fox wasn't even in custody in Turkey any more. This was something other sources had claimed, but I hadn't been able to confirm it. Neither the prosecutors nor the police officers at Noa could tell me whether he was in custody or not. There were several rumours going around, including the one that he supposedly bribed his way out of the prison he was being held in. Allegedly, the Fox's mother had been able to arrange a visit with him. She found out who it was she needed to talk to, booked a meeting with the person in question, and 'explained the situation'. After this, reportedly, he was released.

I wondered if that was really possible, given the crimes he had been accused of.

'These are corrupt countries we're talking about', my sources pointed out.

Several other sources had claimed that 'millions' had been paid to secure his release. It was also rumoured that he had moved to an apartment complex in Istanbul, where several of his friends were also staying.

My sources in Turkey were looking into this for me. The Turkish legal system was keeping silent about it, and so were the local journalists who had initially covered the story of the Fox's arrest. There had been no follow-up stories about the suspected drug smuggler in the Turkish tourist resort that had been such a huge news item when it first happened.

Since Hasse believed that the Swedish justice system was broken beyond repair, he had no confidence at all in the courts, the police or the prosecutor. As a result, he was unable to believe that the Fox really was the man that was portrayed in news reports. Hasse told me he was prepared to accept that the Fox liked to present himself as some 'super-gangster'. He kept returning to the fact that the Fox's partner had asked for a small amount of money when they needed to leave Sweden in the spring of 2020. She had asked for 20,000 kronor. He found it hard to believe that somebody who was making loads of money selling drugs would be asking for a sum like that, or that his mother would be out selling *Situation Stockholm*.

Hasse was angry with the Fox. He hadn't just put Hasse in this situation, he had also dragged his own mother into it, and she was somebody Hasse still cared a great deal about. Hasse gave me a message for the Fox, in case I ever got to speak to him:

'Tell him he's a wannabe criminal.'

39

On 28 September 2022, I suddenly received a message on the encrypted Signal app. It came from an alias I didn't recognize.

'Hi there', the person wrote to me.

I noted that it came from a Turkish number. In the past few months, I had conducted interviews with family members, criminals, lawyers, prosecutors and police officers. I had thrown out feelers to as many people as I possibly could, to try to get word out that I was keen to meet with wanted individuals who were hiding in Turkey. Rumours about the Fox being released from custody were still going around, but even the Swedish police didn't seem to know if they were true or not. This was quite an indication of how frosty relations between Swedish and Turkish authorities had grown.

'Hello! Who's this?' I asked.

The answer came quickly.

'You have questions. You can get all the answers you need if you write them here in the chat. I'll pass them on. And then you'll receive a letter.'

There's only one person this could be about, but I still asked if the Fox was out, and said that I'd prefer to meet with him instead of having to go through an intermediary.

'He's never going to meet with anyone. I can't confirm whether he's out or not. But you will get your questions answered.'

At this point, I had no idea how the messenger had acquired my number, or whether this person really was in contact with the Fox as he had claimed. In a series of messages, I explained how important it was for me to be in direct contact with him.

'Bro this comes straight from him', the person wrote to me.

In the same message, he explained that this was the only option I'd be given. Not even he got to meet the Fox. They only communicated through proxies.

I didn't relent, and continued to emphasize the importance of direct contact. Talking to me would be an opportunity for the Fox to correct any untruths and respond to the various accusations that had been levelled against him. If I were in his shoes, I wouldn't have wanted anybody else to speak for me. 'I want to be fair and accurate', I explained, and added a question to try to keep the possibility open.

'Could he at least talk to me on Facetime?'

Three minutes later, the person wrote back:

'I'll ask him, but I doubt he'll accept. I'll get back to you within 2 days.'

*

It would be almost a month, however, before I was once again in contact with the person who had asked me to write questions to the Fox. This time, I decided to call back. One late evening in the autumn, I dialled the number, hoping that I could speak to somebody. I didn't want to have to write cryptic messages and then maybe have to wait for a response for several weeks. After a few ringtones, a male voice answered. This person, whose identity was unknown to me, spoke perfect Swedish. He told me that he was in Dubai, but that he would soon be travelling to Turkey. I insisted that I needed to speak to the Fox. It seemed to me that the Fox would also have an interest in making sure I 'got the facts right', since I would be writing the book either way.

'I know who he is deep down. He's not the person everyone's talking about', the friend said to me.

'Wouldn't that depend on who you asked?'

'He's no monster.'

'What does that mean?' I asked.

'I'd like him to talk to you. If that can't be arranged, he'll have to answer your questions some other way instead.'

The same week that the Fox's friend was going to travel to Turkey, I was also planning on going there. I explained that I would be there working on a story about people from Sweden who had fled there because they were wanted by the law.

'I would very much like to meet the Fox. I don't want to have to go through intermediaries.'

40

Shortly after the new Swedish government took over in the autumn of 2022, a delegation of officials from the Ministry of Justice went to the Turkish capital Ankara with a delegation of Finnish colleagues. Ahead of the meeting, the Turkish minister of justice, Bekir Bozdağ, told Turkish media that he expected to secure extraditions of individuals with ties to the PKK and the Gülen movement.

The Swedish delegation didn't offer much by way of comment, but stated that the Ministry of Justice was engaging in negotiations on various levels to get people who were wanted for serious offences in Sweden extradited from Turkey. As far as was known, several of these individuals were not Turkish citizens – at least, not yet. The Fox, an Iraqi Kurd, was an obvious addition to the list. The extensive drug-smuggling operations he had been linked to had made him a bargaining chip in the ongoing political game. Several Swedish government sources indicated that they hoped to have him sent to Sweden.

When I travelled to Turkey a few weeks later, those wanted individuals were precisely the people I wanted to meet with for my story. Besides the Fox, my list also included Maximilian Rivkin, the ANOM vendor from Malmö. He had emigrated to a small village in Serbia several years ago, but the police had stated that he was in all likelihood currently in Turkey.

The Fox Hunt

The thing that the Fox and Rivkin had in common was that neither of them had a Turkish background. This meant that they didn't have the natural protections a citizen would enjoy when it came to matters of extradition.

The third name on my list would be more difficult: Orhan. He was a young man from Botkyrka in Stockholm who was a suspect in the murder of a twelve-year-old girl, Adriana. Also suspected of involvement were Maykil Yokhanna, the man the Vårby network had been planning to shoot to death in Västerås, and two other individuals.

This story is a tragic one, which illustrates how innocent people can be affected by gang violence.

*

On a balmy summer night in early August 2020, the twelve-year-old Adriana had walked out of her father's home in Norsborg with the family dog. She met some friends, and the group headed to a McDonald's restaurant that was open at night. Outside the fast-food restaurant, there were two guys in bulletproof vests who were hanging around next to a car park by the side of the motorway. Until recently, they had been members of a local group that had ended up disbanding after an internal conflict. The guys outside the McDonald's had become allies of the Vårby network, while several of their former friends had joined up with Maykil Yokhanna. In some circles, this group was referred to as 'the Turks'. Orhan was a member. After the split, a violent sequence of events began, including several shootings and other acts of violence.

Just before Adriana had arrived on the scene, several members of the Vårby network had been seen inside the petrol station next to the restaurant.

Late that night, a white Audi had driven over to the petrol station and turned around. In the car park outside McDonald's, the passengers in the car had spotted the two guys in bulletproof vests who had aligned themselves with the Vårby network. While these individuals were by no means the main enemies of the other side, they were still considered valuable targets.

A large number of bullets were fired from inside the car, from two different weapons, one of which was a Kalashnikov.

Once the panic at the scene subsided, it was confirmed that the two intended targets had survived. But twelve-year-old Adriana was still on the ground. She had been standing nearby, and was hit by the burst of bullets. One of the young men who had been shot tried to stop Adriana's bleeding, and he stayed on the scene until the police and Adriana's father arrived after a little while.

The man who had tried to stop the bleeding made what he thought was an anonymous call to emergency services two days later, identifying Orhan as the person who had shot Adriana. After this, the police focused their suspicions on the Turks.

While the investigation was under way, the intended targets began to plot their revenge, and began looking for a *goare*, somebody who could lure the Turks into a trap. One of them offered a *kanin*, 'a rabbit', a slang term for 1 million kronor, as a reward to anybody who could tell him where they were. The offered reward would later grow even larger.

'Just tell us where they are and you'll get anything you want.'

Eventually, they were approached by Filterlösa grabbar, or FLG, a group of younger individuals who had been loyal to Shottaz in their much-publicized conflict with the Death Squad in Järvafältet.

A little over a month after Adriana's murder, FLG helped set a trap for the Turks, and one evening at eleven o'clock, about thirty shots were fired in the central square in Vällingby. One of these shots hit Orhan in the arm, but most of them hit the neighbouring buildings, some of which were residential. The fact that nobody else was hit was something of a miracle.

After this assassination attempt, the wounded Orhan had fled to Turkey, where he stayed in his parents' home town of Kulu. He remained in Turkey, and during his time there, an international arrest order was issued for him in relation to Adriana's murder. A whole year after the tragedy outside McDonald's, when investigators gained access to the Sky ECC accounts of the people involved, they added Maykil Yokhanna and two others to their list of suspects.

*

With the assistance of local journalists, I discovered that the Fox, Rivkin and Orhan had all entered Turkey, and that none of them had left. However, my search for Rivkin was to prove fruitless almost immediately.

'I haven't heard anything about him. Is he even still here? He could just as well be in Iran or Dubai.'

The person across from me who told me this was another Swedish criminal who was in hiding in Turkey. He had agreed to talk to me in exchange for a promise of total anonymity. We were sitting in a restaurant near the tourist areas. Word on the street, and in police files, is that he is a dangerous individual. However, like so many others of the criminals I've met, he was friendly and articulate in our conversation. His parents did their best for him, but they couldn't do anything to change his desire to pursue a criminal lifestyle. He told me he spent most of his time in Turkey doing 'legal stuff'. He wanted to stay under the radar, so he wouldn't get into trouble with the Turkish state police or security services.

'Turkey isn't a sanctuary for criminals, in case anybody's given you that idea. The police here have everything under control. If you're caught with an AK47 here, you end up getting charged as a terrorist, because of the history here with the PKK', he explained.

Many known criminals have made their way to Turkey. This fact is what has caused Swedish police and prosecutors to begin to refer to Turkey as 'New Spain'.

When Spanish police began to take significant action against Swedish criminals who were living there, many of the leading figures were arrested and sent home, particularly after the encrypted services had been cracked. As a result, many decided to go to Turkey instead, ending up in cities like Istanbul, Bodrum and Izmir.

'All of the criminals who managed to evade capture during the phone raids are there', another source would tell me.

*

My task, then, was to find two specific wanted individuals among the 85 million people who live in Turkey. My targets were the Fox, and Adriana's suspected murderer, Orhan. As Maximilian Rivkin hadn't left much of a trail for me to follow, I ended up removing him from my list. However, I would very much have liked to hear what he had to say about the accusations other criminals had levelled against him after he convinced them to use ANOM. The anger against him was apparent from the way others would mention him, usually with some derisive reference or other to his weight. Many of the people who were subsequently convicted seem firmly convinced that he was actually cooperating with the police, and find the idea that he might still be on the run from Europol and the FBI laughable. Noa and the FBI have both denied that he was a secret informer. Swedish police officers tend rather to describe him as a 'useful idiot'. As they see it, it was his greed that led him to convince others that ANOM was a secure means of communication.

The Fox Hunt

All I had to go on as I tried to track down the other two people on my list was a list of places where I knew each of them had been. I was hoping to uncover further clues in those locations.

My photographer colleague from SVT (Swedish Public Service Television) and I travelled to Marmaris together. We went there during the off-season, and there were only a few British tourists in the resort. They were spread out among the beach clubs, which all blasted '90s disco at the highest possible volume, even though they were all right next to one another.

We sat down at one of the bars and ordered a drink, and watched as an older British woman danced very closely with the bartender. It wasn't far from here that the footage of the Fox with handcuffs around his wrists had been shot. Naturally, I very much wanted to know what the status of that case was now, and whether or not any charges would be made. However, journalists aren't granted the same access to legal proceedings in Turkey as they are in Sweden.

As we walked back to our hotel, the Brits continued singing along with the disco music.

*

Several local journalists in Turkey assisted me, particularly when it came to gaining information from official sources. I learned from them that the Fox had used genuine Iraqi identity documents when he first entered Turkey. I also learn that he has since managed to receive Turkish citizenship.

My sources told me this was an unexpected development, but something that was 'possible in Turkey'. The Swedish police had received intelligence suggesting that the Fox had become a Turkish citizen, but that kind of information was always uncertain and difficult to verify when it came from Turkey. In Sweden, all you'd need to do would be to place a call to the Swedish Tax Agency. I knew that the Fox being granted Turkish citizenship was a major setback for Jacob, Niklas, Denny and the rest of Team Foxtrot.

All the sources I spoke to about it, who all wished to remain anonymous, were in agreement that once somebody was a Turkish citizen, you could forget all about trying to get them extradited.

The Swedish justice system, then, would be reduced to the option of trying to have him tried in Turkey instead. This was the route they chose in the case of Denho Acar, the former leader of Original Gangsters. He was one of the first known criminals from Gothenburg to flee to Turkey, where he was a citizen, to avoid prosecution in Sweden.

After many years of persuasion from Swedish authorities, he was put on trial in Turkey, but ended up being acquitted in 2018. After that, he wanted to return to Sweden, but his residence permit had been withdrawn by then, and the Migration Agency refused him a new one.

Timur Soykan, an award-winning Turkish crime reporter and author, has covered organized crime in Turkey for a long time. He has reported on the corruption that exists at the state level, and on the various organized crime rings that operate within the country.

'This is a possibility in Turkey right now', Timur Soykan told me when I asked him if it was really possible to become a citizen despite being suspected of crimes and having an Interpol warrant issued in your name.

There were several explanations for why this was the case. One was that there was no longer a reliable census in the country, as millions of refugees had entered it, first to escape the Syrian civil war and then to escape the Islamic State. Another reason was that it was possible to invest your way to citizenship by, for example, buying a home for at least 400,000 USD. Before the summer of 2022, the amount had been lower, too, at 250,000 USD. In order to bolster the country's strained economy, the government had also introduced what was referred to as a 'wealth amnesty' programme. 'People who bring foreign capital, gold or other assets into the country no longer have to declare where their money came from', Soykan explained.

The most common buyers of expensive residential properties are Russians, Iranians and Iraqis, many of whom are specifically seeking citizenship so that they will have an alternative country to live in if they need it, a Turkish estate agent explained to me.

'This has also made Turkey an attractive country in which to carry out money laundering', Soykan said.

Investigative journalists such as Timur, as well as opposition politicians, have criticized the way this system has facilitated the laundering of criminal profits. However, another point of criticism has been the opportunity it has opened up for foreign criminals to invest their way to citizenship. Doing this can allow them to eliminate their risk of being extradited.

I asked him if Turkey had become a safe haven for criminals. He answered without a trace of a doubt: 'Yes, it has.'

Ibrahim Kalin, a spokesperson for the president of Turkey, however, would strongly deny this when I interviewed him. When I asked him why no action had been taken against Swedish criminals who had fled to Turkey, and why the country was beginning to be spoken of as a new hub in the international cocaine market, he accused me of serving the interests of the PKK and the Gülen movement. After that, he ended our interview.

The interest that Turkey has begun to attract from criminal organizations has also come to be reflected in an increasing number of cocaine seizures in Turkish ports, where shipments had been sent directly from the cartels in South America. According to Timur Soykan, this was a consequence of a series of successful police operations in Europe, in which many leading criminals had been arrested and convicted as a result of the police gaining access to their encrypted chats. However, the number of arrests that had been made in Europe hadn't had any effect on how much cocaine was being smuggled into the ports – last year, a record-breaking amount of cocaine was seized.

In addition to cocaine that was found in shipping containers in Turkish ports, a private jet was stopped in Brazil as it was about to take off for Brussels with a load of 1.3 tonnes of cocaine that had been packed into a large number of suitcases. That particular aircraft had been used by Turkish government officials in the past, and, according to media reports, it was used to fly President Recep Tayyip Erdoğan to safety during the military coup of 2016.

The drugs that were smuggled to Turkey were redistributed to Europe in minivans, as well as to the Gulf States, where a gram of cocaine can fetch several times the price it does on the Swedish market.

*

The thing that makes the Fox's case especially interesting is the fact that he was released despite the serious suspicions against him. Even if he wasn't guilty of any crime in Turkey, he was wanted by Interpol, the world's largest international police organization, at the time of his arrest. Turkey is a member of Interpol, and has been criticized by human rights organizations for supposedly abusing the red list by adding domestic critics and political opponents to it. As a result, journalists have been arrested in airports in various European countries.

Sweden and most other countries use the red list for individuals who are wanted for serious offences. When a red-listed person lands at an airport, is stopped in a border checkpoint or an ordinary traffic stop in any of Interpol's 195 member countries, they are supposed to be immediately apprehended. After this, an extradition procedure is supposed to be initiated. However, according to my contacts in the Swedish government apparatus who work with these issues, it isn't always that simple when it comes to Turkey. Several of them claim that it's far too easy for red-listed individuals to enter the country, and that, afterwards, they are able to move about more or less freely. Any attempt to get Turkish authorities to act on a situation like this and, say, arrest a wanted individual involves time-consuming legal procedures.

It would take a long time for the process to run its course, and by then, the individuals in question might have managed to make their way to another country, arranged a false identity for themselves, or even gained Turkish citizenship. The most common outcome, according to my sources in Swedish government agencies, is that Turkey does 'nothing at all', even in cases related to suspected murderers and drug traffickers who are in the country.

Whether the Fox had become a Turkish citizen, and how he went about it if he had, was something only he would know. I hoped that he was going to respond to the enquiries I had left with his relatives and friends. In Turkey, however, I did eventually get the names of three lawyers in Istanbul who had represented the Fox. One of them answered my call, and promised to get back to me after speaking to his client.

The more calls I made, the more the fear began to grow among my fixers, who were all local journalists with their own contacts.

'This person must be very well connected within our justice system, and have a lot of money', one of them said to me when we were discussing the Fox.

Nobody wanted anything to do with the case. I was welcome, however, to ask for any help I might need regarding other matters.

'If you want to identify any Russian oligarchs who are here, feel free to get in touch', one fixer told me.

*

We headed farther north, to another popular tourist resort: Bodrum. This long street of restaurants by the Aegean Sea, just north-east of the Greek island of Kos, was mainly frequented by domestic tourists at this time of year, but there were also some Russians in town, either there on holiday or avoiding being conscripted and sent to the war in Ukraine. Orhan, Adriana's suspected murderer, had reportedly been in Bodrum a few weeks earlier, according to government sources. When I showed a picture of the young man to somebody who been working in local restaurants for more than a decade, I was surprised to hear him say that the man in the picture looked familiar to him.

'I saw him a few months ago. I never forget a face', he claimed.

That was all we managed to learn, except that there was some drug-trafficking activity there, as there is in many other tourist resorts. Instead, we travelled on to the suspect's home town, Kulu in central Turkey, in the hope that we might make contact with him there. Many residents of the city either have lived in Sweden or have family members who currently live or have lived there. We headed straight to the Olof Palme Park, and walked through the two stately iron gates that led to a green area with trees, shrubs, statues and a restaurant with outdoor seating.

At the restaurant, we met several local AKP politicians. With typical Turkish hospitality, they offered to help us connect with one of Orhan's few relatives who was still living in Kulu. The rest were in Sweden, most of them in the Botkyrka area. One of the men called the relative, and asked him if he would speak to us.

'No', was the curt reply.

I showed them a picture of twelve-year-old Adriana, and told them that she was the person Orhan had been accused of murdering. They shook their head and gave me troubled looks.

'The trial is already under way. If he had been in Sweden, he would have had his day in court, and maybe even been acquitted of the charges.'

A little later, a man who had lived in Sweden before being deported after serving a term in prison came to the restaurant. In broken Swedish, he explained to me that Orhan and several of his friends had been in Kulu just a few months earlier.

'He's innocent of this. He's not a murderer', the man insisted.

'Where do you think he might be now?'

'He's in Istanbul. They have a little group there.'

*

After returning from Turkey, I was frustrated that I hadn't managed to get any closer to the Fox, Rivkin or Adriana's suspected killer. However, I had returned home with a far greater understanding for the frustration that police and law enforcement must experience when they see that people they have spent thousands of hours trying to catch are able to live out in the open in Turkey. It's as though criminals were able to buy 'get out of jail free' cards, and all the police can do is watch it happen.

41

Mere hours after my return, I suddenly received a call on the encrypted Signal app. It was the Fox's friend again. It felt typical that he would be calling me just as I had gone to meet a friend at my local. This time, he told me that he was sitting next to the Fox. Then, he handed the phone over. A few seconds later, I heard a voice that was speaking perfect Swedish.

The first words the person on the other end of the line said to me were 'I hear you've been calling all kinds of people and asking questions about me.'

My mind was reeling. I walked away from the noise inside the restaurant, and decided not to give any information away until I had been able to confirm that it really was the Fox.

'Did you get top grades for any subjects in secondary school?' I asked.

'Yes. Personal sales', he replied immediately.

That was true. He failed seven subjects, but received eleven VG grades (pass with distinction) and a G (pass) for the rest of his classes, apart from one MVG (pass with particular distinction), the highest possible grade at that time. We discussed the possibility of meeting, for the book. He wasn't interested in giving a televised interview, he told me. What he did want was to comment on something that was important to him, and which he didn't really want anybody to be writing about: his murdered cousin, Shad, and the allegations that he had been somehow involved in the murder. I explained that my work was based on the existing allegations, and referred him to an account that had been made public in the course of the investigation against the King and the Prince, the two lawyers who had been giving their clients secret tip-offs on Encrochat.

The Fox sounded troubled by this, but told me that he wanted to make it clear that the idea that he had been involved in the murder of his cousin was 'bullshit'. Some of his cousin's family members had got it into their head, certainly. But he advised me to contact Shad's brother, who was serving a life sentence in prison, to ask him what he thought.

I did just that. The brother had been sentenced to life for a double murder committed in Kista in 2017, and was being held in the Fenix ward at Kumlaanstalten prison. He told me that, because of the severe restrictions he was under, he had only received limited information concerning the allegations against the Fox, and that he would prefer to wait until he had seen the full report before making a statement.

*

The Fox confirmed that he had changed his name in Iraq, and that he had been using his new passport when he was arrested in Marmaris. He also confirmed that he was free, but didn't offer any details regarding whether his case was still under investigation.

'How is it you could be released when an international arrest order has been issued for you?'

'I'm a Turkish citizen', he replied, as if this were the most natural explanation in the world. 'If you invest in this country, they make you a citizen.'

It's not that his answer surprised me. Nevertheless, actually being given the information that so many have tried to get confirmation on gave me a bit of a shock. He claimed that his citizenship application had been submitted before the arrest.

I asked him if he had bought any properties, but he didn't want to tell me what investments he had made. He simply stated that everyone knows that you can become a citizen of Turkey by investing in the country, and that it was also common knowledge that Turkish citizens weren't extradited.

'Some people might say that you bribed your way out of prison', I told him.

'They would be wrong', the Fox replied.

When I told him that I was curious to learn how he had managed to build the vast drug-smuggling network he was suspected of running in such a short period of time, he raised no objection to the premise of the question. He also said nothing to confirm its truthfulness. He wasn't prepared to admit to having used the Encrochat aliases Foxkurdish and Foxplanet.

'I deny any and all accusations. I'm a mama's boy', he insisted.

'Plenty of other people have been convicted on the basis that the courts believe you to be the person you're accused of being, and that you were the one who coordinated everything. If you're denying the accusations, don't you think it would be a good idea to stand trial in Sweden and be acquitted?' I attempted.

'Nah. I could never get a fair trial, it's all a foregone conclusion.'

It was difficult to dig any deeper into this issue over the phone. He told me he would consider my request to meet in person instead. I asked him to get back to me as soon as possible with information on when it would be convenient for him, so that I could book a flight to Turkey. When we hung up, it suddenly struck me how many questions I had that remained unanswered. I was annoyed with myself for not taking my computer with me.

*

Knowing that the Fox was a free man was particularly painful for his relatives in the Järva area. The family of his murdered cousin Shad had also heard the rumours that he had 'bribed his way out'. Their deep resentment towards the Fox and his mother remained. They had both been ostracized – by parts of the family, at least.

However, the Fox's father was still accepted. He wasn't thought to be as culpable for the Fox's chosen path. I've been told that the Fox's father had a very special relationship with Shad's parents. Almost every day, he walked from his flat to a travel agency in Husby, which was run by Shad's father. He walked inside, made a pot of tea in the small kitchen inside the office, and went out to sit down next to Shad's father. Behind the desk, there were two large portraits of the murdered Shad.

While Shad's dad helped customers with address changes and travel bookings, the Fox's dad would open a desk drawer and take out a plastic tub of biscuits, often a sweet variety that Shad's mother baked. He enjoyed his biscuit and drank his tea, seemingly untroubled by the accusations that several of Shad's relatives had levelled against his son.

When I asked one of Shad's relatives if there was a blood feud between his family and the Fox, I was told that there wasn't. Others had claimed that there was, however.

'That's not the kind of person I am', this person told me. 'I want him to be punished and suffer in prison for what he did to Shad. Death would be too quick, too easy. I want him to suffer.'

42

Evidence implicating the Fox continued to be turned up all over the country. Several charges were brought against individuals with links to the Fox. Meanwhile, the police's suspicions were further strengthened. One piece of evidence that contributed to this was intercepted phone conversations in which it was claimed that the Fox was still organizing large-scale drug-smuggling operations in Sweden.

He found new customers through a friend who had been serving time in Kumla prison since 2018. This friend had authorization to call his girlfriend, and she would in turn connect his calls to the Fox and other parties by holding two phones together.

However, problems soon arose in dealing with at least some of these buyers. In Stockholm, the police seized a large quantity of drugs, and the individual who was recorded in the wiretap – whom the police suspected of being the Fox – was demanding more than a million kronor for the lost goods.

'You're the one who introduced me to these shitty people', the Fox said in a conversation with his friend in Kumla.

He didn't want an apology – he wanted his money. He also demanded they give him the buyer's family's addresses. His friend tried to reassure him.

'They'll have to borrow from their parents and siblings until they've paid it all back', the Fox stated.

The Fox Hunt

The Fox's friend in Kumla also connected him with buyers in Östersund. The local police there had noticed that larger quantities of drugs had been entering the city. After an extensive surveillance operation, they managed to identify a large network of sellers and mules who were picking drugs up in Gothenburg and Stockholm.

The Fox's name would also appear in the winter of 2022, in an indictment that was filed against some teenage boys in southern Stockholm. The suspicions against them involved serious weapons offences, vandalism and harassment, but when the police began to investigate their communications, they also came under suspicion for dealing drugs for the Fox's network.

These are just some of countless examples.

The Fox wasn't suspected of any crimes in relation to any of the mentioned investigations. According to police officers who had kept updated on the Fox, these cases didn't just reveal that he was actually an even bigger player than had previously been suspected – they also revealed that the drug market was much larger than anyone believed.

And, as we know, more drugs meant more conflicts – and thus, more violence.

*

In the early morning hours of Christmas Day 2022, a young man was shot dead as he was leaving his parents' home in Rinkeby. The victim was Dumle, who had recently been featured in a controversial interview in the *Expressen* newspaper. Police intelligence described him as an affiliate of the Death Squad, but others have insisted that he wasn't in any way involved in the Järva conflict. Dumle had been informed that he was suspected of having been an accessory to the murder of Einár. It was alleged that he had lured the rapper into a death trap. However, there hadn't been sufficient evidence to detain him.

Over the next few days, Stockholm became the scene of an escalating cycle of violence. The next event in this sequence was another murder, in Vällingby. This was followed by a bombing at an address linked to the rapper 1Cuz after he had posted a video on social media that had reportedly been interpreted as an act of mockery aimed at the murder victim.

In the southern suburbs of Stockholm, there was a series of bombings targeting a young man called Scar, who had also been implicated in the Einár murder, and the rapper Haval, who was convicted for his involvement in the Einár kidnapping. The common denominator between several of the targets was the existence of either suspicions or evidence that they had committed crimes of some variety against Einár. The violence intensified further. Two teenagers, aged fifteen and sixteen, were arrested after firing a large number of shots at the front door of the home of an elderly man who had nothing to do with the ongoing gangland conflicts.

Events like these continued to occur, one after another, at a rate that soon had the public, including myself, losing count. What nobody realized at the time was that all this was still only the beginning.

PART 7
WHEN NO ONE LISTENS

JANUARY 2023 – MARCH 2023

PART 7

43

Many of the people I had spoken to within the justice system believed that the successful Encrochat, ANOM and Sky ECC operations would turn things around. At the time of writing, more than 400 people have been sentenced to more than 2,300 years in prison based on evidence gathered from the encrypted chats. After asking around in other countries, I determined that there had been a lot of convictions there too, and that the German Supreme Court, the Bundesgerichthof, for example, had found no obstacles to the admission of Encrochat evidence during criminal proceedings. However, it was also obvious that there were still some ongoing legal disputes concerning the use of the encrypted chats.

Anyhow, the cases don't seem to have done anything to improve the situation in the streets. Paradoxically, the success that the police found in their chat operations would ultimately have the opposite effect.

The many arrests of leading criminals created a power vacuum. This produced something of a Wild West situation, in which younger criminals were 'running around like headless chickens', to quote one of Sascha's sisters. This new generation of criminals is armed, and prepared to use violence, but they don't have the same sense of consequence or experience with weapons as their elders.

In many cases, the situation is further exacerbated by the fact that mainstream society – especially businesses and public services – has ended up withdrawing from areas plagued by frequent violence. In the areas where gang crime is at its most pervasive, it's common to see single mothers left alone to raise their children, sometimes up to seven or eight of them, and, sometimes, the absent fathers' behaviour only adds to their burdens. Poor language skills, unemployment and failed educations often combine to keep people excluded from society.

'Busting' or 'crushing' the gangs doesn't help, either, since any organization can quickly disperse and regroup. It's also not uncommon for former rivals to become 'brothers' overnight. This is the conclusion Magnus Sjöberg arrived at after spending the last few years working for the tactical council of Noa, where his areas of focus were deadly gang violence, terrorism and extremism.

He advocates refusing criminals all room for manoeuvre, to prevent them from committing crimes in the first place. He argues that the criminal networks are social structures, in which individuals commit crimes together and violence is ever-present. It becomes an ideology of sorts, empowering the group as well as the individuals within it. Violence is contagious, because any act of violence will cause more people to be offended and want to seek revenge. For every individual the police arrest, others will line up to fill the void.

Sjöberg agrees that the acccess to information that criminals enjoy has sparked new conflicts and triggered acts of vengeance. One example of this is 41-year-old Atte in Helsingborg. According to his family members, his murder was an act of vengeance committed in response to the publication of the preliminary investigation against his older brother, who was charged and later convicted of conspiracy to murder a former associate. The case was built on evidence gathered from messages on Encrochat. The convicted brother claimed that, in questioning, he had given very clear warning that the allegations made would put his family members in danger. According to the police and prosecutors, the danger wasn't deemed to be serious. A complaint has been submitted to the Parliamentary Ombudsmen, but has not resulted in any action on their part.

The void left by all the arrests blew the market wide open, allowing people like the Fox to claim larger shares of it. Some police officers who worked these cases even feared that this opportunity for growth might give major players the capacity to infiltrate and threaten state institutions.

Could this have been avoided? Magnus Sjöberg believes it could have. In his opinion, these effects were predictable in areas where many people ended up getting arrested, and should have been taken into consideration during the encrypted chat operations. He believes that there could have been plans in place, ready to be put into action in the hours following the raids, and that this could have been arranged without giving anything away. Municipalities, schools and other local institutions could have been informed and given time to prepare.

'Of course, it's easy to say that with the benefit of hindsight', Sjöberg admits.

He remains optimistic that the escalation of violent crime can be reversed, but claims that this would require a 'total realignment', in which all of the institutions of society would have to be mobilized to perform their own specific duties to help prevent organized crime. The role of the police in this ought to be to provide security and ensure that all other institutions can carry out their long-term efforts safely.

He points to several different causes that have contributed to the current situation: freedom of movement within Schengen, the opportunities for drug smuggling across the Öresund Bridge, and the attitudes of consumers when it comes to drugs. The Noa director also points to a factor that he believes to be unique to Sweden: the strong protection of privacy that's in place, which means that there are boundaries of secrecy in place between different authorities. He feels that this has to be changed completely, to allow exchanges of information between schools, the healthcare system, mental healthcare providers, social services and the police. However, he also believes that we need to be prepared to discuss weaker groups in society, where there is an increased risk that children will end up in a life of crime. We mustn't allow ourselves to be hindered by fears of stigmatizing people or being accused of racism.

'We need to be able to address problems directly if we're going to take responsibility for them. Failing to do so would be both arrogant and cowardly', Sjöberg says.

Within all the complexities of these problems, there is also the issue of prevailing norms that will require a long-term approach: honour, status and indignation. Primary schools in the Järva area have actually started to work on this. Programmes have been introduced in fourth grade, with the aim of teaching ten-year-old children how to resolve conflicts in a productive way, both at school and at home.

Peter, who survived being shot nine times in Viksjö, told me that one thing many people in the criminal underworld have in common is having been subjected to violence by their elders – both in their homes and in their neighbourhoods. Although this didn't go on in his family, he believed that absent parents were the single most important reason why young people ended up on the streets.

Even though we've seen constant power struggles and more shootings than ever since the chats were made public, Magnus Sjöberg still believes that it was necessary to act. He believes that the problem was that too many people believed, or hoped, that these operations would somehow solve the growing problems related to crime.

'Nobody realized which forces might be set in motion when the old hierarchies dissolved and the power vacuum appeared', he says.

44

A lot has happened since all the raids were carried out against the suspects who had used the encrypted chat services.

By the autumn of 2020, the police had gathered sufficient evidence from Encrochat to take down Danni in Malmö, who had been in a deadly vendetta with the Boxer and ran into his rival Salle at that hotel in Ängelholm. When the police questioned Salle, the Boxer's friend, he didn't have much to say except that he was living 'family life' now. Since he was unemployed, his relatives were helping him with his living expenses, he said. He refused to comment on the assassination plot against him, but stated that he wasn't afraid of 'cunts like that'. When asked about Danni in an initial interview, he refused to utter his name, consistently and exclusively referring to him as 'the rat'.

Fifteen men would eventually be charged with crimes related to elaborate plans to murder rival gang members in what would be the largest ever organized-crime trial in Malmö. In early February 2022, during a hearing in the District Court, the news reached the court that Salle had been shot dead while spending a Friday evening in Vesterbro in Copenhagen. Two of the suspects in this case were young boys from the Malmö area who the police suspect had been hired to do the job by an older criminal in the city.

All of the convictions in this gang trial ended up being referred to the Court of Appeal, which delivered its final verdict two days before Christmas Eve 2022. Danni and Kitekiller, who had planted the GPS transmitter on Salle's car, were convicted of conspiring to kill Salle, as were Haraketamal and Juggen. The person behind the alias Kitekiller was sentenced to seven years' imprisonment for two counts of conspiracy to commit murder and a serious firearms offence. Danni was sentenced to two years in prison, which were to be added to his existing five-year sentence for the smuggling operation that Customs officials intercepted on a ferry in Rostock.

Three men were cleared of all criminal charges, including Niff, the partner of Karolin Hakim, the intern physician who was murdered. He had been charged with conspiracy to commit murder on suspicions that he was involved in a plan to avenge Karolin's killing. He was acquitted in both the District Court and the Court of Appeal, despite having confessed to using the alias Stiffherb on Encrochat. He had claimed that his intention had been to try to uncover information about who it was who had murdered his partner, to find out who it was he needed to protect himself from. He never intended to seek revenge, he said, but he may have implied that he did, because that was what people would have expected him to do.

Allegedly, there is good evidence available regarding the identities of the people who plotted and carried out the murder of Karolin Hakim. The investigation is at an advanced stage, and the investigators have such good 'knowledge of the events and the people involved' that they expect to be able to bring charges in the near future.

'The Encrochat materials have confirmed many aspects of the previous findings of the investigation', a source told me.

*

Although some specific sentences have been quite severe, Helena Ljunggren, a prosecutor at Rio in Malmö, feels that sentences that are handed out for conspiracy and preparation to commit murder are far too lenient.

'But before we can worry about that, we need to be able to convict the perpetrators', she tells me.

Ljunggren says that lawmakers need to realize that it won't make any difference that the police can hack servers and phones and find conversations about murder plots if the legislation that's in place prevents them from getting convictions.

In the case of the murder plots against the Boxer and his allies, the Court of Appeal found that the messages provided evidence that Niff and two others had wanted to see their rivals dead, and that they had engaged in some degree of planning when they agreed to strike when an opportunity presented itself. However, the court determined that the chat logs contained no reference to a specific time and place at which the victims were to be attacked. According to the court, no firm conclusion could thus be drawn regarding whether any *decisions* were made to take the lives of the intended victims based on those chats.

Helena Ljunggren is frustrated by the fact that even specific information like this doesn't constitute a decision.

'Do they have to put it in writing and sign it for there to be a conspiracy? The legislators have work to do here', she said to *Sydsvenskan* in response to the announcement of the verdicts.

When I contacted her, she told me she stood by that statement. And she's hardly the only person to feel that way. Several prosecutors I spoke to mentioned the same issue. They felt that the current legislation needs to be brought up to date in relation to planned crimes, and the specific offences labelled conspiring, preparing, and aiding and abetting. If nothing was done, they claimed, the legal system would be powerless against the leaders who order the killings. They all pointed to the inadequacies of current legislation and court practice.

In many other EU countries, there is law against criminal associations, and this is something that several prosecutors suggested might 'close the gap' and make it less difficult to prosecute criminals in leadership positions who 'leave the dirty work to others'.

The original plan had been to also charge the person behind the alias Sadking with crimes related to the conversations with Niff and others about having the Boxer's allies killed. Sadking was extradited from Spain at a later stage, so it wasn't possible to prosecute him along with Danni and the others. However, following the Court of Appeal's verdict on preparation, conspiracy, and aiding and abetting – which acquitted both Niff and Hamid in Örebro – the prosecution has decided not to pursue the case against Sadking, as the prospects of securing a sentence are considered too poor.

*

In the spring of 2023, the Boxer was still detained in Málaga, where he had been since being extradited from Dubai. He and three accomplices are suspected of involvement in two murders that were committed in 2018.

'I'm innocent', was the response the Boxer gave to these accusations after his lawyer Gonzalo Boye had come to visit his client ahead of the upcoming trial.

The lawyer explained that there was no forensic evidence, such as DNA evidence or digital records, that could tie the Boxer to any of the crime scenes. He claimed that there was evidence that connected both murders to other gangs.

'During the trial, it will be made clear that all of the accusations against my client are based on nothing but the assumptions of the police', his lawyer said.

One of the Boxer's friends said that he was always careful on Encrochat, and that he doesn't believe that the police will have particularly strong evidence. The lawyer claimed that the investigation in Spain didn't include any evidence gathered from the cracked encryption services. Nor was any mention made of the Dutch-Moroccan mafia leader Ridouan Taghi, whom the Boxer had allegedly collaborated with.

The lawyer said that the Boxer had already made his way to Dubai when his friends were arrested. From there, he had been in constant contact with his former lawyer, who had tried to negotiate terms for a voluntary surrender with the judges and prosecutors, with the main demand being that he be released on bail while the investigation was being completed. This offer was rejected.

Whatever the outcome of the trial ends up being, police in Malmö have claimed that the Boxer used several Encro phones during his time in Dubai, and that the logs from these constitute a 'huge body of material' that was of great interest to Swedish investigators. The Boxer's Spanish lawyer said that he hadn't received any evidence from Sweden that in any way linked his client to the two murders he was suspected of having involvement in. He claimed that the case seemed weak, and even alleged that the evidence had been tampered with – and claimed he had evidence to support this allegation.

During one of my conversations with the lawyer, I naturally felt compelled to ask if the Boxer had anything to say about the conflict in Malmö, which had claimed a total of ten lives in Sweden and England.

'He doesn't want to talk about that until after the trial', the lawyer told me, and added that his client had nothing to do with those murders either.

Most of the killings in Sweden, and the murder in London, had been committed while he was in Dubai, far from any of the crime scenes. The lawyer rejected all allegations that he had remotely coordinated and instigated the murders.

'If that had been the case, surely he would have been charged with those offences by now, after having spent almost three years in custody? I can confirm that he has not been notified of any such suspicions anyway', the lawyer went on.

Police sources in several countries were unsurprised to hear the Boxer's lawyer proclaim his client's innocence. However, there was a degree of concern that the lawyer may have been right, and that the Spanish police had shortcomings, specifically regarding their ability to investigate a crime of this kind. One explanation that was offered was that the country has two separate police forces, between which there is a degree of competition that sometimes causes them to 'trip each other up'.

A friend of the Boxer doubted that the Spanish police had much of a case.

'I think he's going to be released. I just have this feeling.'

*

At first, they had been seeking a life sentence. However, the court rejected some of the electronic evidence, and when they became worried that the Boxer and the other three might be acquitted altogether, the prosecution offered the defence a deal that's possible in Spain: they could confess to the offences in exchange for greatly reduced sentences. In the case of the Boxer, to the surprise of Swedish police, this would mean he could be released by the end of April.

However, moments before the Boxer was due to be released, he was told that he had to remain in custody, as a European Arrest Order had just been issued for him. He had been arrested *in absentia* on suspicions of serious drug offences supported by evidence from Encrochat.

In the spring of 2023, he was extradited from Spain to stand trial in Sweden. The Swedish police officers were relieved.

45

One of the people who would eventually be arrested because of evidence found in the cracked chats was Donvar. When he realized that several serious drug charges would be brought against him, based on evidence from Encrochat, all he could think was 'fuck'. Like many of his friends, Donvar was sentenced to several years in prison for serious drug offences. He was one of many convicts who have since questioned the legitimacy of the Swedish courts' decision to treat the Encrochat messages as admissible evidence.

Donvar described his life in prison as 'disastrous'. He felt like he was just being stored – the wings were overcrowded and the activities available were substandard. He ended up waiting for more than ten months to finally be admitted to a training programme he had applied for to give himself something meaningful to do while he was in prison. With conditions as they were in the country's prisons, he had doubts that anybody could possibly be rehabilitated and readied for a return to society. He thought it was more likely that prisoners who were released would go right back to committing crimes. Many people he knew in prison weren't even allowed visits from their partners, because they were considered 'network affiliated', and hindrances to successful reintegration into society.

'How the hell is getting to see your girlfriend supposed to make it more difficult for you to reintegrate into society?' Donvar wondered.

He said he was smart and would be fine, but he realized that he'd have a hard time finding a job with a criminal record that contained serious drug offences.

'Who the hell would want to hire me? For all practical purposes, my life is ruined.'

*

Sara kept her promise to herself and stopped selling drugs. Today, she's a mother with a young child, and works in customer service. The criminal lifestyle is firmly in her past.

I asked Sara whether she had any regrets. She told me she didn't. Her customers would have done drugs either way, whether they bought them from her or from someone else. At least she had been able to treat her customers well, and talk to them. However, she had also seen some of her customers fall victim to addiction. One of her customers had been evicted after failing to pay his rent for several months. He had been buying more drugs than he could afford.

'It made me feel guilty. I never had that criminal, ghetto mindset. It gave me anxiety. I felt like it was my fault that he had nowhere to live. At the same time, I knew that it wasn't my fault that he chose to spend all his money on drugs.'

*

Maja, the social worker, still works with young people who are struggling with issues related to substance abuse and organized crime. These last six months, she's kept herself clean. According to her, she stopped using drugs because she 'couldn't stand the hypocrisy any more'.

Staying away from drugs has been easier than she thought, because she has changed her social circles, and she doesn't encounter drugs the way she used to. When she and her friends drank alcohol, they used to move on to drugs to keep the party going. But Maja felt that she'd had enough of being 'two-faced', and doing things that were so incompatible with her professional identity.

She felt better now, too.

This was probably because she had received an ADHD diagnosis. The medication she was taking, which is a controlled substance, had made her less of a thrill-seeker than she had been before.

'I think I've probably felt like a bad person because of how I was carrying on. It's easier for me to feel proud of what I do now', she explained.

46

'Hi, are you that journalist?'

Late one evening in the middle of an intense spurt of work keeping up with all the shootings and bombings in Stockholm, I received that message on Signal.

A while later, I called the sender back. This was the older brother of the wanted suspect Orhan. He wanted to get in touch with me to talk about my trip to Turkey.

It was early 2023, and the trial of Maykil and two others who were suspected of involvement in Adriana's murder had begun. Evidence gathered from encrypted chats on Sky ECC had been crucial for bringing charges against the suspects, according to prosecutor Anna Svedin. Defence lawyers had called the case 'weak', and claimed that it was based on circumstantial evidence. The fourth individual suspected of involvement in the murder was Orhan, who was detained *in absentia* and internationally wanted for murder and attempted murder.

Orhan's brother told me that they didn't like that I had visited their parents' home town and gone around asking questions. They had been contacted by relatives they hadn't spoken to in 'forty years'. They felt that had been a transgression on my part.

'You had some balls going to Kulu to poke around', the brother told me.

When we had discussed this for a while, he claimed that his brother Orhan was innocent. When I said I wanted to hear him say that himself, the phone was suddenly handed over to Orhan, who had been listening in while we spoke.

'I had nothing to do with Adriana's murder', he told me.

I answered that, if he wasn't involved, there seemed to be no reason why he couldn't come back to Sweden and state his case in court instead of hiding over there in Turkey. It was his best opportunity to clear his name. However, both Orhan and his brother told me that they had friends who had been found guilty of crimes they hadn't committed, without any evidence. Orhan didn't want to spend two years in solitary confinement waiting to be acquitted when he could 'lead a life of luxury in Turkey'.

'I know, 100 per cent, that I wasn't in that car. I'm here in Turkey while I wait for the others to be acquitted', he said. He had recently turned twenty-five.

Chats from Sky ECC revealed that one of the young men who had been targeted when Adriana was killed had begun to mention Orhan and start looking for him the day after the murder. He and his friends became convinced that he had been involved in the shooting, and offered a reward of 1 million kronor to anybody who could provide information on the whereabouts of those involved – most specifically, Orhan. Another fact that strengthened the suspicion that Orhan had been present in the Audi was that one of the targets – a former friend of Orhan's – made an anonymous phone call to the police in which he identified Orhan and two of his friends as Adriana's killers. The caller was identified in a later stage of the investigation. All suspicions against Orhan's two friends who had also been named were later dropped, but he still remains a suspect. So far, however, he has managed to evade prosecution as he isn't in the country.

He told me that Adriana's murder hadn't been why he went to Turkey. He claimed that he had to leave Sweden after being shot during an attempt on his life. According to the investigation, this attack was an act of vengeance orchestrated by the rivals of Orhan who had been the real targets when Adriana was shot.

Orhan's mother and other family members had urged him to leave the country after he survived a bullet wound to the arm. Several of the people involved have since been sentenced to several years in prison for this attempted murder. His former friend, who had been unharmed during the attack outside McDonald's, had been involved in planning the revenge plot, and received a sentence of 15 years and 10 months in prison. Orhan and his friends were paid damages for the attempt on his life that he survived, and he said that he respected the court's decision.

'If the court said they should be sentenced, they should be sentenced', he told me.

He didn't have much to share about the conflict with his former friends that had led to the shooting on that evening in August. He had no idea why 'people choose to form alliances with others'. There were some things that he hadn't known about, which he had learned of like everybody else, by reading the chats that were made public when they were presented in court.

'I'm learning about all this, just like you.'

He admitted that he had been to the filming of a highly publicized music video the day before Adriana's murder, for the rap song 'Blue Cheese'. Once investigators gained access to the raw footage from the video shoot, they were able to determine that both Orhan and Maykil had been present during the filming, and it was when this evidence was submitted to the court that he had been detained *in absentia* for his suspected involvement in Adriana's murder. This happened in July 2021, when he was in Turkey. Sometime later, more evidence from Sky ECC had been introduced to the case.

Several live firearms were shown in the music video, including a Kalashnikov, and this turned out to be the specific gun that was used when Adriana was shot dead. The alleged ringleader, Maykil Yokhanna, and two other people were eventually convicted of serious weapons offences committed during the music video shoot, and Orhan also remained a suspect in that case.

I asked Orhan what he felt about being accused of murdering a child.

'Even the most vicious person in the world would have felt guilty about that. What can I do about it? I mourn Adriana's death, but it had nothing to do with me.'

*

In Room 11 at Attunda District Court in Sollentuna, Susanne Yakes sat next to Adriana's father as they listened to the charges against her daughter's suspected murderer.

She was Adriana's mother, and she looked straight at Maykil and the two other young men who were suspected of involvement in her daughter's murder. Maykil was in the front row, in the middle, with the lawyers to his left. He was dressed in black, and wore black Louis Vuitton shoes. His hair was long and tied into a ponytail. To his right, several witnesses, including two boys who were Adriana's age and had been her friends, recounted their memories from the night of the murder. Throughout this testimony, Maykil sat still, looking straight at the screen in front of him. He was wearing black-rimmed glasses. On occasion, he leaned over to his two lawyers, who were seated to his left, and whispered comments to them.

Susanne was struggling to maintain her composure, and decided to leave the room when the children were going to be heard. She couldn't bring herself to sit through their testimonies, but she returned when Adriana's father testified about how he had arrived at the scene ten minutes after his daughter was murdered. He told the court how he had struggled to understand what had happened, how he had ended up having to bring the dog Adriana had walked out with back in his car and how the weeks of his life that followed had seemed to collapse into a mess of grey sludge. When he was able to deal with people again, two or three people he considered reliable got in touch with him. They gave him the names of those who had been responsible for his daughter's murder. One of the people named was Orhan, who had allegedly been driving the Audi, and the other was a young man who had subsequently been cleared of all suspicions. Later, he also learned that Maykil had been in the car with them. To the prosecutor's surprise, however, the father didn't want to name the people who had told him these things, because he claimed that this would put their lives at risk. He didn't want to subject them to that. Maykil and his fellow suspects had consistently denied all wrongdoing.

'I'm innocent, and I hope the court will give me a fair trial', Maykil Yokhanna wrote to me in a letter. He didn't answer any of my other questions about the conflict with the Vårby network, his relationship with Sascha, or any of the other things in this book that relate to him.

In late April 2023, he and the two other defendants were given life sentences for the murder, and for the attempted murder of seven other people who had been present outside the fast-food restaurant. The legal teams representing the defendants have announced that they intend to appeal the case to the Court of Appeal.

*

Susanne said that there had to be some lines that even criminals wouldn't cross. When an innocent child was murdered, surely the rules of the street couldn't apply? Surely telling the police what you knew in a case like that couldn't count as snitching? Adriana's mother said that she believed that criminals observed a false honour culture, which caused them to value material possessions more than human lives – the life of her daughter, Adriana, in this case.

'They talk so much about honour, but where was the honour in this? If you want people's respect, this is the wrong way to get it. Doing this doesn't make you a gangster, it makes you a child killer', she said, and directed the following questions to the male suspects:

'Was it worth it?'

'Did it get you the respect you wanted?'

'Do you deserve that respect?'

47

One Friday in early January 2023, I met with Jacob, who had returned to the role of investigative lead for Team Foxtrot. He was leading a team of twenty-one investigators and analysts, working out of two office spaces, and their focus remained the continued hunt for the Fox.

Along the short side of the room, there was a large whiteboard with photographs of about thirty people who were believed to be associated with the Fox in various ways. Some of them were already serving prison terms, while others might have been the next in line to be arrested. At the top of the board was a picture of the Fox.

Although the Fox had gained Turkish citizenship, and was unlikely to be extradited to Sweden, there was always the possibility of having the case prosecuted in a Turkish court. That would be complicated, as much of the material would require translation, but Jacob insisted that 'the Swedish legal system isn't going to give up'.

He was very much aware of all the traces of the Fox's involvement that were being discovered in investigations all over the country, and he was also aware of the Fox's growing influence in rap music.

In October 2022, a rap group from Jordbro which was tied to allies of the Fox released a music video that featured a group of masked individuals who were carrying guns and wearing T-shirts with clear printed messages. One of these was 'Free Wizz', which was supposedly a reference to an individual who had been convicted after the raid on Lidingö in which more than 300 kilos of drugs were seized.

In the video, we also see a man dressed in black, who raises a gun and points to his chest. 'Free Fox' is the message, and beneath it is a picture of a fox.

A few seconds later, in the last shot of the video, we see two people dressed in summer shorts. Their faces are covered up with Fox emojis. One of them is wearing a thick, gold chain with a fox charm that has the same colours as the Kurdish flag.

*

By now, so many drug investigations had been linked to the Fox that 'the cup was already full' as far as Team Foxtrot was concerned. They had enough to seek the maximum penalty in a prosecution: fourteen years in prison for several counts of exceptionally serious drug offences. According to the police, the Fox was a suspect in about fifty serious and exceptionally serious drug offences. Because of this, they had shifted their focus to gathering evidence of acts of violent crimes that the Fox was suspected to be linked to.

Denny, the detective, felt that the case against the Fox was a good example of how important it was that the police took action against drug traffickers, as it was also a way of curtailing the violence. However, even though he had been present for seizures of a total of about a tonne of drugs that the police suspected could be linked to the Fox, he hadn't seen any evidence that drug smuggling or drug use was slowing down.

'I don't think the users understand their role in this', he said. 'When they do a line at Stureplan at the weekend, they're really contributing just as much to this bloody conflict as the people who carry out the shootings do. They just don't realize it.'

As I sat down to talk with Jacob, I asked him how many bites of the elephant still needed to be eaten. He smiled, but quickly turned serious when he thought of all the murders that had occurred in the Fox's conflict with the Bandidos, and all the weapons that had been seized. Anybody who becomes a bigger player ends up having to defend their new power.

Two years earlier, he had tried to convince his colleagues at Noa to spend more resources on catching the Fox, but they hadn't felt that he was a sufficiently dangerous target.

'We might not have been able to stop him, but perhaps we could have slowed him down. Now, we're back at work, trying to bring this case in, again. It's unfortunate that he's grown so violent', Jacob says, and then adds: 'It didn't have to be like this.'

Despite that, Jacob and his Team Foxtrot are continuing their hunt, one bite at a time.

'It's just that this elephant keeps growing. We haven't even started eating it, to be honest, at least not when it comes to the violent crimes.'

*

Just two days after our meeting, bombings and shootings began to happen in various parts of Stockholm and Uppsala. What soon began to come into view was a conflict involving the Dalen network, which was led by the Greek, a 24-year-old former hockey player. The rival side was suspected to be the Fox and his allies, as there were indications that they were behind a bombing at a restaurant in Södermalm, as well as several of the shootings. Reportedly, the conflict was at least initially sparked when the Greek's network decided to send a message to the Fox when 'his drugs' turned up in Sundsvall, a market that was controlled by the Greek. Several of my sources told me that Sundsvall was a gateway for onward distribution of drugs to the north, as well as for onward smuggling to Norway and Finland. The Fox already had contacts in place in those countries, to whom he was selling drugs. The strategic importance of Sundsvall was also confirmed by sources in the criminal underworld, who likened the conflict to the one that Hells Angels and the Bandidos had fought for several years back in the 1990s.

By mid-March, this conflict alone had produced a series of bombings and shootings in the Stockholm area, which had already claimed several lives. A man in his forties, who may have been mistaken for somebody else, was shot dead outside a restaurant in Solna, and a fifteen-year-old, who was linked to the conflict by virtue of having participated in activities targeting the Fox's network, was shot in the head inside a sushi restaurant in Skogås. The suspects included a trio of teenagers who were suspected of carrying out the murder. One of these teenagers had allegedly lured the victim to the restaurant, where a fifteen-year-old boy was suspected of firing the shots. They all came from difficult circumstances, and now these child soldiers had been recruited to carry out a retaliatory strike. An even more distinctive feature of this power struggle was that both sides were choosing to target people in the orbits of the respective leaders, the Fox and the Greek. The targets included family members, as well as others who were more loosely affiliated to the bosses.

People I spoke to were beginning to wonder where all this was headed. How far were things going to go?

A shooting happened, that shooting was avenged, and so on, and so on. In early March 2023, the television programme *Efterlyst* published pictures of two young men from southern Stockholm who had been arrested *in absentia* for a shooting they had previously carried out in Uppsala, in which relatives of the Fox were the targets.

That same night, there was a knock on the door of a house in Tullinge in southern Stockholm, where the parents of one of the wanted men lived. The father opened the door, and was shot dead.

'Real criminals look down on people who go after somebody's parents. That's an absolute taboo', an older criminal told me. In his eyes, anybody who ordered something like that was a 'miserable coward', who would be 'quiet as a mouse' in the presence of 'real gangsters'.

When I asked people from the criminal underworld how they could stop this from happening, they told me that this kind of attention was actually a positive, in a way. A reputation for violence is *good* for business. It kept people talking about the Fox's network, it kept people paying on time, and it made groups in neighbouring countries aware of the gang, which had begun to use its name, 'Foxes', in music videos as well as in the logos they added to their drug shipments. The violence deterred other gangs from retaliating against them, and if somebody chose to retaliate anyway, even their families wouldn't be spared. Targeting people's families was a part of this escalation of violence – a way of hitting your rivals where it hurt. The whole situation reminded me of a subculture undergoing rapid radicalization – only in this case, violence was a means within the power struggle, a way to take out your enemies. Even if the gangs' members themselves found targeting rivals' family members distasteful, they turned a blind eye to the consequences, as they had already made their gang their new family.

Police officers I spoke to felt that the violent acts that had been linked to the Fox should have been treated like cases of domestic terrorism. After the murder in Tullinge, many began to say that the time had come for the Swedish government to summon Turkey's ambassador and demand responsibility for all the bombings and murders that had been orchestrated in Sweden by the Fox, who was now a Turkish citizen. 'The government has to defy NATO and challenge Turkey's inaction', one police officer who had spent a lot of his time trying to track down the Fox told me.

Apart from the violence, the police had also begun to monitor the increasingly ambitious branding efforts of the gangs, which usually revolved around music. Rap artists made reference to the Fox in their songs and videos, publicly announcing their support for his network. As the conflict escalated, a popular rap artist from Upplands-Bro posted pictures on Instagram of people covered in fox emojis. He also posted a music video in which he was seen wearing a thick gold chain with a fox charm. In another picture, the rapper was sitting with a silver gun in his hand, with hundred-dollar bills arranged in the shape of the word 'FOX'. In mid-March, this rapper's relatives in Hässelby were targeted in a bombing that was linked to the escalating spiral of vengeance.

Despite the many articles and news reports that were published that spring about the Fox and the deadly conflict that had caused so much terror, particularly in Stockholm, there was still one person who didn't want to believe a word of what was being written: the Fox's mother's friend, Hasse.

'People have spun this mystical fairy tale around him. It's just not accurate. I find it very hard to believe that I could be such a bad judge of character and be so incredibly wrong', Hasse told me.

Team Foxtrot was monitoring the escalating violence, of course, as were other police officers who had now become involved with the many investigations that were simultaneously ongoing. The team that had been on the Fox's trail for almost three years watched hundreds of colleagues get called in from all over the country to help curtail the growth of the Fox's network.

'I've said "I told you so" so many times now. And now, here we are', Denny said late one night when I asked him for a reaction to the recent developments. He was very obviously annoyed.

I contacted Christoffer Bohman, who had written the operation plan for Team Foxtrot in response to his colleagues' warnings about the Fox's capacity for violence back in the autumn of 2021. He believed that the police had been struggling with a limitation in their methodology that had been exposed to the public by the events that had occurred in recent years.

'If you don't work to address identifiable future challenges, and focus exclusively on urgent issues in the present, those future challenges will eventually hit you right in the face', Bohman told me.

As examples of this, he cited the failure to anticipate the delays in digitalization which had hampered the police's internal work, and the investigative activities, which were facing increasing criticism for failing to keep up with the escalating violence. It had been just the same with the Fox, he claimed. Several colleagues had been sounding the alarm, at the top of their voices, that this was bound to become a bigger problem down the road.

'We need a cultural change in our management and governance', he said.

However, that will have to happen without Christoffer Bohman. He had reached a point where he realized that he simply couldn't make the difference he wanted to as a police officer. More police officers were certainly needed, but another thing that was needed was more people who could work to ensure fewer people ended up becoming criminals. Bohman didn't see how he could make a difference when everybody he arrested had ten people waiting to take their place. It wasn't even that unusual to see twelve-year-olds getting involved.

'If we don't resolve this now, we can only guess what things will be like tomorrow', Bohman stated.

Because of this, he would be leaving the police force and his position as head of investigations in Sörmland, where he had been working on cases involving gun violence in Eskilstuna and elsewhere. His next position would be with Skandia's Ideas for Life foundation. He looked forward to tackling security issues from a national, long-term perspective in that role.

'Lots of people could do what I'm doing in the police force today. I'm comfortable with entrusting this to others. I'm needed in another sector now', he concluded.

*

The investigator Niklas, who had repeatedly tried to convince the brass to make taking action against the Fox a top priority with Jacob and the other members of the team, would finally manage to bring Team Foxtrot back. The result of his efforts was the assignment of half a dozen officers to a team that would be 'grudgingly permitted' to focus their efforts on the Fox. None of the commanding officers had taken the concerns of this small group of police officers seriously. According to them, there were other matters that were more important at the time.

The tidal wave of violence that was erupting around the Fox now had been inevitable, an evolution of sorts, and they had tried their best to raise the alarm, but to no avail. Instead, they were viewed as troublemakers, unable to let that one case go and move on to the next. In my final interview with Niklas, I asked him what he thought about the recent developments. He paused, and thought about it for a moment. After this, he began by emphasizing that the failures of the police had been caused by an issue within the management culture, which had made the leadership unable to address problems of this kind. After the recent, controversial reorganization, the idea was for crimes to be handled by the local police districts, which had 'occasional access to one specialized skill set or other'.

Several of the officers I interviewed stated that they found their commanding officers to be anxious and unwilling to take decisive action, and that coordinated efforts were the exception. The lack of coordinated efforts was particularly troubling, as crimes related to the Fox had been investigated by different regions and police districts, in which there wasn't always a good understanding of how they could benefit from pooling their investigative findings. Access to this information could help colleagues draw better conclusions, and find better support for their suspicions.

On top of this, there was the 'usual bickering' about whether the police ought to be prioritizing gun violence over tracking down the drugs and the money. The ability to make the right decisions here was also in short supply within the police force. Niklas sighed, and started to pack his things up, as he would soon have to hurry on to his next meeting.

'This is what happens when nobody listens', he said, and looked me in the eyes.

48

In the spring of 2023, just before this book was due to go to print, I reconnected with the French prosecutor Alexandre on Signal. I was in my home in Stockholm, and he was in his office in Lille. We discussed everything that had happened since this whole story began. He told me that thousands of convictions had been made all over Europe thanks to the investigation he launched against Encrochat, and the later one he authorized against Sky ECC. He was satisfied, but he noted that there had been no significant effects on the trafficking of cocaine from South America to Europe. The trade routes that passed through the major ports of northern Europe were still the main avenues. He was currently investigating cocaine smuggling to the French ports along the English Channel, where 12 or 13 tonnes of cocaine had been seized each year for the last two years – that is, since Encrochat was hacked.

'It just keeps growing', he told me, and asked me to look farther east, towards the ports of Antwerp in Belgium and Rotterdam in the Netherlands.

The authorities in these two countries had recently announced that 160 tonnes of cocaine – an all-time record – had been seized in those two ports in 2022 alone. Most of that, 110 tonnes, had been intercepted in Antwerp, which is thought to be the main gateway for drug smuggling into

Europe. The port is located less than an hour from the centre of European political power in Brussels, which houses the European Parliament.

Both countries promised to continue their cooperation, and invest in more Customs staff and more modern scanning equipment to help them fight 'the war on drugs'.

'It's *business as usual.* The war continues', Alexandre told me.

*

The United Nations has estimated that the cocaine trade is a multi-billion-dollar industry, and that global cocaine production reached 1,982 tonnes in 2020.

This was a new record, despite the ongoing pandemic.

Belgium and the Netherlands are currently subjected to particular pressure by organized crime, and considered to be at high risk of having their political system and other parts of the state apparatus infiltrated. According to Belgian media reports, the Belgian minister of justice, Vincent Van Quickenborne, who was also deputy prime minister, had to be placed under 24-hour protection after plans to kidnap him and use him as a bargaining chip in a prisoner swap were exposed. He has drawn comparisons between organized crime and the Islamic State, which rocked Belgium during two attacks in March 2016 that claimed a total of thirty-two lives.

'Organized crime is the new terrorism. It's incredibly difficult to combat it', the minister of justice told Politico.

The same alarm has been sounded in the country's neighbour to the east, the Netherlands. Here, politicians have called for action against the Mafia, which has 'compromised the democratic rule of law'. For years, the president of the Dutch police union has argued that the country is really a narco-state, where a parallel economy is competing with the official one, and where legal businesses are being taken over by criminals who use them to launder their illicit profits. The fear is that this will ultimately undermine both the democratic system and the economy of the country, as well as put more people at risk of being coerced, exploited, threatened and murdered.

One example is the Marengo trial that was held in the Netherlands, in which the Boxer's alleged boss, Ridouan Taghi, was charged with six murders and several attempted murders.

In the course of this major trial against organized crime, the brother and the lawyer of the main witness were both murdered. Later, crime reporter Peter R. de Vries, who had aided the witness after the lawyer was killed, was also murdered.

*

The intelligence department of the Swedish Police Authority has estimated that there are ten times as many drugs being smuggled into Sweden as was previously believed, which means the correct amount is up to 150 tonnes a year.

'People in Sweden aren't used to the massive amounts of money that drugs bring, or the things it can do to people', said a man who has been linked to one of the most violent conflicts in the last decade, who also made countless appearances in the encrypted chats.

When I talk to police officers in various parts of the country, they tell me they aren't seeing any changes in the scale of drug smuggling. What's changing is the violence, even though both Gothenburg and Malmö were fairly peaceful at the time of writing.

No matter what, however, the drugs keep flowing in to meet the demand. *Business as usual.* When I asked Alexandre if he remained optimistic even though the seizures kept growing bigger, he mentioned the threat that organized crime poses to state institutions, and told me that 'Democracy is at stake.' That's why 'We need to focus on our fight against the poison we call organized crime.'

'In other words, we need to stay optimistic, ambitious and committed. And we'll handle the new people who take over, too', Alexandre said, and added that the operation had 'obviously' been justified and well worth the effort it took.

Thousands of arrests were made, hundreds of murders were prevented, and tonnes of drugs and half a billion euros of criminal assets were seized. However, perhaps the most important win of all was the extensive intelligence data that was gathered from Encrochat and Sky ECC, as well as ANOM. He called it 'a goldmine'.

But, despite all that progress, the criminal underworld in Sweden is in turmoil, and both the perpetrators and the victims involved in the shootings seem to keep getting younger. Older criminals have described this situation as 'chaos'.

'My lawyers like to joke with me and tell me that if I had been out on the streets, I could have brought peace to Södertälje in a few hours', said Berno Khouri of the Södertälje network about his home town, which was the scene of seven fatal shootings in 2022.

Several leading figures who are in Swedish prisons told me that their relationship with the Fox is a good one. Others who hold influence in the underworld told me they believed that his days are numbered. Targeting outsiders, internal division and debts incurred in the wake of big seizures have harmed the Fox's reputation, rather than strengthened his brand as a reliable business partner.

'I don't think he's going to be around for too long. Or, rather, I know he won't', said one of the older figures in the world of Swedish organized crime.

Another alleged gang leader who's currently serving a long prison term was troubled by the harm that had been caused to innocent bystanders.

'When I was out on the streets, we had rules, and nobody would ever dream of involving innocent people in a conflict', he said.

He is personally thought to be linked to fatal shootings, and had friends who were murdered. The stuff that's going on now has made him feel 'disappointed' with his own people. Next year, however, 'twenty or so friends' are due to be let out as the first wave of releases after the encryption case convictions arrives. Things will change then, he tells me.

The question is just how they'll change.

AFTERWORD

My work on *When Nobody's Listening* actually began in the summer of 2020, when the news that Encrochat had been cracked first broke. I began reporting on the raids that followed, including the one against the Boxer, but later on, I also covered the trial against the Vårby network's kidnapping of Einár, in which a long list of individuals from several different organizations received lengthy sentences, largely because of evidence from Encrochat. It was obvious that they had felt completely shielded from any outside scrutiny. Chihab Lamouri, the leader of the network, who was in hiding in Spain, gave his identity away by posting pictures of himself in the chats.

I conducted my first interview for this book in December 2021. That was a conversation with Alexandre, the French prosecutor, who was visiting Sweden to meet with his Swedish colleagues. Since then, I have read investigative reports and verdicts, tens of thousands of pages in all, and conducted more than 100 interviews with people all over the country and abroad.

The most challenging part of this project was gaining insight into the police operations involving the encrypted services. The secrecy involved meant that information about the operations was only given to a very small number of individuals. I spent many hours in interviews with people working in the justice system – mostly police officers, but also prosecutors and lawyers – to get a better understanding of what had actually happened.

As far as the work at Noa is concerned, no single person had access to the whole picture, so I had to piece that together from the things I learnt in my interviews. I had to work my way through several layers of intelligence officers before I finally got to meet with Putte and Cattis, two of the police officers who worked on the first batches of Encrochat intelligence.

In seeking to understand the complex web of people, and the many layers and clues involved – like the shipping waybills or the way that Spex the cat ended up helping the police arrest individuals with ties to the Fox or Rivkin – I have been greatly helped by many different people who have taken the time to explain various matters to me. I have also spent more than a year trying to piece things together to help me gain an understanding of the motives behind specific actions. My main resource in this work has been my interviews and correspondence with twenty or so convicts, wanted people, and others who are currently or were previously involved in these events in different ways. Several names and details have been altered in order to protect my sources and the people mentioned. Many of the people I have written about in this book have not responded to my attempts to contact them, and others have declined my offer to participate.

Several of the family members I spoke to, particularly Sascha's family, Adriana's mother and Shayan Gaff's family, helped me understand their tragedy and put it into words.

I think, however, that it would be more accurate to call it *Sweden's tragedy*.

*

Afterword

After the Second World War, many people found it hard to believe that seemingly well-functioning and well-adjusted people could ever commit horrific crimes such as murdering and torturing civilians. In an attempt to better understand this, psychologist Stanley Milgram would later conduct a series of famous experiments at Yale University. In his experiments, Milgram studied people's propensity to submit to authority in carrying out actions that their sense of conscience would never otherwise permit them to. In the most famous of these experiments, Milgram asked his subjects to administer electric shocks – which they believed to be real – to a person who was seated in another room. All forty of the participants, who were all men, proved to be prepared to administer potentially lethal electric shocks to a fellow human being when encouraged to do so by an authority figure, the experimenter.

Considering Milgram's findings, it may not be too surprising that many seem to be prepared to take another person's life, even without being paid for it, as in the case in Viksjö where the sixteen-year-old attempted to take Peter's life, or that of the seventeen-year-old who was hiding outside Maykil's home in Västerås. However, as far as I know, there aren't any research findings that can explain how an adult can stomach using phrases like 'stop being a baby' to convince a child to murder somebody.

I think of all the murder and drug smuggling that's already going on, where small-business owners and middle-aged men who live in quiet neighbourhoods serve as mules and wholesalers. I also see the many people who place orders for drugs on the dark web, always keeping safely out of the way of the violence their money fuels. There are other enablers, too, of course, like the people who help exchange money or funnel income from criminal activities into cryptocurrencies, luxury items and residential properties, in Sweden and abroad.

Afterword

Police are watching new alliances and internal conflicts play out, and more and more of what goes on is now being remotely coordinated from Turkey and other countries. At the very bottom of the food chain are the teenagers, the 'child soldiers' and hitmen who are waiting to be given their missions. One young drug offender argued that children are used for the simple reason that the tougher gun laws have encouraged older criminals to avoid risk by having 'kids' carry guns instead.

Because of the constant influx of new children to these networks, it's difficult for the police to keep their information up to date. This no longer applies only to boys from disadvantaged neighbourhoods, who make up the vast majority of the membership of most violent networks. The networks are also recruiting young men from middle-class backgrounds, whose parents were born in Sweden. Girls, too, are seeing an opportunity to earn some money.

Gang culture has a powerful allure for many, and rap music serves as the framing for this fantasy.

One convicted gang leader told me that it annoyed him that he couldn't control the young ones who were out there any more. They did as they pleased, and they had warped the macho culture their elders had taught them to the point where they felt compelled to avenge 'the tiniest offence by shooting somebody'.

Another older individual who is allegedly the leader of a gang noted that the chats themselves had sparked new conflicts, and that 'Blood demands blood.'

Personally, I find it incredible that there could be such a seemingly endless supply of teenagers who are ready to die or be killed. And as you read these very words, tonnes of drugs are being carried towards the Swedish border by fishing boats, cargo ships and trucks.

THANKS

First of all, I'd like to thank my wife Linda and my daughter Agnes, who was born when this book was still just a mountain of information with a mess of jumbled names and details attached to it. While I became a father, I was also working on the most difficult project I had ever taken on. You weren't always too happy with the obsession that working on this book aroused in me, but you did find the patience to accept it, along with the lion's share of the responsibility for our daughter. You will always have my gratitude for that.

Of course, I'd also like to express my sincerest thanks to everybody who has taken the time to talk to me, often on many different occasions, to assist me in understanding the story and getting the facts right. This applies equally to the police officers, the prosecutors, the family members, the lawyers, the prison officers and those of you who are incarcerated or wanted by the law. It's my impression that all of us would prefer to live in a society in which people's family members were safer.

I would also like to thank my employer, SVT, for trusting me to work on in-depth journalism and go beneath the surface, rather than just focusing on the iceberg that's towering over it.

Having recently become the father of a young child, I can't overstate how much easier the generous book award I

Thanks

received from the Natur & Kultur Foundation has made my life, and I am deeply grateful for that.

In closing, I would also like to express my deepest respect to everybody at the Mondial publishing house, which has helped me see this project through. I am particularly grateful for the work of my editors, Gustav and Anton – you guys are the best! – and my publishers, Olle and Simon, who have helped me make this narrative digestible and relatable. Behind the scenes, Emma has helped me in more ways than she will ever know, and I've also appreciated the support of their great colleagues Adam, Alba, Nikki and Matilda, who has been my main point of contact.

Of course, there are many others I owe thanks, but I would like to particularly acknowledge the colleagues who have taken turns checking my mailbox, and my family, who have helped me in every way imaginable.

This was only possible thanks to all of you and the efforts you've made on my behalf.

Diamant Salihu
Stockholm, March 2023